WHAT OTHERS ARE SAYING ABOUT
THE HEALING CONNECTION

Who better than a career emergency department physician to report on the quality of healthcare offered by systems run by non-physician business interests, as is the current trend in the United States? As if common sense and 40 years of clinical experience were not enough, Dr. Remignanti marshals abundant research evidence pointing to the unnecessary physical, emotional, and financial costs to patients and providers alike when the doctor-patient *relationship* is forced to take a back seat to quotas and other profit-driven economies of scale. A true *tour de force*, *The Healing Connection* solidly documents the value of a stable long-term relationship with one's doctor—which allows for the development of trust, openness, collaboration, and (not coincidentally) enhanced emotional well-being, leading to superior and more cost-effective health outcomes.

—**Stephen A. Buglione, PhD**
Clinical Psychologist
North Salem, New York

Dr. Remignanti has made a valuable contribution to the discourse regarding how to improve the delivery of healthcare in general, but with particular relevance to how it is done in America. His 40-year career as an emergency medicine physician, the entire time of which he was also a patient suffering from a debilitating chronic disease, enables him to share critically important insights gleaned from both ends of the stethoscope—insights that are supported by extensive research and conveyed with considerable humor. Healthcare professionals, patients, and policymakers, indeed, society in general, will be better off for having read this book.

—David Rutstein, MD, MPH

Yes, you and your health insurance company invest financially in your primary care physician for his or her care. But your most enduring insurance is your care for yourself, your investment in yourself and your health, including mental wellness, emotional quotient (EQ), and spiritual attitude. Dr. Remignanti points to the urgency of attention to all these factors that undergird your physical well-being. More than that, he emphasizes the incalculable value of a long-term relationship with your primary care physician. He asks for patience from his patients in learning what might be called 'the art of partnership wellness.' Then you may never have to walk through the door of the emergency department which he knew so well. Some of his stories are quite dramatic, but they may prompt new mindfulness for health as a lifestyle choice itself. My long-term primary care physician had retired about a year before I read Dr. Remignanti's book. Reading it got me immediately on the phone to make an appointment with a new PCP for my annual checkup!

—Rev. Dr. Michael Caldwell
Retired pastor in the United Church of Christ and
a member of the international, ecumenical Iona Community

Dr. Remignanti passionately explores the great importance of the physician-patient relationship and the power and spirituality that it embodies. It is the most significant therapeutic aspect of the practice of medicine. In his well-researched presentation, he gives evidence for the healing power of the physician-patient relationship, a relationship which is being threatened by the misguided direction US healthcare is being taken by corporate America. He presents his case, reviewing scientific research, and relating riveting personal experiences from both the physician and patient side of the bed. In doing this, Dr. Remignanti also gives the nonmedical person an honest glimpse of the challenges, struggles, and joys of being a caring physician. He has the courage to lead us to the inevitable conclusion that the patient-physician relationship is a "near sacred encounter," a beautiful, spiritual act, that is our best hope not only for our own personal optimal health outcomes but also for changing the destructive course the US healthcare system is currently on.

—John V. Romano, MD, MPH

In his book *The Healing Connection,* Dr. Remignanti takes a fresh, very personal, and compelling look at the nature of the modern patient-physician relationship. He has experienced both sides of this relationship in very profound ways. He has had a long career as an emergency physician who has dealt with countless very stressful and life-saving challenges in his everyday work. I consider myself very privileged to have both trained and worked alongside him early in our careers. Dr. Remignanti has also been a patient who has confronted and struggled with multiple, very serious life-altering medical problems. Through these two lenses, he has examined and presented a detailed and thoroughly researched analysis of the current state of medicine as it pertains to the patient-physician relationship. Moreover, while weaving in fascinating stories about facing and overcoming adversity as an emergency physician and as a patient, he provides guidance on how to rebalance and regain trust in this relationship in order to optimize medical outcomes for all involved. The reader is taken on a very thoughtful journey and is left with real hope for the future of medicine.

—Don Middleton, MD

Drew Remignanti, in his book *The Healing Connection*, skillfully weaves compelling stories from his medical career and his own experiences as a patient suffering from chronic disease with extensive research into all aspects of the physician-patient relationship. The result is a meticulous dissection of modern medicine that lays bare the flaws and failures of our current healthcare system and makes the case for a renewed emphasis on primary care and the connection between doctors and their patients. This book is a clarion call and a guide for reform at all levels of healthcare delivery to prioritize and protect the sacredness of these healing relationships and should be widely read by medical providers and patients alike.

—**Karen M. Wyatt, MD**
Hospice Physician, Podcast Host, Spiritual Teacher, Speaker,
Author of Award-Winning Book *7 Lessons for Living from the Dying*
End of Life University – Real talk about life and death (eolupodcast.com)
www.eoluniversity.com
www.karenwyattmd.com

Leonardo, like great artists, drew lines. He drew lines to illustrate. When he filled the lines with color, he illuminated. Like the artist, Remignanti draws the lines to illustrate. He takes our eye to the data, the science. He offers the facts. He illustrates. Then he adds the rich colors of his experience as a physician, the stories of hurt and healing. There he illuminates. He crosses the lines of illustration, draws our minds into a new vision, and then blends his own deep spiritual insight to create his masterwork. Remignanti makes the conversation personal. Rather than critiquing a health care system in distress, he guides the reader to place himself in the portrait. He tells us where we fit in the picture and how we may behave to make art of our own lives. This is a book that changes the way one lives.

—**Jeffrey Salloway, PhD**
Professor Emeritus, University of New Hampshire
After a career of teaching and research in medical schools, nursing schools, and as a chairman of health management, Dr. Salloway has turned his efforts to writing. His novel, *The Binding of Isaac*, is published by Winter Goose Publishing. The Binding of Isaac: Salloway, Jeffrey: 9781941058930: Amazon.com: Books

THE HEALING CONNECTION

A Partnership for your Health

Drew Remignanti, MD, MPH

Printed in the United States of America
First Printing: 2023

ISBN: 978-1-954102-15-6
Library of Congress Control Number: 2023942744

Edited by Beth Rule, Eileen Maddocks
Cover design by Veronica Coello
Interior design by Amit Dey

Published by:
SOMETHING OR OTHER PUBLISHING LLC
Brooklyn, Wisconsin 53521
For general inquiries: Info@SOOPLLC.com
For bulk orders: Orders@SOOPLLC.com

"*Illness is the night side of life, a more onerous citizenship. Everyone who is born holds dual citizenship, in the kingdom of the well and in the kingdom of the sick. Although we all prefer to use the good passport, sooner or later each of us is obliged, at least for a spell, to identify ourselves as citizens of that other place.*"

—Susan Sontag, *Illness as Metaphor*

To the memory of my parents Jack Werner Remignanti and June Kelsey Remignanti for the love and education that they gave me. Also, to my wife Darby Johnson and our son Cooper Remignanti for their continued love and support throughout this entire process.

CONTENTS

AUTHOR'S NOTE

For those readers who, like me, prefer to read with a book in your hands, please do yourself a favor and have the companion ebook alongside for easy access to hyperlinks for the more than 250 digital references in this book which confirm and elaborate upon the points that we will be considering. Every digital reference has been hyperlinked within the body of the text for ease of access—no need to go to the Notes to find the web address (URL) and type in yourself.

As a critical starting point, I want to say that I have the utmost respect for and concern still for the patients that I have encountered throughout my career. I want to express my extreme gratitude for the lessons that they were able to teach me.

If in the moment, I fell short of the standard of conduct with them that both they and I would have preferred, I can only sincerely apologize for that at this current moment in time. There's a long-standing tradition in medicine to present patient cases in an anonymous fashion to our colleagues in conferences, or in professional or lay publications, so that we can all learn and improve our medical skills from that particular patient encounter, necessarily including that patient's unique suffering and course of illness.

The ability to learn from these presentations hinges upon the very specific details unique to each patient. In the course of this book, I will present multiple such patient encounters. Due to the nature of my emergency medicine work, I cannot now know, or learn these patients' names at this point, to facilitate any efforts to seek those specific patients' permissions to describe their cases.

My concern now is that these specific, unique details may by extreme coincidence allow a reader to indirectly identify themselves or someone else they know. If that turns out to be the case, at this point I can only profusely apologize for any distress that may cause you or them.

In similar circumstances, I have found my medical colleagues somewhat cautiously resorting to the strategy of calling these 'hypothetical' patients. I have chosen to reject that strategy under the belief that it seems to me even more disrespectful to be referred to as 'hypothetical' than seeing your own real suffering portrayed. To strip those patient portrayals of the details of their real and fully felt suffering seems equally disrespectful to me, so I have chosen to leave the details intact in order to reflect the inherent lessons that I think accompany them. I have been equally, and perhaps even more so, frank about my own health details, perhaps veering into TMI (too much information) at times. I wish all readers well, whether we have met before or not.

I want to now add here the entire text of a retirement note that I sent to my coworkers at my final job. I particularly wanted to share these similar sentiments with all of those individuals with whom I've had the honor and pleasure to work throughout my entire career in medicine.

April 19, 2020

Hello folks,

Turned 67 years old today with the sobering realization that I'm now substantially closer to 70 than to 60 (which I fought back with the philosophy that I adopted back when I turned 50, that it's not until age 90 that you're really old, and even then only if you give into it). Also, happy birthday today to Mary A. who shares 4/19 with me.

With only two shifts left, 4/20 and 22, I also realized that I might not see some of you before I leave. I have been thinking about this ever since the dinner gathering was proposed several months back, in the time BCE (before the corona era), that is, any parting comments I might want to make and came up with several dozen or so. That seemed excessive, so I've narrowed it down to just three.

Firstly, I think it should be pretty clear by now that patience and subtlety are not my strong suits. So, I want to clarify that if anything I've ever said or done, or written in an email, came across to anybody as a personal attack, be reassured that it's never been my intention to call into question anyone's character, intelligence, or commitment.

Next, looking back over my jobs since finishing residency, I counted 10 different jobs involving 12 different hospitals (couple of dual hospital positions in there). You guys will probably have fewer I'm guessing, since I ended up bouncing around a bit following my stroke in '92 (absent my stroke I might've spent the balance of my career at what I'll now call MSH). But probably the most surprising statistic in there is that I was only ever fired from one job!

Little bit of a long-winded way of getting around to my second point which is, if at any time since finishing my residency in '83 you had ever told me that I would be spending 13 years of my career at (what I'll now call MLH), I would've been very skeptical and asked why would I, and how could I, put up with that? The answer to that is you guys! Not just you guys of course; the nurses especially, secretaries, interpreters, EMS, and all the various ED tech and ancillary people who keep the department running were a very important part of my time at MLH too, but mostly you guys. That's because truly only we know what it's like to do what we do in emergency medicine (the nurses of course have the closest similar insight, and no doubt have their own unique stressors and indignities to deal with). It's a heavy burden of responsibility for other people's well-being that I'm ready to put down after 40 years (I am exercising major restraint here not to go on and on about this and related themes). You folks currently have the additional challenge of that burden now being able to reach back out and literally harm you, in addition to its ever-present ability to figuratively drive you crazy. You have all made this time in my life very tolerable, and even fun at times. So, thank you for helping to carry me through these final 13 years of my career.

This third point I would not have spontaneously brought up myself, but the original emails that went out about the possible dinner gathering had pointed out the coinciding of my retirement with the one-year anniversary of Medichart, and I could not bring myself to let that go unremarked upon. Again, if you had predicted to me that an EMR (electronic medical record) company and product would come along that was less responsible, less rational, and less healthcare literate than our patient population, I wouldn't have believed that was possible. However, I would have reassured myself by the thought that there's no way we would ever touch such a thing with a 10-foot pole. Shows you the severe limitations of my powers of prediction. Thanks again for carrying me through this final year.

Lastly, yes, I realize that's four, but related to my second point, I feel like I'm not very easy to impress but the way you folks have been operating both individually and as a department in this constantly moving target environment of COVID-19 has been truly admirable. Watching you all gear up and intubate left and right without hesitation does appear truly heroic (loose use of that word heroic usually makes me cringe, but in this case it's fully justified!). I loved that Cortext picture caption "Michelle K. MD/astronaut". I'll be forever grateful that you younger folks were willing to uncomplainingly shoulder part of the additional burden of covering for and shielding us, your older colleagues; that is truly selfless and generous beyond comparison. A final thank you for your assistance in shepherding me safely through these last days of my career. I can't help but feel like I'm bailing out on you all now and parachuting to a lower and safer level of existence.

So, rock on you MD/PA/NP/astronauts and all the rest of the department too. Plus be safe out there!

Luck and love (yes, love) to you all, Drew

FOREWORD

In his book, *The Healing Connection: A Partnership for Your Health*, Drew Remignanti, MD, MPH, an emergency medicine physician offers a frank and 'no holds barred' commentary about both the strengths and weaknesses of the US healthcare system based on his 40 years of clinical practice experience. He describes how we continue to incentivize fragmented and episodic sick care while devaluing primary care, disease prevention, and health promotion.

Dr. Remignanti goes beyond this, however, to share his remarkable professional and personal life journey in coping with the experience of health and illness—both *in caring for patients* and *as a patient*—in an often-dysfunctional healthcare system. His compelling story illustrates the power and importance of the five Rs—reflection, relationships, recovery, resilience, and resolve. Cultivating connectedness and authentic healing relationships with each other is crucial for positive outcomes.

In its seminal 2021 report, *Implementing High-Quality Primary Care: Rebuilding the Foundation of Health Care,* The National Academy of Sciences, Engineering, and Medicine states:

> *High-quality primary care is the foundation of a high-functioning health care system…. [It] provides continuous, person-centered, relationship-based care that considers the needs and preferences of individuals, families, and communities. Absent access to high-quality primary care, minor health problems can spiral into chronic disease, care management becomes difficult and uncoordinated, visits to emergency departments increase, preventive care lags, and the nation's health care spending soars to unsustainable levels.*[1]

Unfortunately, the Millbank Memorial Fund subsequently documented in the "first national primary care scorecard…a chronic lack of adequate support for the implementation of high-quality primary care in the United States across all measures, although performance varies across states."[2]

In this well-written, important, and timely book, Dr. Remignanti issues a clarion call about the critical need to strengthen our primary healthcare infrastructure. In particular, he discusses the negative impact of the increasing commoditization of healthcare. As we move to value-based models of care, there is a need to change the financial incentives to fully support primary care, address the social and environmental determinants of health, and transform our health profession's education and training programs. Embracing 'high tech' can and should go hand-in-hand with 'high touch' care.

As a family physician, medical educator, and primary care health services researcher, I would completely agree! We need to meet the Quintuple Aim of improved patient experiences, better population health outcomes, reduced costs, increased clinician/staff well-being, and greater health equity. Recognizing the centrality of person-centered care and the patient-practitioner relationship; fostering empathy and compassion; making appropriate use of health information and digital health technologies; and pursuing justice, equity, diversity, and inclusion (JEDI) in health and healthcare also needs to be emphasized.

Rather than just providing an academic discussion of the above issues, Dr. Remignanti reflects on and shares his personal and professional experiences with health and illness. He weaves together a mix of compelling real-world stories relating to himself, his education and training, his family, his patients, his professional colleagues, and the hospitals and healthcare settings in which he has worked. In the tradition of narrative medicine and the health humanities, this book is also a *pathography* that includes his own autobiographical accounts, perspectives, and lived experiences with various illnesses and their treatment.

Drew and I first met as undergraduate students at Dartmouth College in 1973 during a Foreign Study elective in the Kingdom of Tonga in Western Polynesia. He was majoring in Geology/Earth Sciences, and I was majoring in Anthropology. Our long plane trip to Tonga was quite eventful. We arrived just after a major Pacific storm had struck the island and made the first night landing in the island's history on a muddy dirt runway lit up by lanterns and flares. We later learned there was only a limited amount of fuel left so it was either land or ditch in the ocean. Drew and I were sitting next to each other during the long flight. I recall saying that we were fortunate to be alive and living on "borrowed time." Our three-month stay in Tonga was otherwise an extremely meaningful and transformative one. After graduation, we both went on to pursue careers as physicians—Drew in Emergency Medicine and Public Health, and myself in Family Medicine.

Dr. Remignanti discusses his own experiences with a host of significant chronic illnesses, complex treatment regimens, multiple surgeries, residual disabilities, and the psychosocial sequelae. The long-term toll of these illnesses on his professional work and personal and family life, as well as his recovery, resilience, and resolve, is powerfully described. He also reports on his positive and negative encounters receiving care from a variety of medical specialists, rehabilitation professionals, behavioral health clinicians, and other social service providers. He notes the critical importance of having a primary care physician who serves as a trusted healer, guide, and advocate in helping him receive the needed care and navigate through the complex service delivery system.

Dr. Remignanti also makes the real (and not television) world of emergency medicine come alive by sharing memorable clinical case vignettes about the wide variety of patients he and his colleagues have cared for in their busy, stressful, and often chaotic emergency rooms. These include patients of all ages with serious and life-threatening conditions; physical, sexual, and psychosocial traumas; acute and chronic illnesses; mental illness and addictions; pregnancy-related issues; rare diseases; distress related to social determinants of health (e.g., housing, food, and financial insecurity), and the 'worried well,' to name just a few.

The challenges of working in emergency medicine are candidly discussed, including dealing with clinical ambiguity and uncertainty; prioritizing and appropriate triaging; multi-tasking and addressing competing demands; performing procedural interventions under challenging conditions; transporting high acuity and complicated patients to other healthcare facilities; communicating about death and dying; risk management and responding to complaints from angry patients, family members, medical colleagues, and health care administrators; and coping with compassion fatigue, burnout, and moral injury. At the same time, the joys and satisfaction of being an emergency medicine physician including the variety of patients seen, frequent saving of lives, ability to 'fix problems,' and positive *esprit de corps* of working as a valuable member of an interprofessional team are also well described.

Dr. Remignanti's writing style is forthright, engaging, and authentic. You experience his 'ups and downs' throughout the narrative including his uncertainties and fears, his frustrations and anger, his sadness and aloneness, his desire for connection and relationship, his search for meaning and purpose, his hopes and dreams, and most of all his resilience and resolve. The clinical case scenarios shared are grounded, and at times quite stark and raw. You can almost see, hear, taste, smell, and touch what is going on. He mixes pathos with humor which at times is self-deprecating, dry, and dark, but always well intended.

Dr. Remignanti also discusses published research that addresses issues including the US healthcare system in comparison to other countries; the politics and economics of healthcare; the history of medicine and the doctor-patient relationship; the biopsychosocial model of care; strategies for eliciting patient health and illness beliefs; *compassionomics*; clinical reasoning and potential biases; the placebo and nocebo effect; complementary and alternative medicine; the COVID pandemic's impact; medical errors, making apologies, and malpractice lawsuits; the value of interprofessional teamwork; overuse and underuse and cost-effective clinical practice; burnout and moral injury in the workplace; and ethics, spirituality, and religion in healthcare.

The Healing Connection: A Partnership for Your Health will be of significant interest to both professional and lay audiences, especially those who are working to strengthen our primary care infrastructure and transform our healthcare delivery system to provide more comprehensive and integrative person-centered care. This excellent and informative book should be read by physicians from all medical specialties, residents, medical students, clinicians from other health professions' disciplines, health care administrators, and policymakers.

Dr. Remignanti's observations and recommendations about primary care and our healthcare system are well worth heeding. His inspirational professional and personal life story demonstrates courage, determination, fortitude, and resilience. There are many powerful and enduring lessons for us all to learn!

—Robert C. Like, MD, MS
Emeritus Professor of Family Medicine and Community Health
Rutgers Robert Wood Johnson Medical School
Founder and CEO, JEDI Health Care and Education, LLC
(JEDI = Justice, Equity, Diversity, and Inclusion)
Website: www.jedihealthcare.com

INTRODUCTION

To start with a warning, I am by nature an impatient person. Therefore, I feel guilty (but only marginally so) for petitioning the reader's patience in considering the following prolonged argument. My goal is to convince the reader to carefully choose a qualified primary care physician through whom they can fully understand and agree to all diagnostic and treatment decisions. Besides the inherent personal satisfaction of establishing such a meaningful connection, the reader stands to benefit in three ways. Firstly, they can reduce their mortality rate risk by 50% (seriously, multiple published scientific studies will be presented later to support this claim). A second benefit is avoiding or successfully controlling many common chronic disease conditions. The third and final benefit is increasing the odds of avoiding having to consult an emergency physician such as myself!

At the start of my college education, I had only distant and dispassionate thoughts about health and healing, consistent with my lack of any significant illness experiences or interest in medicine as a career. It

was therefore eye-opening and memorable to see in an abnormal psychology class images of skulls from thousands of years ago that had
undergone trepanation, the process by which a hole is created in the
skull, speculatively to 'let out bad spirits' for treatment of conditions
like headaches, seizures, and mental illness. The evident signs of bone
healing and even repeat episodes of these procedures on the same skull
show that the patients actually survived these experiences. Of course, all
of the attendant details regarding the how and why of such aggressive
interventions are lost to history, along with who was nervy enough to
conceive of and attempt such a violation.

Again, curious but distant and dispassionate thoughts. What a surprise then to find myself some eight years later making a diagnosis that
required this exact procedure. I was a fourth-year medical student doing
my emergency medicine rotation when I saw a particular six-year-old
child. She was brought in by her mother who had been told by the
child's pediatrician that she "likely has just a viral illness" (a very common and, more often than not, very accurate conclusion). Her mother
was concerned, though, because the child was becoming progressively
more listless and was more specifically listing to one side. My examination showed that she was able to keep herself seated upright on the
stretcher but was clearly leaning to her left side.

I don't recall her having any specific complaints or the mother
providing additional information, but she had definite physical exam
findings of an extremely enlarged right pupil with a distinct abnormality on the back of the retina referred to as papilledema or a 'choked disc.'
This condition occurs when pressure within the skull impinges on the
back of the retina causing swelling around the optic nerve as it leaves
the eye. My speculation remains that these findings were either not yet
present, or nowhere near as advanced, when she was in the pediatrician's
office as they were now, just a day later, in the ER.

In fairly quick procession, after my findings were confirmed by the
attending emergency physician, a CAT scan of her head showed the
unusual finding of a unilateral (one-sided) hydrocephalus (excessive

fluid within the brain's ventricles) of the right side of her brain, and the neurosurgeon was soon at her bedside. After explaining his findings to her mother, which included her distinctly worsening lethargy in our presence, along with a slowing heart rate and rising blood pressure, he recommended an emergency procedure immediately, to be followed by more definitive surgery later.

So, right there in the ER (it was still just one really large room in 1980, unlike today), in her own little curtained-off cubicle, he shaved off a patch of hair over her right frontal scalp, injected a local anesthetic, and made an incision through her scalp right down to the surface of her skull. What he did next was likely only made possible in that setting by the degree of her abnormal sedation. He took a hand-cranked drill and bored through the skull with a drill bit, as parts of her skull were forced up through the grooves in the bit. Then, taking a narrow flexible red rubber catheter with a side hole near the tip, he inserted a thin metal reinforcing rod in parallel with it and pushed the combination right down through her brain into the enlarged ventricle space.

Up until that point, I had been a stunned, speechless observer, and it was both somewhat reassuring and also unnerving to see that the neurosurgeon was perspiring a little bit as well. Trying to make sense of and clarify what I was seeing, I couldn't restrain myself from asking, "Aren't you going right through the brain there?" He came back with, "Yes, but it's a silent area of the brain." I thought to myself, but did manage to restrain myself from saying, "Well, it sure is now." To clarify, the frontal lobe of the brain that this tube had to pass through does not have an assigned specific sensory or motor function but is involved in emotional processing. So, presumably, the loss of the limited number of cells that the tube had to cleave through in order to get into the ventricle would not be immediately apparent and would be able to be overcome. The advantage achieved was that with finger-pinch pressure he controlled the catheter drainage of cerebrospinal fluid from her right ventricle. As he did this, we could all see her right pupil gradually shrink down to its normal size from the relief of the pressure on its motor nerve, as well as her becoming progressively more responsive. She successfully underwent the more extensive and complete cerebral shunt procedure the next day, and I decided that emergency medicine might just be the right place for me.

Even more inconceivable and disruptive was to find myself some twelve years later, at age 38, being offered a more refined and complicated version of a skull opening procedure by my own neurosurgeon. I had awoken at daybreak from a brief catnap in the physician call room where I was now an emergency medicine attending physician, at the very end of my night shift, only to have my staff tell me that I needed to take off my white coat, get on a stretcher, and become a patient. Turns out that, unbeknownst to me, I was in the midst of having a major stroke!

My newly acquired personal neurosurgeon was explaining my x-ray and physical exam findings, along with the option of immediate surgery. I had already experienced four of my seven abdominal surgeries, so I had no qualms about the general anesthesia risks or 'going under the knife.'

However, I found myself distinctly squeamish and resistant to the prospect of having my skull opened with somebody mucking about in there. I had foolishly managed to ignore some stroke-warning symptoms and had subsequently completely clotted off my right middle cerebral artery at its origin (one of the major arteries deep in the right side of the brain), and so the on-call neurosurgeon was collegially offering to go in there to manually remove the clot (at that time…March 2, 1992…clot-dissolving thrombolytic drugs were still investigational, and intra-arterial catheter clot removal was decades away). Given my lack of enthusiasm for this suggestion and some visible, though minor, improvement, rather than any worsening in my condition, we jointly opted for medical management over surgical, a decision that I have never regretted.

This is a book consisting of reflections on health and healing, and the crucial importance of those distinct moments of joint decision-making between patient and physician. I only very briefly considered making this a completely objective and dispassionate review. Having had a lifetime of experiencing and encountering illness both personally and professionally, I quite quickly concluded that I no longer felt particularly distant or dispassionate about this topic.

Dispassionate data does tell us the following, though:

1. In 2010 the US spent 17.6% of its gross domestic product on health care (19.7% as of 2020), which was 1.5 times as much as any other country and nearly twice the average of the 38 Organization for Economic Cooperation and Development (OECD) nations. I am intentionally using somewhat dated and thus pre-COVID data here.[3]

2. A 2011 Commonwealth report found that the United States had the highest percentage of respondents saying that their healthcare system was in need of fundamental change or complete rebuilding (>70%).[4]

3. Currently over 50% of physicians report burnout in their profession;[5] physicians have the highest suicide rate by profession (see Chapter Ten); and suicide is more common in medical school than in any other school setting.[6]

4. Estimates (in 2017) ranged as high as over $200 billion per year being spent in the US on "unnecessary and wasteful" testing and treatment interventions.[7]

5. Studies show that patients understand only half or less of the medical advice that they are given.[8]

This data makes it clear that serious trouble involving both sides of the physician-patient connection is brewing within the US healthcare system. My goal in this book is to sketch out some of the reasons why we have arrived at this sad state of affairs and also to propose some possible solutions. To state it most succinctly, we have lost sight of the critical importance of the patient-physician relationship, and we have allowed dollar-driven decision-making to override patient-centered decision-making. We must therefore commit ourselves both personally and societally to the extremely difficult but necessary work of reversing both of those trends.

In the United States we are suffering a crisis of confidence in our healthcare system. Having experienced the system extensively from the inside, I can admit that there are definite reasons for concern and caution. This appears to leave us, when we are ill, feeling uncertain about where to turn. In fact, returning to our opening consideration of trepanation, I've learned that there is actually an International Trepanation Advocacy Group (ITAG) endorsing the recovery and modern use of that 'lost art.'[9] Apparently, some devotees advocate doing this only in a medical setting, while amazingly not just one but several people have performed self-trepanation at home!

Without informed or expert knowledge and guidance, we can make some unusual and inadvisable choices as patients. How have we ended up in this position where we now distrust professional medical judgment so much that some of us have ended up drilling holes in our heads at home in order to feel better?

Americans consistently report that their greatest concern regarding our healthcare system is how they are going to get their healthcare paid for (a concern that I do share). However, I believe that there are even more imperative issues. In fact, I would go so far as to say that we are experiencing a near public health emergency in the United States currently. We, as both patients and/or as physicians, are under both overt and covert pressures to interact with our healthcare system in ways that are potentially harmful to our health.

Fortunately, many of us will neither develop a severe structural abnormality as my young patient did, nor develop a chronic disease process as I myself did. On the other hand, the number of structural abnormalities and the variety of disease processes that we are subject to as human beings is truly staggering, and medical suffering of one form or another inevitably finds us all.

My specialty is emergency medicine, which I see as the mud wrestling equivalent of our profession. We do not often see people when they are at their best, nor do we always find ourselves as our best selves. I have been a physician both learning and practicing emergency medicine for 40 years. But I've also been a patient for longer than that, having first become chronically ill at age 19.

Lest the reader feel sorry for me, let me quickly clarify that I haven't been ill for all, or even most, of that time. It is true, though, that I was symptomatic with my ulcerative colitis to one degree or another every single day of the entire decade of my 20s. I have a lengthy abdominal scar where my surgeons have gone in seven different times, plus a similar number of nonoperative hospitalizations, leading up to but not culminating with that stroke in 1992, at age 38.

I mention this to additionally establish my credentials as a patient, in order to demonstrate that I've had experience from both sides of the bed, that is both inside and alongside the patient care bed. Therefore, I have divided loyalties, both to us as patients, and to those of us trying to assist patients.

I remain disappointed that after all that experience, I don't have greater clarity on a lot of the relevant issues, and an alternate subtitle to this book could have been, 'Things that continue to confuse and disturb me about health and healing.' Unfortunately for you, as you may have already realized, I will not herein present heartwarming tales of health and healing. However, I did conclude my career entirely convinced that there is a great healing power and potential within the physician-patient relationship, a relationship that can be more effectively pursued outside of the emergency department.

I plan to advance and support the following thesis regarding what is best for us to do to address our healthcare needs:

1. We all need to consult with the most competent physicians that we can find and access.

2. We should do substantial independent investigation of what we are told and ask all the questions that are necessary in order to dispel our doubts.

3. We then need to, in partnership with our physicians, precisely follow that mutually agreed upon plan, without fail.

I know that may sound terribly anachronistic and paternalistic and the following questions arise: What about nurses, nurse practitioners, and physician assistants? What about nonmainstream complementary and alternative medicine (CAM), and its practitioners? What if I don't agree with my physician's advice? Why so much emphasis on physicians?

A quick set of responses on my part would be yes, you can supplement your healthcare with any number of healers and healing measures, but you can't just leave out the physician. If you disagree with a recommendation, you can get a second or third physician opinion, but you must ultimately choose and follow one. The uniqueness of the physician's role will be explored and discussed at length, along with the critical importance of our becoming fully informed and involved participants as patients. What separates this from the paternalism of the past is that uniquely important step number two. In that step, we choose to commit ourselves to engage with our physicians to the extent of our capabilities, so that we can educate ourselves to be confidently 'all in' with regard to our healthcare.

Absent achieving this new paradigm of a patient-physician partnership, I believe that US healthcare will continue along its merry way of going to 'hell in a handbasket'!

CHAPTER ONE

WHERE ARE WE AND HOW DID WE GET HERE?

In the course of this book, I will expand on my claim that US healthcare is going to hell in a handbasket. At this point, let me share a quote from Dr. Raymond Tallis from his 2004 book *Hippocratic Oaths: Medicine and Its Discontents,* in which he states:

> *I believe that medicine is in danger of being irreversibly corrupted. This threat comes not from within (where its values are struggling to survive) but from society at large. ... The patient's indifference to the cause of the doctor's hurry—not infrequently the needs of another patient—points to something that has rarely been noted. In a condition of scarcity, every patient is the direct or indirect enemy of every other patient. The current demand for time (and the attention that goes with it) is potentially limitless and the quantity available is finite. Over the last few years, the*

gap between expected and available time is widening—and it
will get wider.[10]

Instructive here is that Dr. Tallis is not writing about the US healthcare system. Instead, he is a British physician (a neuroscientist, specializing in geriatrics) who spent his lengthy clinical career working in the National Health Service of the UK. It is thought-provoking that a physician working in a healthcare system that is financed in an entirely different fashion than ours in the United States has apparently identified a similar dilemma.

Public confidence in the US healthcare system is low, with only 23% expressing "a great deal or quite a lot" of confidence in the system (Gallup 2014). Indeed, the level of public trust in physicians as a group in the United States ranks near the bottom of trust levels in the 29 industrialized countries surveyed by the International Social Survey Program (ISSP) from 2011 to 2013, according to *The New England Journal of Medicine*:

> *The United States is unique among the surveyed countries in that it ranks near the bottom in the public's trust in the country's physicians but near the top in patients' satisfaction with their own medical treatment.*[11]

I find this lack of confidence in our healthcare system discouraging, but not surprising. My own opinion here is that I do not reflexively trust 'the system' either. There are fairly intense feelings of distrust, disappointment, and anger on both sides of the patient-physician relationship. I hear those feelings on both sides, and I get it!

The part that I find immensely encouraging is that the United States ranks high in patients' satisfaction with their own medical treatment, and I believe this is the foundation upon which we can build a better healthcare system. The system is as it is, but I can't change it as a patient or solely as an individual doctor, either. However, I can choose to change how I act as a patient with my doctor and together we can change our small system. Then ultimately the entire system might have to change in order to accommodate what the majority of patient and physician systems together want.

During the course of researching this book, I received a written reply from someone working in the book-publishing industry stating:

> *I receive 2-3 queries similar to yours each week which is extremely distressing. Healthcare professionals writing about the poor quality of the health care system in the US. There are already a lot of books out there and soon to be published as well. Maybe there needs to be an online forum where health care providers can communicate with each other and figure out how to make a difference. We desperately need change.*

In response to her, I wrote:

> *I regret having to unfortunately add to your 'distress.' Both broadly amongst the physician community, and within my own EM specialty, there already are such forums, along with a significant consensus of how and where changes should be made. It's a perfectly logical thought and hope within the non-medical community that physicians should be able to confer amongst ourselves, identify, and then improve upon the shortcomings of our US healthcare system. The sad fact of the matter though is that we physicians are no longer steering the healthcare ship, the helm of which is currently in the hands of administrative and financial folks (only some of whom are physicians) with little to no direct clinical medical experience (or even interest!).*

Many of those decision-makers are making money hand over fist (six- to nine-figure annual compensation at the executive level at health insurance and pharmaceutical companies, as well as at hospitals, even at the 'nonprofit' ones).[12, 13, 14, 15] So, not surprisingly, there is little evidence of substantial incentive to make changes. Politicians themselves appear preoccupied by maintaining their elected positions and complying with partisan political dogma. Thus, they similarly lack motivation to bring about substantial change. In essence, those who have the incentive to alter US healthcare (patients and physicians) lack the power to do so, while those who have the power to do so (politicians and administrators) lack the incentive.

Dr. Paul Batalden (pediatrician and Professor Emeritus of Pediatrics at the Geisel School of Medicine at Dartmouth College) made an observation that is apropos here, "Every system is perfectly designed to get the results it gets." So, if we prioritize high-tech, high-cost, acute-curative interventions over lower cost preventative and health-sustaining interventions, then we end up with the system that we have right now.

The following are two conclusions from a more recent 2020 Commonwealth Fund report:

- *The U.S. spends more on health care as a share of the economy— nearly twice as much as the average OECD country,* and
- *has the lowest life expectancy and highest suicide rates.*[16]

Casual readers would have picked up the same information from a *Time* magazine headline in 2014, "US Health Care Ranked Worst in the Developed World,"[17] which was based on that year's version of a similar Commonwealth report. But it would take a closer reading of the just mentioned 2020 report to encounter these additional conclusions:

> *The U.S. has one of the highest rates of hospitalizations for preventable conditions and the highest rate of avoidable deaths. ... the U.S. continues to have the highest rates of premature deaths from causes such as diabetes, hypertensive diseases, and certain cancers — all considered preventable with timely access to primary care and good chronic disease management.*[18]

The U.S. has the highest chronic disease burden and an obesity rate that is two times higher than the OECD average. [19]

Deeper research would then reveal this other telling data.

1. From a Journal of the American Medical Association (JAMA) 2019 article:

   The United States spends more on health care than any other country, with costs approaching 18% of the gross domestic product (GDP). Prior studies estimated that approximately 30% of health care spending may be considered waste. Despite efforts to reduce overtreatment, improve care, and address overpayment, it is likely that substantial waste in US health care spending remains. [20]

2. From Statista regarding 2017:

   America has the highest drug-death rate in North America and the world. 'A problem in many countries, the harm caused by opioids is particularly evident in the United States of America,' the United Nations Office on Drugs and Crime (UNODC) concludes in its (2017) report. [21]

3. From a Commonwealth Fund issue brief, October 8, 2015:

   In the US, healthcare spending substantially outweighs spending on social services. This imbalance may contribute to the country's poor health outcomes. A growing body of evidence suggests that social services play an important role in shaping health trajectories and mitigating health disparities. [22]

I have the same reaction that most people likely do to reading these kinds of headlines and study results, which is that we are certainly not getting our money's worth here. However, I also have another reaction, that is, we need to do, and can be doing, a much better job as both patients and physicians, and that healthcare is as much a responsibility as it is a right.

Neither as physicians nor as patients do we have much direct control over healthcare costs or administrative- and governmental-level decision-making. But we do have quite specific control over what we choose to do individually as patients and as physicians, and even more importantly what we choose to do in partnership with each other.

Three more observations:

1. In the last quarter of 2017, for the first time in history, healthcare surpassed manufacturing and retail to become the largest source of jobs in the US.[23]

2. It is fairly widely known that historically hospitals began as nonprofit humanitarian, usually charitable, religion-based institutions. Less well known though is that the health insurance industry itself also began as a nonprofit venture, originally with Blue Cross in Texas in 1929 (recall the aforementioned current executive pay scales).[24]

3. Nearly half of US hospital-based healthcare now takes place in emergency departments.[25]

Due to these last three factors, top-down changes are unlikely to ever happen spontaneously in the US healthcare industry, given that so many people benefit from its current structure and functions.

We patients have certainly contributed to the creation and perpetuation of this predicament. The *JAMA* 2015 article "The Arc of Health Literacy" notes:

> ...*only about 12% of US adults had a proficient state of health literacy whereby 'individuals can obtain, process and understand the basic health information and services they need to make appropriate health decisions'.... US adults scored below the international average for literacy, numeracy, and problem solving in technology-rich environments.*[26]

So, we definitely have our work cut out for ourselves both individually and societally as patients. But I firmly believe that our physicians are more than willing to meet us halfway and help us to become more knowledgeable/literate and, as the phrase goes in the medical literature, 'activated' as patients (i.e., having the knowledge, skills, and confidence to play an active role in the management of our own healthcare).

Let's now briefly move back in time some 2,500 years for a whirlwind historical perspective on where we started. There are surviving ancient Egyptian documents (e.g., the Ebers and Smith papyri) addressing medical ideas and treatment interventions dating back to 1600 BC. However, Hippocrates in Greece in 460 BC is considered the 'Father of Medicine.' He proposed that diseases were caused naturally, and he separated the discipline of medicine from religion.[27]

Hippocrates believed and argued that disease was not a punishment inflicted by the gods, but rather the product of environmental factors, diet, and living habits. He promoted the principle of 'First Do No Harm'[28] and first systematized the existing humoral theory of disease.[29]

Humoral theory proposed the four basic humors within the human body as blood, yellow bile, black bile, and phlegm, corresponding to the four natural elements of air, fire, earth, and water, and the four human temperaments of sanguine, choleric, melancholic, and phlegmatic. Though clearly not 'evidence-based' in the modern scientific meaning, there is speculation that perhaps observation of the natural separation over time of collected blood into a darker clotted blood layer, an unclotted red blood cell layer, serum, and possibly a white blood cell layer may have lent credence to this otherwise far-fetched theory.

Either way, this humoral theory led to a long tradition of bloodletting and other interventions to 'balance the humors.' Bloodletting enjoyed a three-thousand-year popularity up until the late nineteenth century. One example of the application of this medical theory is the following condensed version of the recorded treatment of King Charles II of England in 1685:

> *The king apparently collapsed with a seizure on a Monday morning, and he had no fewer than fourteen royal physicians. His 'emergency treatment' consisted of being bled off sixteen ounces of blood. His chief physician, Scarburgh, felt this was insufficient and then drew off an additional eight ounces. Unfortunately for the king, he stirred, and this 'auspicious sign' was taken to mean that he would benefit from more fluids being extracted from his body. This Scarburgh did with a 'voluminous emetic' that induced vomiting. Again, his royal majesty stirred, and this time he was given an enema to extract still more ill humors. After a second enema, he was flipped back over, and force fed an oral purgative. He grew breathless. Again, he was bled. But on Wednesday the king suffered more fits. He was bled, then given a draft made from the pulverized skull of an 'innocent man' who had met a 'violent death'. The treatment smacked of homeopathy in that 'forty drops of extract of human skull were administered to allay convulsions,' as Scarburgh wrote, thus attempting to cure a symptom with a 'like' substance. Charles had a fitful night's sleep, though no more fits. At eight-thirty Saturday morning, after 5 days of 'treatment', his speech faltered and failed. At ten he was mercifully comatose. At noon he finally died, a testament to the stamina of the human body.[30]*

Quite at variance with the 'First Do No Harm' principle, wouldn't you say? Also, a pretty specific prescription there that the pulverized skull had to be coming from an 'innocent man' who had met a 'violent death,' as opposed to just any old skull! It's not clear what's more surprising here—that the monarch of England could be treated in this fashion, or that his physicians were so confident in their treatment that they recorded the details this precisely.

If there is a divine creator, can't you just imagine God witnessing such treatments and thinking, "My word, what are they getting up to now? You can't even look away from these people for a minute. They are in serious need of some healthcare instruction, and a greater respect for science!"

Since it was not until the seventeenth century that science itself was first developed as a formalized and critical way of thinking in the Western world, physicians before that time can be understood and forgiven for what now appears to be appallingly deficient, and at times downright harmful, therapeutics.

Nonroyals may have benefited from being spared the same degree of aggressive treatment. Other popular remedies of the day consisted of powdered mummy, unicorn horn, and usnea (which is the moss scraped from the skull of someone who had been hung). Reflecting on this, one modern physician (Arthur Shapiro, MD) wrote, "One might ask how physicians maintained their position of honor and respect throughout history in the face of thousands of years of prescribing what we now know to be useless and often dangerous medications?"[31]

I think it would be equally valid to ask, how did we survive such treatment as patients, and as a species? Shapiro went on to conclude that "the patient responded to something inherent in the doctor-patient relationship." Shapiro also adds, "The effectiveness of the placebo effect lies in the action, ritual, faith and enthusiasm on the part of both the doctor and patient." (Findley, T 1953).

A current and more science-based placebo investigator Fabrizio Benedetti, MD, states it this way: "Humans are endowed with endogenous systems that can be activated by verbally induced positive expectations, therapeutic rituals, healing symbols, and, more generally, by social interactions."[32]

Intriguingly, there are many physicians who have anecdotally reported patients with entirely unanticipated survival from serious illness, or resolution of their cancers without proven focused treatment methods. A well-known example of this phenomenon was reported in a *New York Times* article in 1998, "Placebos Prove So Powerful Even Experts Are Surprised; New Studies Explore the Brain's Triumph Over Reality," which includes description of the case of a 'Mr. Wright.'[33]

I tracked down the original 1957 report by Dr. Bruno Klopfer[34] that this *New York Times* article was based on and confirmed that the details were accurately reported. In this case a patient had cancerous lymph nodes (lymphosarcoma) that waxed and waned in parallel with the strength of his belief in the effectiveness of his ultimately proven ineffective cancer treatment with a drug called Krebiozen. At one point, his cancer nearly vanished after he received an infusion containing only a saline solution, after being told that it was a doubly potent dose of Krebiozen. When he learned of the falsity of that claim, his cancer promptly returned and caused his death.

So as not to rely on anecdotal data, Chapter Seven will present multiple published studies which provide support for Shapiro's conclusions, by way of data and actual brain imaging studies that delve into mind-body interactions and the placebo effect phenomenon. In that same chapter, additional compelling study findings will demonstrate the benefits of closely adhering to medical advice, with the conclusion from one such study in 2011 stating, "High placebo adherence was inversely associated with most outcomes including hip fracture, myocardial infarction, cancer death, and all-cause mortality."[35]

In other words, those patients who chose to adhere more closely to the regimen of the study's placebo medication had far fewer adverse medical events. In fact, over the course of this study, those participants who adhered more closely to placebo use had half the mortality risk of those who were less adherent.

The journey from treating patients with heroic bloodletting, pulverized skulls, and/or skull moss to the point where we can now see images of the specific areas of the brain that are involved in healing illnesses, whether by placebo effect or otherwise, has been tumultuous, but relatively short. The above study/researcher's conclusions, and similar ones, look less surprising when we take into account that for most of our existence as humans there was not only no scientific medicine, but there was also no science at all. The late arrival of science to the stage is described by the historian David Wootton as, "There were no persons called scientists before 1833."[36] In point of fact, medical science arrived even later to the stage, due to religious/societal restrictions against dissecting the human body.

Later chapters will additionally be exploring, in essence, the 'battle for the soul of medicine,' as we both individually and societally try to balance the essential truths of both pre-and post-scientific medicine. During the course of this exploration, I will also point out that religion arrived on the scene many millennia before either science, or medical science itself, only being preceded by injury, illness, and disease themselves. The repercussions of that timing persist until this day. The implications of these facts will be examined, and I will attempt a synthesis of these considerations of human suffering, medical science, and religion in the final chapters.

Humoral theory ultimately gave way to germ theory through the efforts and findings of medical scientists including, but not limited to, Joseph Lister, Ignaz Semmelweis, Louis Pasteur, and Robert Koch, the last of whom convincingly demonstrated the presence of the specific microbes that cause cholera and tuberculosis.

Although we did benefit enormously when some 3,000 years of humoral theory gave way to germ theory and science-based medicine, we have unfortunately adopted the expectation that all medical ailments should be able to be identified as having a single cause and single treatment. This single-cause/single-cure formulation did produce near miraculous results but has not served us well across the board. This is especially true with regard to conditions that have, or may ultimately end up being identified as having, a causal chain rather than a single causative factor. These causal chains can include contributing elements such as genetic susceptibility, possible lifetime environmental exposures, and then a final precipitating event. These medical ailments include autoimmune conditions such as type one diabetes, multiple sclerosis, lupus, ulcerative colitis, and so forth, along with many cancers. I speculate that this type of a causal chain may ultimately become the prevailing explanation in even currently less well understood conditions such as autism and Alzheimer's disease. Regrettably, the single-cause/single-cure formulation can lead us to try to shoehorn a complex disease process into a single more satisfying explanation. I will use my own illness experience here as an illustrative example.

Nineteen-year-olds typically feel bulletproof with respect to their health, since in the normal course of events they tend to be infrequently and only briefly ill. I know that I certainly felt nearly impervious at that age, having completed a year and a half at Dartmouth College, including two successful seasons on the soccer team. This included an enormously satisfying undefeated 1971 freshman soccer season (a 9-0 record, with 38 goals scored and only one goal allowed). It never occurred to me then that I would ever be anything other than 'well' up until the day I dropped dead, preferably on the soccer field itself while playing vigorously at an unreasonably advanced age. This was not fated to be my experience.

Figure 1: Me at age nineteen with my new puppy Dusty. This photo is one that always induces nostalgia in me, being the last picture in which I was fully healthy with all of my original body parts in full working order. In those days, I had a nineteen-year-old's typical mindset of feeling 'bullet proof.' Now I have to leave 'The 70s' behind and deal with my own 70s.

Figure 2: The 1971 photo of our undefeated Dartmouth freshman soccer team (9-0 record with 38 goals scored and only one allowed!). For the sake of friendship and completeness, this rogue's gallery includes, left to right in back: Coach Dud Hendrick, Keith Mierez, Andy MacDowell, Scott Stenhouse, Jack Foley, Al Barstow, Kevin O'Brien, Craig Thompson, John Pittenger, Dean Queathem, Pete Verity, Don Dixon, and Steve Buglione. In front (L-R) is Ron Cima, Michael Caldwell, Mark Porto, Davie Coles, Frank Gallo, Drew Remignanti, Herb Childs, and Bill Keefe. Not pictured: Stu Rolfe.

In mid-February of 1973, I found myself scrambling up the side of Tofua, an active volcanic island in the South Pacific nation of Tonga, in search of the outhouse. I was in the initial stages of a dysentery-type diarrheal illness, and in my distress could not recall the precise location to head off towards, other than the vague notion of diagonally uphill through the dense vegetation.

Having failed to reach the outhouse in time, I stopped and squatted in the full moonlight to relieve myself. Other than the roiling in my bowels, it was an otherwise peaceful scene. I was now on a sparsely vegetated and rocky open space looking across the narrow finger of the Pacific Ocean that separated Tofua from its sister island Kao, a classic peaked but inactive volcanic island. This very stretch of water was near the location of the actual mutiny on the *H.M.A.V. Bounty* in 1789, and we had earlier been shown what the islanders had told us was the gravesite of a British sailor, John Norton. Norton was one of the 18 *Bounty* sailors who were set adrift in a small open boat along with Captain Bligh, and he'd been killed by hostile Tongan islanders after coming on shore.[37]

Figure 3: We are sitting on top of Tofua looking towards the inactive volcano Kao with its snagged clouds and overlooking the strip of Pacific Ocean where the 'mutiny on the Bounty' *loyalist sailors came ashore in 1789. In the forefront is Howie Hawkins (the future Green Party's 2020 presidential nominee) next to Maka'afi who is bearing my red backpack, one that he liked so much that he wouldn't allow us to take turns carrying it, so I gifted it to him when we left. Take note of the palm frond hats that he wove for us on the spot. Repeating history, in 1973 we also appeared unannounced, likely on the very same beach that Captain Bligh and his loyalists came ashore. We had a much better reception though. Maka'afi and his family immediately housed and fed us for a full week, whereas the* Bounty *quartermaster John Norton was killed when the* Bounty *party was attacked by the hostile islanders of that era.*

Figure 4: Maka'afi's cousin and a friend showing us the location that oral legend identifies as John Norton's gravesite on Tofua.

While letting events take their own mutinous course in my own 'below decks,' I was marveling that in the moonlight the clouds that always seem to be snagged on and obscuring Kao's peak throughout the day were still present even now. We were two days into our week-long stay in a small compound of thatch-walled and corrugated tin-roofed huts on this remote tropical island and had yet to see Kao's completely exposed peak. I briefly considered whether it wasn't maybe steam instead that was constantly oozing out of the mountain top, suggesting that it was threatening to come back to life. Tofua itself was less impressive in height, its peak having collapsed into itself forming a central caldera lake, while a new cinder cone was being actively formed along the lake's edge.

Both my thoughts and actions seized up as several snorting, semi-domesticated pigs came cavorting over, having taken notice of me, or more likely my odor. I always have and would still love to see the video replay of this scene, no doubt reasonably well-lit by the ambient moon-light, as I ineffectually tried to shoo them away with flailing arms and

Figure 5: This is me and our local guide Maka'afi surveying the actively steaming new cinder cone on the inner aspect of the collapsed caldera of Tofua. We are trying (and failing) to figure out how to collect a steam sample, as part of my geology independent study project.

the "No, no, no" that you would use with a disobedient family dog. Not surprisingly, this does not work with your semi-feral pig. Mind you now, I did not fear for my safety, but for their, my, and the rest of the compound's ultimate health. These pigs were clearly hell-bent on rooting around in my mess, and no doubt, one day soon, one of them would be set out on our dinner table.

Cooking a pig on an island with no electricity, running water, or routine transportation to or on it proved to be an interesting trick when we first witnessed it ("we" being just a fellow Dartmouth student and I, off on our own from the 15-student contingent on this foreign study program). First you start by digging an appropriate, relatively modest-sized hole in the ground within which you build a substantial fire after covering the bottom with stones. Once the fire has burned down, you cover the resulting embers and heated rocks with seaweed, upon which you place the unfortunate pig that you have dispatched. This is followed by another layer of seaweed before the dirt is placed back over it level with the ground, and *voilà* you have created an 'earth oven.' No doubt that process would have burned off any and all germs and foulness that I may have inadvertently donated to my moonlight friends.

Figure 6: Here is our 1973 Dartmouth foreign study program to the Kingdom of Tonga pregame soccer team photo. From left to right in back are Professor Jon Appleton, George Reynolds, Wayne Waggoner, Ralph Fletcher, Tom Streeter, Gordon Wallace, Clark Cunningham, Matthew Keats, Alan King, and our Tongan liaison. In front L-R are Darrell Vange, Frederic Cann, Howie Hawkins, Drew Remignanti, Doug Vaughan, Andy Krakoff, and Bob Like. Our scrimmage record against the Tongans was a presentable 1-1-1 with our matches played in front of the king, who appeared pleased when we won.

Although I couldn't know it at the time, in retrospect, I suspect that this was the onset of my lifelong chronic illness with ulcerative colitis (UC). UC and Crohn's disease are jointly known as inflammatory bowel disease. Although now somewhat confidently thought to be autoimmune diseases in individuals with a predisposing genetic susceptibility, at that time the etiology was imprecisely understood, with even a psychosomatic etiology as a consideration. This could have been my first bout with the disease itself, or more likely the infectious insult that triggered the autoimmune process that took nearly a year before manifesting itself fully.

UC manifests itself as chronic, intermittent, abdominal cramping with frequent diarrheal episodes, often bloody. Imagine if you will a bad case of gastroenteritis, also known as the GI blues, fortunately minus the vomiting, but with the addition of worse abdominal pains, occasional fevers, and intermittent blood loss. For the fortunate, it is a disease that is manifested by exacerbations and remissions. For the less fortunate, as in my case, it means belonging to the 20% to 30% who never go into remission. Currently there are a number of effective medications available, but still no cure. My fate was one of being allergic to the sulfa-based medication that was the only one available as a specific UC treatment back in 1973. I often thought to myself that it was a condition that 'I would not wish upon my worst enemy,' not that I had any enemies that I was aware of.

At any rate, I was hospitalized for the first time when I was 20 years old, and my formal diagnosis of UC was confirmed. I spent the entire next decade without ever feeling fully well and without ever sleeping completely through the night without a bathroom visit. My ulcerative colitis was considered 'cured' only after I went through the first of my abdominal surgical procedures at age 29, when I had my entire colon removed. I made this choice due to the poorly controlled persistent symptoms, along with a substantially increasing risk of colon cancer at the ten-year mark. Beforehand, I did undergo multiple tests for a possible persistent amoebic infection as a cause for my illness. Both my doctors and I were, not unreasonably, searching for a simpler, more easily treatable solution, given my previous year's experience on Tofua. I had unwisely just earlier that day of my illness slaked my thirst with some untreated post rain groundwater that 'looked safe' in that risky tropical environment. I can still recall my intense disappointment when the 'one-cause/one-cure' diagnosis of an amoebic infection had to be abandoned and replaced by the poorly understood and difficult-to-treat UC diagnosis.

Although it was far more startling and threatening when I subsequently had my stroke, I did find it inherently more satisfying to receive an immediately confirmed diagnosis of a large blood clot blocking off my entire right middle cerebral artery, to explain my near-complete left-sided paralysis. The less satisfying part did manage to raise its ugly head again, though, when none of the typical coagulopathy (abnormally active blood clotting) conditions could be confirmed by testing. All of my involved doctors concluded that my coagulopathy was caused by my UC disease that I had already been 'cured' of ten years earlier!

Said conclusion certainly felt like a kick in the teeth, as it did again in 2019, when I was told that I now have an autoimmune hepatitis condition, again related to my supposedly long-gone UC. The surgeons were correct in that my total colectomy did indeed cure my illness (one cannot have colitis without a colon), but the autoimmune disease process apparently still persists.

CHAPTER TWO

ILLNESS VERSUS DISEASE

A useful and critical distinction that has been made is between illness and disease. Although both can involve significant suffering on the patient's part and one should not necessarily outrank the other hierarchically, the distinction between them is not an arbitrary one since the approaches to their resolutions can differ substantially. In this distinction, illness is what the patient subjectively experiences, while disease is an objectively identifiable pathological structure or function. Fortunately, much of what we suffer through in our lives is illness and not a disease process, though it is still suffering, nevertheless. Many of us will never develop a structural abnormality as my young patient in the ER did, or develop a chronic disease process as I did.

As patients, we really don't care whether we have an illness or a disease; we simply know that we don't feel well and want to feel better. As physicians, that is predominantly what we want for our patients as well, but making the distinction is critical when deciding how to proceed.

The challenge of arriving at accurate diagnostic conclusions and effective treatment plans can be daunting.

Dr. Eric J. Cassell has more colorfully described this distinction as:

> *The word 'illness' to stand for what the patient feels when he goes to the doctor, and 'disease' for what he has on the way home from the doctor's office. Disease, then, is something an organ has; illness is something a man has.*[38]

In his book *The Nature of Suffering and the Goals of Medicine*, Cassell elaborates:

> *The uncomfortable fact remains that doctors cannot get at diseases without dealing with patients – doctors do not treat diseases, they treat patients. Further, the same disease in different individuals may have a different presentation, course, treatment, and outcome depending on individual and group differences among patients – from personal idiosyncrasies to genetic or anatomic variations. The scientific basis of medicine does not recognize nor provide a methodology to deal with such individual variations on the level of patient-doctor interactions. Such issues were relegated to the "art" of medicine or to individual judgment.*[39]

In contrast to the unusual hydrocephalus case presented earlier, a more common confusion regarding illness versus disease is one that I would venture we have all experienced. This is best exemplified by the medical suffering visited upon us by acute respiratory tract infections (ARTI). The following data and comments preceded the recent COVID-19 pandemic which, although not changing the essence of these observations, has made it a far more complex topic. Studies across the US and internationally show that ARTI are always among the top 10 reasons, and in some studies the leading reason, for physician visits. Data for the US in 2018 revealed that 84.3% of adults and 93.6% of children had contact with a doctor or other healthcare professional in the past year, and undoubtedly many of those were for this very reason.

Additionally, upper and lower respiratory tract infections in the US are estimated to be responsible for approximately $15 billion annually in direct treatment costs. On top of this, losses in income of employed persons who miss work because of infection are calculated to exceed $9 billion per year.[40] It is worth noting that these figures are from a 1985 article, and while they are no longer current, their inclusion provides a pre-COVID baseline.

To clarify, respiratory tract infections are indeed a disease process, but more often than not, especially prior to COVID-19, they are one of the more minor disease processes that we can experience. However, the subjective experience of illness they produce can result in a truly disproportionate amount of nearly intolerable associated symptoms, engendering memorable medical suffering. It is natural then for us to assume that such suffering must represent a significant disease process. Who can forget the inability to breathe through the nose, the inability to lie down without coughing, or the discomfort when swallowing, which makes sleep nearly impossible, and thus makes recovery agonizingly slow?

There is universal agreement that most of these ARTI illnesses are the result of benign viral infections (ironically, it is the family of common coronaviruses that is often the culprit here), most of which will be self-limited, and for which antibiotics are inappropriate treatment unless a secondary bacterial co-infection has occurred.

Making that diagnosis of a secondary bacterial coinfection accurately can be surprisingly difficult. Nevertheless, many patients expect and insist on being prescribed antibiotics. They frequently say things like, "Because I always feel better when I take antibiotics when I am sick like this." Here they are quite often erroneously attributing the spontaneous resolution of their viral illness to taking the antibiotics, thus committing the post hoc fallacy (more on this later). Many physicians feel pressured to prescribe the requested antibiotics and do comply (estimates as high as 40% of the time).

This is not good decision-making at either the individual level or in terms of the public health perspective. At the individual level, using antibiotics unnecessarily (they have no effect on viruses) or prematurely can result in eliminating susceptible bacteria (sensitive to the antibiotic and therefore readily eliminated), while selecting for the survival of antibiotic-resistant bacteria. If that individual were then to proceed to a lower respiratory tract infection such as pneumonia, they run the risk of becoming much sicker with a more difficult-to-eradicate bacteria for their pneumonia. In turn, this has cumulatively contributed to our current global antibiotic-resistance public health problem.

For some statistical insight into the scale of this problem, consider the 2019 Antibiotic Resistance Threats report by the Centers for Disease Control and Prevention (CDC)[41] which estimates:

> More than 2.8 million antimicrobial-resistant infections occur in the U.S. each year, and more than 35,000 people die as a result. When Clostridioides difficile—a bacterium that is not typically resistant but can cause deadly diarrhea and is associated with antibiotic use—is added to these, the U.S. toll of all the threats in the report exceeds 3 million infections and 48,000 deaths.[42]

Looking more closely at a hypothetical patient-physician interaction, you, as the emergency department (ED) patient, and I, as an ED physician, really don't know each other, having usually just met for the first time. This provides an incentive for me to do more rather than less in evaluating your complaints (so I don't miss anything serious and cause you harm, along with the secondary concern that you may then sue me). My doing more in turn makes you happy, and more reassured as well. For example, for your sinus and chest congestion which convincingly sounds like just a minor cold virus, I decide to comply with your urgent request to have a chest x-ray due to your concerns about possibly having pneumonia. This chest x-ray is then vaguely interpreted by the radiologist as showing "possibly an early small infiltrate" (meaning pneumonia), "correlate clinically" (meaning consider if this is consistent with what the direct evaluation of the patient indicates). This happens nearly every day, no exaggeration!

So now I have to either start you on an antibiotic (useless for your viral infection, of course) or admit you to the hospital, or both. Each of these choices could lead to significant harm to you (gastrointestinal side effects, medication allergic reaction, antibiotic-caused C. difficile diarrhea, and/or a longer hospitalization during which you become deconditioned and confused, fall and fracture your hip, go to the operating room, have a stroke, heart attack, or pulmonary embolism, etc., etc., etc.).

In an alternative hypothetical scenario, if you and I have established a close and trusting primary care physician-patient relationship, I assure you that these are most likely just symptoms of a limited viral illness and provide the information, my evaluation results, and thought processes that have caused me to come to that conclusion. It is then your turn to ask whatever questions you have so that we can address any concerns and alleviate any doubts that might persist. I then agree to treat your symptoms to minimize your suffering (codeine as a cough suppressant and for discomfort can work wonders) and also reassure you that I will be available to see you, should you take a turn for the worse. You are reassured, go away happy, recover uneventfully from a minor illness, and much potential pain, cost, and suffering are avoided. The challenge for us all as patients and physicians is coming to the disappointing realization that some illnesses simply have to be endured until their natural resolution or whatever range of responsiveness to symptom control is achieved; that we cannot hope to bring risk down to zero at all times; and that we must jointly engage in the difficult balance of risk versus certainty in our shared decision-making to find an acceptable equilibrium.

Throughout my career, I consistently chose to present these distinctions to my patients and explain why antibiotics for their acute upper respiratory tract infection, likely a viral infection, were not only NOT a good idea but possibly a dangerous idea. In my experience, more often than not they would appear to listen quite intently, and then when I had finished would immediately say, "and so you're prescribing me antibiotics, right? Why not?" Depending on circumstances I would often repeat the entire discussion, with the same result.

I ultimately adopted what I considered an acceptable compromise. I would prescribe something for symptom control like Robitussin with codeine or Tylenol with codeine for cough and discomfort control. I would then additionally, in certain circumstances, provide a backup prescription for an antibiotic with the strongly stated advice that it should not be initiated immediately. My accompanying advice would be that if they subsequently developed a new fever or their existing fever got higher or some greater degree of coughing with more discolored phlegm occurred, they could then initiate the antibiotic, with the additional proviso that if they were significantly worse, they should return to the emergency department or see their own physician promptly.

Of course, I could not know how many of those people immediately went out and started the antibiotic anyway, though I suspect that many did. I could at least find some consolation in the fact that I had given the proper advice. But by doing this I was also going out on a limb to a certain degree. In one dangerous scenario, their additional symptoms could theoretically be from something more dangerous like heart disease which can cause fluid to progressively collect in the lungs and lead to worsening coughing, even if this wasn't readily apparent on the initial evaluation, with or without a chest x-ray. The patient could then erroneously conclude that I had said starting the antibiotics was an appropriate treatment for that condition and have a bad outcome. Again, the secondary fear is that they could then make this as a claim against me in a malpractice suit (i.e., that I had meant that antibiotics were appropriate treatment for congestive heart failure)! All this serves to confirm that the better plan all around is simply to have a personal physician who knows you well and with whom you have a good communication process and ability to follow up with as discussed above.

Health, as defined by the World Health Organization (WHO), is "a state of complete physical, mental and social well-being and not merely the absence of disease or infirmity."[43]

That definition is both annoyingly idealistic, as well as wonderfully egalitarian. By this standard, none of us is completely healthy, or at least not for very long. It does also usefully encapsulate the biopsychosocial model of illness. The biopsychosocial model of illness was first proposed by Dr. George L. Engel, back in 1977, to stand in contrast with the existing purely physical biomedical model. Dr. Engel was uniquely trained in, and had University of Rochester medical school appointments in, both internal medicine and psychiatry. He wrote:

> *The boundaries between health and disease, between well and sick, are far from clear and never will be clear, for they are diffused by cultural, social, and psychological considerations. The traditional biomedical view, that biological indices are the ultimate criteria defining disease, leads to the present paradox that some people with positive laboratory findings are told that they are in need of treatment when in fact they are feeling quite well, while the others feeling sick are assured that they are well, that is, they have no 'disease.'[44]*

On one level we all believe in his biopsychosocial medical model when we offhandedly say things like, "All of this stress is definitely getting me down, no wonder I keep feeling sick." Or, as we occasionally rationalized to ourselves in medical school, "I'm not going to morning lectures today, because I really need to take a mental health day off." However, as a society, both within and outside the medical profession and to our great detriment, we have never wholeheartedly embraced the biopsychosocial model. When push comes to shove and we feel truly unwell, along with a concern that something serious is wrong with our health, we all most definitely want a quick-fix, biomedical intervention.

Personally, as a patient, I fully understand that point of view, having had far more patient experiences than I would have preferred. Additionally, professionally, it is the very reason that I gravitated towards emergency medicine (EM), with its higher proportion of quick-fix, biomedical interventions. What a joint disappointment it is then to both patient and physician when, even in the emergency department, a quick fix is either unavailable or inadvisable!

It is not at all unreasonable for us as patients to want as satisfying an explanation and solution for our physical symptoms as can be provided. But the reality is that this cannot always be determined and offered. Fortunately, a portion of these symptoms will ultimately resolve spontaneously, some studies say up to 74% as per a 2003 *International Journal of Methods in Psychiatric Research* article.[45] A corollary to this is that due to the post hoc fallacy (*post hoc ergo propter hoc*, Latin which means 'after this, therefore because of this'), we will inevitably attribute our improvement to whatever it was that we had initiated immediately before improving.[46] These interventions may include taking an antibiotic for an underlying viral illness or following some form of alternative medicine, dietary change, or medical advice from a family member, friend, other layperson, or even the internet.

Awareness of the post hoc fallacy has been with us ever since the time of Aristotle and fellow Greek philosophers of antiquity. However, even today as patients, not falling prey to its influence requires a profound act of willpower and commitment to scientific neutrality. I catch my own susceptibility to this post hoc fallacy at times even while trying to stay on guard for this reflex. It only makes sense that this cognitive error is so deeply ingrained in us humans. Those of us who could not easily make accurate cause-and-effect associations would have been strongly selected against by evolutionary pressures. For example, if you don't take notice that those very colorful and tasty, but poisonous, berries make you slightly ill when eaten in small quantities, a larger quantity feast may go on to kill you.

Within the emergency departments where I spent my 40-year career, we do have a higher proportion of patients with problems requiring urgent intervention. However, even in the ED, self-limited illness and minor injury can account for close to half of our patients. The challenge here, of course, is determining which half you are currently encountering.

The following case example will help illustrate some of these issues. In a memorable case that I still find unsettling more than ten years later, I was seeing a 37-year-old gentleman (let's call him Thomas, not his actual name) who had what sounded like a number of minor complaints when he registered. At triage, his chief complaint was listed as "fever/nausea/postnasal drip" with vital signs showing no fever and just minimally elevated blood pressure and pulse. I picked up his chart at the very end of my shift with just 20 minutes remaining, thinking that this sounded fairly benign. I did this so that I could "try to see just one more patient at the end of your shift," as my ED administrator had been haranguing me about, while implying that keeping my job depended upon it. (A more extensive discussion of how the 'unholy three P's' of *productivity*, *performance*, and *patient satisfaction* have put us all at risk will be addressed in later chapters.) Present in the triage notes was the notation that Thomas was a hemophiliac, so I was aware of that but didn't see its relevance to any of his listed complaints. He went on to tell me that he had not been feeling well for the past four days, but at the moment he looked quite well other than talking rapidly and somewhat circuitously.

As I was trying to efficiently elucidate his symptoms, he reported to me that he had taken his temperature just once and got a reading of 98 degrees, and in terms of the nausea he reported vomiting just once two days ago and again a second time that day, but without any blood in it or accompanying abdominal pain. He then reported that his postnasal drip was due to chronic sinus congestion, which he thought was "slightly thicker" than usual for him. He denied any other complaints on a complete review of systems. All in all, not very revealing or alarming and making me wonder why he had even bothered to come to the ED just then. Given that he was a hemophiliac I asked about any bleeding complications, recent falls or head injuries or any significant headache. He reported that his right ear felt "a little uncomfortable," but not anything else relevant. He did go on to anxiously and in great detail describe a left lower molar tooth extraction he had undergone at a somewhat nearby major metropolitan hospital several months back, and the fact that he had chewed food in that region recently, which he had been advised not to do after being cautioned that "the bone there is tissue-paper thin."

I was feeling very frustrated interviewing him because he was so vague and was jumping topics frequently. I was having great trouble relegating him to one of the more common categories we see in the ED, such as 'wanted antibiotics,' 'wanted pain medicines,' 'wanted an out-of-work note,' or 'too anxious to know what he wanted.' Then in reviewing his upper respiratory tract infection complaints of fever and postnasal drip, I asked about coughing and shortness of breath. To this he answered, "I feel like my body just doesn't want to breathe." That meant exactly nothing to me and had in fact just used up my last ounce of patience with him. In my frustration, I chose to turn on my heel and leave the room with a decision to prescribe him some Tylenol with codeine for his described minor right ear discomfort and minor coughing.

Thank God, or the stars, or whatever you want to invoke, right by the door to his room was a wheeled stool which, in my dissatisfaction with 'the feel' of that resolution (in EM we often refer to this as our 'spidey sense tingling'), I sat down on and turned to ask just one more question, "Gee, Thomas, you seem to have a lot of things on your mind today, what is the thing that is most worrying you?" To which he responds, "You know what it is Doc. I'm a hemophiliac and I'm worried that I'm bleeding in my head." To this, my competing thoughts were, "You've got to be kidding me, get out of here!" and "Oh good, we have a test for that."

Fortunately, whatever it was that made me sit down also made me go with the "Oh good, we have a test for that" thought. After reconfirming the absence of any head injuries, significant headache, prior episodes of bleeding in his head, or other recent abnormal bleeding, I did briefly explain to him that a head CT scan was an expensive test which involved a moderate degree of radiation exposure and didn't seem to be pertinent to his symptoms. But I decided to order it anyway, mostly to address his main concern and bring our interaction to a conclusion.

So now I'm still trying to grease my exit from the emergency department by the end of my shift, so I simultaneously ordered a head CT scan and wrote up a discharge plan with a prescription for Tylenol with codeine. As I'm handing this to his nurse to discharge him, I'm saying that he absolutely can't be let go until the relief physician, whom I will sign out and describe my patient and thoughts to momentarily, has confirmed that his head CT scan is indeed negative, as I'm sure it will be.

Then I'm sighing with relief as I see the CT technician already guiding him back into his room. The techs are terrifically good and usually come right to us to report any abnormal findings, even before the formal radiologist reading. As I am sighing my relief though, the tech spins around and makes a beeline right to me saying, "This guy has blood all over the entire right hemisphere of his brain!"

'Working in a mine field with clown shoes' is how my emergency medicine colleagues and I refer to this process of trying to take only the correct steps in identifying dangerous disease states and living with the knowledge of being at the constant risk of making a misstep. Then, having solved, or more accurately stumbled onto, the diagnostic riddle solution, I now had to address the multiple treatment decisions. I had never treated a hemophiliac before, though I knew from my training that he needed an immediate transfusion of the appropriate hemophilia factor. I quickly learned that option was not available in our hospital, so he would require transfer some 30 miles to the major urban hospital, where he had received his hemophilia-related treatment in the past. I internally debated whether ground transport by ambulance or medical helicopter was best. Airflight would be faster, but the flight paramedics usually insist that the patient already be intubated in case respiratory failure or other significant deterioration intervenes, as they can't read-ily intubate in such tight quarters (there's no pulling off to the side of the road option). The formal radiologist report was that he had acute (very recent) on top of subacute (relatively recent as opposed to chronic) blood, which was compatible with a start of the bleeding corresponding to his first feeling ill four days previously, and his now feeling worse as the bleeding resumed or the accumulation gradually enlarged. However, that could not clarify how fast he was currently bleeding, or what was most likely to happen next.

I ultimately chose to send him by ground transport, thus avoiding the risks of possible complications from the intubation procedure and the associated sedation and paralytic medications that I would have had to give him had I decided to do so in my ED. This would also leave him alert enough to converse with the specialist physicians upon arrival, and they could more easily clinically evaluate his progress. I cringed at the very real risk, though, that this was a wrong choice, with him potentially rapidly deteriorating and possibly even dying en route. I reasoned that the ground ambulance crew with a paramedic on board could easily pull to the side of the road and intubate him if needed. But I also knew that I would be second-guessed if complications ensued (for example, "if you had only flown him here, we might have been able to intervene to stop the bleeding sooner and save his life").

Thomas and I did both survive that experience, though each of us a little worse for wear. Despite the fact that a lack of productivity kept putting my job at risk, I continued to work at the pace that I thought circumstances required. At my next annual review with my ED admin-istrator, when he predictably pointed out that my productivity could be increased, I related this case and commented to him that 'I work to my own standards,' such that 'fast things are fast while slow things are slow.' I don't think he really appreciated my comments, but at least I wasn't reprimanded further.

Here in Thomas' case, he had the underlying chronic disease con-dition of hemophilia, along with an acute disease complication of uncontrolled intracranial (inside the skull) bleeding. In this setting, he presented with a vague illness characterized by a host of minor physical symptoms, which appeared entirely unrelated to either the acute bleeding complication or the chronic disease process, except perhaps the "little uncomfortable" right ear and nausea. Those symptoms, by all rights, should have been a debilitating right-sided headache and unrelenting nausea and vomiting. In retrospect, the only thing that might have been related to his acute disease process was that he was having trouble organizing his thoughts, possibly as a side effect of the blood oozing all over the right hemisphere of his brain. However, one cannot be reflexively ordering CT scans of the brain on everybody who has problems organizing their thoughts or relating their concerns in a linear fashion, because that is a shortcoming characteristic of many people when feeling ill, and even some of us when we are not feeling ill.

Ordering a head CT scan on someone who has what we term 'altered mental status' is standard medical practice. However, this patient did not seem to be truly altered, just mildly odd and unfocused. I strongly suspect, though, that if this gentleman had seen his own physician somewhere in the course of the four days of his illness, that physician in knowing him well would have recognized that this was likely a distinct personality change for him and, therefore, would have suspected something more ominous than I was able to readily recognize in not having ever met Thomas before. I ended up ordering the right test on this patient, but for the wrong reason. To this day, I remain disappointed in myself for having allowed my personal wish to leave work on time after a long shift, as well as administrative pressures, to influence my decision-making, which should have only been influenced by consideration of Thomas' welfare.

Even now I shudder at the thought of his being found cold and dead in his bed the next morning with the bottle of Tylenol with codeine prescribed by me on his bedside table!

CHAPTER THREE

CHALLENGES OF THE
MEDICAL INTERACTION

As patients, many of us are unaware of the surprising fact that common, potentially serious, or even life-threatening conditions that we imagine should be easily diagnosable, such as appendicitis or a heart attack, can present as diagnostic challenges. If these conditions present slowly with mild or minor symptoms at their onset, they are best addressed first with a primary care doctor who knows you well. Certainly though, many of these conditions deserve to be seen, and ultimately will be seen, within the ED for more thorough diagnosis and treatment.

The ability to diagnose significant disease processes more accurately and expeditiously, and separate them from the more minor conditions, depends to a great degree upon how effectively the patient and physician can communicate with each other. That detailed one-on-one exchange between the patient and the physician is the heart of all good medical practice. In fact, in medical school we are taught that if you take a good history from the patient, everything you do after that (the physical examination and all relevant testing) should be a confirmation of what you already suspect is the diagnosis (from the top of a differential diagnosis list that you are constructing in your mind). In my professional experience, this turns out to be mostly, but not consistently, true (recall Thomas). Familiarity with each other is also often, although not always, a benefit in these circumstances (there is the well-recognized hazard of trying to act as one's own or a family member's physician).

It's an inevitability that the patient and physician will start off any medical interaction with unequal knowledge bases and expertise. The patient's expertise will be on how we are feeling (what symptoms we are experiencing, causing what concerns) and what we hope to achieve through our healthcare. It is through the medical interview process that we physicians attempt to use our hard-earned expertise to compare a specific patient's report with the storehouse of information that we have from all of the prior patients that we have seen.

When ill, we most commonly make an association or draw a conclusion about what might be bothering us. This is an understandable reflex, with a survival benefit no doubt ingrained by many years of natural selection. But it is here where the physician's and patient's thinking processes and responsibilities diverge dramatically. Our physician training is to take a careful history, that is, a report of the story of the patient's illness experience (the HPI or history of present illness), and in the course of doing that create a mental 'differential diagnosis' list. This is a complete list of all the potential causes for the symptoms that the patient is reporting. Subsequent to that, the physician then goes about adding information by way of more questions or the initiation of medical testing in order to cross off or possibly even add to that list of potential conditions.

If a patient has an immediate idea or conclusion that their illness is caused by a specific condition, I certainly want to hear that, and sooner rather than later is preferable. (Thomas raising his concern about possible bleeding in his head earlier in our conversation would have been helpful!) However, it is the physician's task to put that speculative cause on the list that we are creating in our mind, but not to jump to that as a causal conclusion. This works best in a trusting patient-physician relationship, where the patient trusts that I will listen carefully to everything they have to say and vice versa. This is necessary in order that we not jointly commit the post hoc fallacy, that is, conclude that two things that are simply associated in time and space have a causal relationship… when they actually don't.

I recall an eye-opening patient interaction that I had relatively early in my career. To my question, "What made you come to the emergency department today?", my patient promptly answered, "I have meningitis again." So, I immediately put that on my differential diagnosis list, but definitely along with a grain of salt and dose of skepticism (given how well she appeared). After further conversation and a physical examination, we spoke of the need for a spinal tap. This would involve me inserting a needle through the low back in immediate proximity to the spinal column itself in order to obtain cerebrospinal fluid for testing—not terribly difficult or dangerous, but certainly more invasive than a simple blood draw—to confirm or rule out meningitis.

When I proposed that we proceed with the spinal tap, she requested that I consult the neurologist who had treated her for her prior episode. I was more surprised that the neurologist actually came in and did the spinal tap himself at her request, than that she was absolutely correct and did have viral meningitis again. There is a famous dictum of the renowned late nineteenth-century physician William Osler who stated, "Listen to your patient—he is telling you the diagnosis." Osler certainly didn't mean that they would provide the exact diagnosis, as both my hemophilia and meningitis patients did, but rather that the things revealed in your conversation with them would lead you to the proper diagnosis.

But here, we must also acknowledge that as patients we can at times mention all kinds of misplaced ideas and conclusions to our physicians. I found throughout my career that patients' stated concerns such as "I have pneumonia," "I have appendicitis," "I'm having a heart attack," have far more often been erroneous than accurate. Even knowing that, I never stopped giving patients' stated concerns full consideration, as most physicians also do, because that is a critical part of the process. I want to hear the most pressing thoughts and concerns that the patient has. However, that innocent and inadvertent misleading of the physician is also accompanied by a not insignificant number of patients who are intentionally misleading us due to a secondary agenda (to obtain narcotic medication, an out-of-work note, etc.).

Although we don't always succeed in precisely understanding what our patients are trying to communicate to us, we physicians have experienced our own illnesses (minor and/or major), so we have some limited insight into what the person on the other side of the exchange may be experiencing. However, I often wonder if a layperson can ever really understand what it means to have the responsibility of the physician's side of that same exchange. In writing this book, I aim to give some insight into what it means to be a doctor...or is this even possible? I'm thinking that with some imaginative effort many people could relate.

Imagine for a moment any arena in which you feel an expertise, whether it be the law, carpentry, policing, social work, book publishing, accounting, teaching, or any unique skill ranging from piloting your own private airplane to knitting a hat or sweater. Then imagine needing for whatever reason to convey to a novice the precise steps involved in completing a key task, while simultaneously presenting a list of uncertainties and possible unpredictable trouble spots which might lead to error. Now try to imagine that your audience has often already come to conclusions about how that task is best achieved. If need be, try picturing your audience being your or almost any teenager, or a particular acquaintance with a greater propensity for speaking than listening.

That might give you just a hint of what it is like trying to obtain critical information from, and communicate it to, an ill patient. And here I'm leaving out the vomiting, writhing in pain, verging-on-death parts, the ambient noise level, and the competing and often simultaneous, discussions on entirely different topics with several other individuals (i.e., nurses and lab, radiology, and EKG techs interrupting you to get an urgent answer to a pressing problem that's come to their attention), etcetera.

But now you have to take the additional imaginative leap that for some reason this task that you've done multiple times before is now uniquely different, and now the result of your not conveying the intricacies of the task correctly is that someone may suffer or even die if you don't make a proper connection, obtain or convey the right information, or prioritize your approach exactly as required! This is not intended to curry sympathy, but to highlight the inherent hazards in this kind of novel and unpredictable exchange, and the risks of going astray.

As a minor example, in the last year of my practice, after seeing literally thousands upon thousands of patients with the complaint of chest pain, I encountered a Spanish-speaking woman in her late 60s who had mentioned her chief complaint as cough and chest pain. I had developed the habit of taking a very detailed history for the HPI. Although I can understand quite a bit of Spanish, I always use an interpreter to ask the necessary detailed questions. It turned out that the patient's main concern was that at that moment she was experiencing quite a bit of chest pain, made dramatically worse anytime that she coughed. That by itself is quite a common story and not usually particularly alarming. However, she was in her late 60s and, despite having no other cardiac risk factors, chest pain being cardiac in origin is an ever-present possibility, even more so in her age group. In fact, the nurses had already obtained an EKG, chest x-ray, and cardiac bloodwork, all of which looked normal (but, you may be surprised to hear, all of which can look perfectly normal even in the setting of an acute heart attack).

So, despite my habit of always trying to keep an open mind, I did start off our exchange with the expectation that she would tell me the reassuring story of developing a respiratory infection with frequent coughing that was then followed by the chest pain. Her initial response though was to insist that, "Absolutely not, the chest pain had come first and then the coughing." Long story short, we had a very lengthy and time-consuming conversation involving a day-by-day recitation of her week and a half-illness progression. The conversation ended reassuringly when she ultimately expressed great annoyance to the interpreter, which I understood myself, that, "Of course the coughing came first and then the chest pain followed it!"

Our interaction was then complicated by the fact that I needed to communicate that although today's chest pain episode did not appear to be worrisome or cardiac in nature, given her age group she could actually still have underlying heart disease. So, I then had to elaborate upon the distinctions between how that would feel in contrast to how she was currently feeling. In these cases, we always give patients the advice to return to the emergency department should their symptoms change or evolve in the more ominous fashion that we just described. Unfortunately, some people neglect to follow through with that advice and can come to serious harm. At any point I could have justifiably cut short our conversation and simply made the decision to admit her to the hospital and let another physician inherit that responsibility. In fact, most of the pressures that are brought to bear in modern medical care, which include the ceaseless admonitions to *be productive*, *keep patient wait times shorter*, and *keep patients more satisfied*, would argue for me to have done just that thing, rather than for me to take the time and make the effort that I did to do what I thought was the right thing and keep her out of the hospital for this self-limited illness.

The easy-way-out decision to simply hospitalize patients brings to bear the downside of the financial costs involved, plus introduces the additional risks of picking up a hospital-based, possibly antibiotic-resistant bacterial infection, or suffering a medical treatment error while in the hospital. These concepts can be difficult to convey in a way that patients and family members can easily grasp.

I took care of an 80ish aged woman brought in by her adult son with concerns about urinary symptoms. In the short version, her urinalysis supported a urinary tract infection (UTI) diagnosis, but all other testing and her physical examination evaluation were unremarkable. We had what I thought was a balanced conversation between the three of us as to whether she was capable of being treated at home or was best off being admitted to the hospital. I gave my usual explanation of the possibility of folks in her age group with even a simple UTI having the potential to take a turn for the worse and get dangerously ill with a spreading infection, so there would be the need for them to be vigilant should she go home on oral antibiotics pending the results of a urine culture (done to confirm that she was on the right choice of antibiotic). The patient favored going home, but her son was favoring hospitalization. He won that mini-power struggle, during which I stayed neutral and gave evidence for each side of the decision and voiced no objection to the more cautious route of hospitalization. Several weeks later, I was informed by my ED director that the hospital had received a fairly strongly worded letter of complaint about me from the son. He was quite put out that I had even considered sending her home since she ended up not having a perfectly smooth hospital course (she apparently spiked a fever and became mildly confused, though was adequately treated for both and ultimately discharged home). I had clearly outlined that as a possibility in our discussion, but now it appeared that he was holding me responsible for the fact that I couldn't reliably predict her future complication (thus reconfirming the truism that hindsight is 20/20, while foresight is far less clear, and overlooking the fact that medicine is practiced in real time).

As a different ED director colleague once succinctly described it, "There's not a lot of 'attaboys' in emergency medicine, Drew. Nobody thanks you for the treatment interventions or hospitalizations that you have helped the patient to safely avoid."

Even with the best intentions on both sides, the patient and physician communication may go astray. Leo Tolstoy perfectly encapsulates this in a line from *Anna Karenina*, after Anna's family is left to repeat to her what her doctor's comments to them had been:

They tried to tell her what the doctor had told them, but it turned out that though the doctor had spoken very well and at length, it was quite impossible to repeat what he had said.[47]

I think it may be somewhat helpful to understand how we can end up talking at cross purposes in medicine by visualizing the patient-physician interaction as being characterized by three prominent, inherent tensions which we will label here as:

1. Uniqueness versus sameness
2. Suffering versus diagnosing
3. Living fully versus just living

Tension #1 – Uniqueness versus sameness

Even when people suffer from the same disease process, each of their individual illness experiences are almost entirely unique, bringing to bear as they do their own particular resources of the moment, their characteristic coping mechanisms, and the skills of whatever physician or other healthcare individual with whom they interact. Your bout with a heart attack, stroke, or lung cancer may look similar to mine from the outside but your experience of it as a patient will be uniquely your own. I am philosophically opposed to using the phrase 'I know how you feel' to anyone who is suffering, medically or otherwise, and replacing it with the phrase, 'I can only imagine (or I'm trying to imagine) how you feel.'

The tension I speak of is created when I as the physician am attempting to identify which disease process you may be encountering by comparing your experience to the dozens, even to sometimes hundreds, of previous patients that I've seen with that same disease process, or similar set of symptoms. As patients we are often immediately on guard or on the defensive about the possibility of our physician not recognizing the extent and uniqueness of our current suffering. I've been there on the patient side a time or two. But I've also been on the other side and know that on that other side, as physicians, we are immediately shuffling through a stack of mental note cards of previous patients that we've seen who have described similar-sounding symptoms, while we are comparing all the nuances of similarities and differences. This is all done in an effort to not come to premature conclusions about the cause of your suffering (the 'art' of medicine that Cassell referred to as quoted in the last chapter).

It would do you no good, as in the Hispanic woman's chest-pain-with-coughing illness above, if I were to try to make you feel more comfortable (more heard and understood) by referring to your subjective illness experience as 'Maria's disease,' for example, as opposed to my more objective and I believed accurate description of 'an upper respiratory tract infection associated with coughing-induced chest wall strain.' As patients, we have a tendency to fight tooth and nail to the very end to maintain and retain our individuality. This is of course understandable but can be dangerously problematic by possibly leading to further unnecessary medical testing and even hospitalization (see Chapters Eight and Nine). Being ultimately told that we have a more minor illness or injury than what we had anticipated and feared is frequently very difficult for us to accept.

My patients have often appeared disappointed, rather than elated, to hear that they do not have the dangerous condition (pneumonia, appendicitis, heart attack) that they had suspected upon arrival. One phenomenon that we encounter as physicians in general, and particularly as emergency physicians, is when the patient objects to our conclusions by saying, "I know my own body." This can unfortunately sound to us physicians like, "The salience of my illness experience trumps your career-long clinical experience."

In the true patient-physician partnership that I am advocating, the physician response could then more helpfully be, "Yes, knowing how you feel is undoubtedly part of your expertise. I'm taking that fully into account and considering the more ominous disease process that could be causing or contributing to your symptoms, but here's what my experience has taught me that we should do to be certain that those more concerning conditions aren't currently present." A very useful consultation can proceed from there and the patient and physician can be united in the process of seeking an accurate and credible explanation of, and resolution for, the patient's suffering.

In this way, we can avoid the patient feeling like they are being 'medically gaslighted,' a phrase that did not exist before I retired. In addition to highlighting the absurdity of just a 15-minute doctor's appointment for any complex medical issue, I agree with what this one physician was quoted as saying about how to handle this predicament:

> It can be helpful to find and stick with a primary care physician that you trust. A doctor who is familiar with your medical history may be more understanding of your concerns, Rosen notes.... But at times, the answer could be to switch your physician or get a second opinion.[48]

However, I also fear the possibilities for dangerous misapplications of the term gaslighting, which carries the implication that this is a purposeful and dishonest psychological manipulation, when a physician may simply be legitimately trying to communicate a different point of view to a patient. Yes, as physicians we can make the mistake of seeking relief from our own uncertainty by appearing overly dogmatic in our confidence. As patients, although we need to be confident that we are being fully heard by our physicians, we should not be asking for our physician to be immediately convinced of our point of view without bringing their own experience, judgment and expertise to the task.

On both sides of the patient-physician interaction, we undeniably prefer certainty. It is very unsatisfying when even the best of these interactions ends up confirming that certainty cannot be achieved at this very moment. As Jared Diamond wisely pointed out in an otherwise nonmedical book *The World Until Yesterday*:

Assigning a cause to an illness, even if it's not the right cause, makes the patient feel better by letting him adopt some action rather than waiting helplessly. [49]

A longer passage by Daniel Kahneman from *Thinking Fast and Slow* reconfirms, but also points out the drawbacks of this as well:

Here again, expert overconfidence is encouraged by their (physicians') clients: Generally, it is considered a weakness and a sign of vulnerability for clinicians to appear unsure. Confidence is valued over certainty, and there is a prevailing censure against disclosing uncertainty to patients. Experts who acknowledge the full extent of their ignorance may expect to be replaced by more confident competitors, who are able to gain the trust of clients. An unbiased appreciation of uncertainty is a cornerstone of rationality – but it's not what people and organizations want. [50]

I believe that the monumental task confronting us as patients and physicians is to interact rationally and honestly, while overtly acknowledging the limitations of what we can and can't know with certainty, and still contribute to the healing of illness and disease. If we fail to achieve that and continue on our current path, we are committing a form of slow-motion national healthcare suicide, as trust within the patient-physician relationship progressively erodes!

Here are two quick illustrative cases. I enter the patient's room to find an apparently pregnant woman, looking reasonably well and with normal vital signs, as evident on her chart. She's accompanied by two young children—one I'm guessing close to two years old restrained in a stroller, and another child maybe eight months old restrained in a car seat. As I begin my evaluation, I take note of the fact that the kids are being admirably and silently stoical about their confinement, while the patient confirms that she is indeed four months pregnant and has been ill with an upper respiratory infection. (This was in the pre-Covid years, so at least that was not a concern.)

Briefly, I come to the conclusion that her illness is likely a viral type of upper respiratory tract infection (ARTI again) without signs of current bacterial complications. Fortunately, she agrees with my assessment that she doesn't require a chest x-ray to rule out pneumonia. I'm straightforward about the speculative nature of my diagnosis and mention low-dose codeine as an excellent cough suppressant being likely safe at her stage of pregnancy and while breastfeeding as well, but which I am reluctant to prescribe without her OB/GYN doctor being in agreement. She counters with her concern that the codeine might be sedating and make it difficult for her to be aware of when her children need her in the nighttime, a reasonable concern but probably not significant with the amount of codeine involved.

Part of this exchange includes a joint acknowledgment of how her mothering obligations are also interfering with her ability to sleep at night. I didn't want to appear judgmental by raising the question of whether there are other adults to assist her in this process, since she is otherwise unaccompanied. She becomes frustrated with the speculative nature of our conversation and interrupts me by saying, "I just want to know exactly what I have, and exactly when I'll feel better!"—a perfectly reasonable desire in an ideal world, and I want that for her too. However, for her current situation, in the real world in which we live, it is also a completely unachievable goal.

She leaves, encumbered by her responsibility for three children, with a palpable dissatisfaction. I had only momentarily considered lying to her by reformulating what I'd already described as "the most likely" and stating more emphatically, "I'm absolutely certain that you have a viral illness, that you and your pregnancy won't suffer any complications, and that you will be fully better within a week!"

Although I didn't practice back then, I believe that this is what was most often done in the days of more overt medical paternalism and that many people actually preferred it that way and even derived benefit from it (see placebo effect in Chapter Seven). When, as I've encountered, you come in as a patient with a self-described 'bad cough and cold,' you will definitely feel much better about your condition, and about your decision to spend the time to consult a physician, especially in the ED, if I give you the more official diagnosis of having 'acute bronchitis' and 'acute sinusitis' and start you on an antibiotic (most likely unnecessary). This you can then more formally report to family, friends, your employer, and to yourself as a 'significant illness,' but what is just alternative medical terminology for a 'bad cough and cold,' and a placebo equivalent, all of which just doesn't carry the same cachet.

I hear the next patient before I see him as he is retching nearly constantly. He does appear miserable, though stable, upon examination. There are also extensive bloodwork results pre-ordered by his nurse that have already returned as normal. After a reassuring HPI and full physical exam, I mention that he seems to have cannabinoid hyperemesis syndrome (a distressing but not dangerous condition related to prolonged marijuana use), a diagnosis that he reports has been proposed to him in the past. He's previously undergone CT scan imaging of his abdomen, has had multiple sets of blood tests, and had a gastroenterologist consultation with an upper gastrointestinal (GI) endoscopy (a direct look into the stomach with a flexible fiberoptic scope). It becomes clear that he's frustrated with these recurrent episodes and wants a more satisfying diagnosis with a treatment plan that makes them go away, especially one that doesn't involve his having to stop his marijuana use.

I explain that cannabinoid hyperemesis syndrome is still a relatively poorly understood condition, due to the fact that while it's well-known that marijuana can be an anti-emetic that treats nausea and vomiting, in certain forms it can confusingly have a pro-emetic effect which promotes the nausea and vomiting.[51] He's quite resistant to that idea and counters with, "I've been smoking marijuana every day since I was 14 (he's now 28), so how can that be the cause?" Treading lightly, I start with, "I make no judgment here about your smoking marijuana, but over years and years of cultivation the marijuana available now often has much higher and varied cannabinoid content than earlier versions. Plus, you're now responding to the IV medications that we use for this condition (which oddly enough include antianxiety benzodiazepines and the antipsychotic medication Haldol), which should really not affect any other specific organic causes for your symptoms."

I add what I think is the hopeful outlook that at least he does not have a condition that can't be cured, like many other chronic conditions, and end with, "I really hope that you'll do yourself the favor of trying the experiment of completely stopping your marijuana use and see if you don't also completely resolve these recurrent episodes." Despite starting with my cautious disclaimer about making no judgement, he ends up saying to me, "Now you're being condescending!" I'm stunned by the fact that he accuses me of the very thing that I'm trying my best not to convey, but I don't retort.

I can only speculate that he thought that I was being paternalistic. Paternalism in medicine is in decline, given that women are now just over half of all medical students (though certainly not nearly at parity throughout all aspects of our profession). It's a definite change for the better in my opinion. But rejigger the lettering and there's an inherent *parentalism* in medicine that can't and shouldn't change. As a parent, if your child came to you with an incompletely informed and/or ill-considered idea about something, could you even imagine just saying, "Sure go for it, if that's what feels right to you!" without even attempting to share your greater experience with them? We might not like it as patients, but the fact of the matter is that, as regards medical considerations, our doctors are flat-out more informed and have spent their careers considering concepts that may be relatively or completely novel to us. Plus, we physicians have that never-ending, near-parental concern for your welfare.

Above and beyond these communication failures are the frustration and danger when disease processes simply don't present as they should (because they don't read medical textbooks). In the case of appendicitis, and without going into too many details, I have made that diagnosis in people who have had the following unusual presentations—a 30-day episode of abdominal pain (rather than the typical several days), a repeat visit within 24 hours for someone who had a normal CAT scan the day before and now has clear appendicitis on a second CAT scan, an elderly man whose chief complaint was, "My wife is trying to poison me," and "by the way, I have right thigh pain."

I did, however, miss an appendicitis diagnosis in a patient who complained of reproducible right lateral chest wall pain (the right-sided nature of his discomfort being the only part of his symptoms that was consistent with appendicitis). Additionally, I no doubt would have missed the diagnosis in a colleague's finding of an episode of 'stump appendicitis' (a condition that I had never even heard of before) in a patient who had already undergone an appendectomy. This patient's first laparoscopic operation apparently had inadvertently left a small fragment of the base of the appendix remaining.

Regarding heart attacks, one 37-year-old woman brought in by ambulance appeared from across the hallway to be having what looked for all the world to be a panic attack, though long experience had taught me to be on guard not to come to premature conclusions. On a different shift, a slightly older gentleman, apparently not having raised much concern on the triage nurse's part (and it being a very busy shift), was triaged back to the rapid medical evaluation section of the ED, where he was as far from critical care attention as he could possibly be, behind a curtain and not on a cardiac monitor, in an emergency radiology hallway. I was spared the risk of missing their diagnoses because their EKGs, which were done and shown to me promptly, declared immediately that they were each having a STEMI (an S-T segment Elevation Myocardial Infarction), in other words an obvious heart attack in progress. My involvement with them at that point was simply to confirm that their vital signs were stable, to initiate the medications that might reduce their pain, and to prepare them to go immediately to the cardiac catheterization lab under the care of the on-call cardiologist. This deprived me of the opportunity to gather information about the sequence of their illnesses, so I don't really know whether I might have suspected that they had heart disease or not, based solely on their history and physical examination.

This realm of uniqueness versus sameness is complicated by two additional phenomena. This first phenomenon revolves around the trite observation that 'common things are common.' The medical version of this, which is more or less drilled into us repeatedly during our medical education and training, is, 'when you hear hoofbeats, think horses not zebras.' In other words, think of common diagnoses first to explain a patient's symptoms before resorting to rarer explanations for them. This serves us all well, patients and physicians alike, in the vast majority of cases, that is, except for the zebras out there.

I was in the midst of examining a middle-aged woman who had come in complaining of right upper back pain, which was reproducible by my pressing on that area and by the patient taking a deep breath, and I was on the verge of concluding that her discomfort might be just musculoskeletal in origin, given the lack of any other concerning symptoms in her HPI or findings on her physical exam. I had already taken a look at her EKG and her lab work results, most of which were already back (with just the odd finding of elevated eosinophils, a type of white blood cell usually seen in allergies or parasite infections), but she had not had her chest x-ray yet, which was the only one of those protocol driven pre-orders initiated by her nurse that I was actually interested in seeing.

At that moment, her nurse came in to show me that her pending troponin level was just now back and elevated (very briefly, troponin is a protein that lives in our muscle cells, most prominently in the heart muscle, and the miniscule level that is normally circulating in our bloodstream becomes elevated when heart muscle is damaged). That the troponin level was elevated was surprising, but even more eye-opening was the fact that it was the highest I had ever seen before at 27, with normal levels being just .04. Long story short, the chest x-ray showed some kind of diffuse infiltrative process throughout all of her lung tissue, and, when as a late addition she described some numbness that she had been experiencing, a head CT scan showed a diffuse infiltrative process also in her brain. I ultimately heard back from the hospitalist who admitted her and then transferred her to a metropolitan teaching hospital that she had a diagnosis of hypereosinophilic syndrome (a condition whereby this class of white blood cells are overproduced and then infiltrate into other body tissues)[52] and was treated with steroids.

This was a diagnosis that I had not considered because I had never even heard of it before. These types of patient presentations lead us in EM to at times joke that patients should have to go through a total body CT scan while checking into the ED, and also have 'one of everything else' done in terms of other available emergency department diagnostic testing. While that approach might have some attraction for us as patients as well, we will review further along how it can lead to overtesting, overdiagnosis, greater healthcare costs, and even greater harm to us as patients.

The second phenomenon is even more disturbing to both doctors and patients, and that is the fact that some patient symptoms fall into the category of MUS, which stands for medically unexplained symptoms! These are physical symptoms for which medical science has reached no scientific consensus in explanation of them, despite extensive medical testing.

The following comments are from a 2003 article addressing this complex and mutually frustrating medical problem:

> *At least 33% of somatic symptoms are medically unexplained, and these symptoms are chronic or recurrent in 20% to 25% of patients. Unexplained or multiple somatic symptoms are strongly associated with coexisting depressive and anxiety disorders.... Somatic symptoms account for over 50% of all outpatient visits, or an estimated 400 million clinic visits in the US alone each year (Schappert, 1992). This includes visits for pain, headache, fatigue and dizziness (Figure 1) as well as other physical complaints. Indeed, somatic symptoms in the general population are*

ubiquitous. An estimated 80% of individuals will experience one or more symptoms in any given month (Reidenberg et al., 1968; Kroenke et al., 1990; Green et al., 2001). These symptoms are often self-limited, because only about one in four patients seeks healthcare for their symptoms (Green et al., 2001).[53]

Studies show that a wide range of 20% to 75% of primary care patient physical symptoms are self-limiting, that is, resolve spontaneously, and lack a precise organic cause even after costly diagnostic testing (including referral to and evaluation by subspecialty physicians). Frustratingly, medications or other treatments are often ineffective. Such symptoms are often attributed to chronic low grade, undiagnosed/untreated anxiety and depression. Researchers who do these studies often refer to this segment of our patient population as the 'worried well.'

The following is from a 2007 article on anxiety:

More than 30 million Americans have a lifetime history of anxiety, and anxiety disorders cost an estimated $42 billion per year in the United States alone, counting direct and indirect costs.... However, despite the substantial disability associated with each anxiety disorder and the availability of effective treatments, only a minority of patients (15 to 36%) with anxiety are recognized in primary care.[54]

In addition, anxiety often goes hand-in-hand with depression, which has been called the 'common cold of mental health.'

This 2004 article comments:

In the primary care setting, a high percentage of patients with depression present exclusively with physical symptoms.... Of the 1146 patients in 14 countries included in the survey who met the criteria for depression, 69% reported only somatic symptoms as the reason for their visit. Unfortunately, depression can often go undiagnosed in these patients, as the physical symptoms associated with depression may be interpreted as symptoms of a somatic illness…. In patients who reported 0 or 1 physical symptom, 2% were found to have a mood disorder, but among patients who reported 9 or more physical symptoms, 60% were found to have a mood disorder. Overall, the presence of any physical symptoms approximately doubled the likelihood that the patient had a mood disorder.[55]

I believe that it is the persisting stigma associated with mental health disorders that often leads us as patients to either not spontaneously report, or to deny when asked, if we have problems with anxiety or depression. Being aware of this resistance, some of us as physicians may even be reluctant to raise these issues, at least studies appear to support that. This often promotes conversational exchanges that are at cross purposes, with patients feeling that we are dismissing their symptoms or, in this new vernacular, that we are 'gaslighting' them. I suspect that the conversational shortcomings in these kinds of exchanges are likely bilateral.

Although this many decades later I can't recall any of the other particulars, I can distinctly recall the dismay I felt the first time a patient said to me, "So, now you're saying it's all in my head!" I've always considered it a form of malpractice not to raise the issue with patients…if I suspected that anxiety or depression might be contributing in any degree to their current feelings of illness. However, I've never even entertained the thought that it's all in somebody's head, much less ever said it out loud. I would have to review the video replay to see if and/or how I may have botched my half of that conversation when I was a very new and inexperienced physician.

Eventually I learned to lead with that concern by stating something along the lines of, "I've just met you, so I don't know you as well as your own physician would. I recommend that you follow up with them to review these results. Our evaluation here today does not reveal a specific cause for your symptoms, and in those cases we need to consider whether stress along with anxiety or depression might be contributing to your symptoms. We do not have a 'stress' test in particular. The only stress test we have is one for putting physical stress on your heart, not a measurable way to determine the amount of stress in your life. This is not to say that this is all happening in your head, it's never all in your head. When you have physical symptoms in this way, your body is feeling the same way it would if you had an organic disease. It's just that in your case, fortunately, we don't find any organic disease process. I realize it's very frustrating not to have a definite explanation, but more often than not, if I can give you a very definite explanation, it's likely to be something that you don't want to hear, like you have appendicitis, a heart attack, pneumonia, a tumor, etc." Some patients respond well to that, even with a palpable sense of relief and acceptance that the possibility of anxiety or depression is out in the open.

Others, not so much. I had one such conversation with a young woman whom I had tried to reassure that her back pain, and additional vaguely described symptoms, did not appear to be from anything dangerous and then discharged her home. At her request, I had asked her nurse to give her copies of her lab test results. Shortly afterwards, her nurse returned to warn me to watch out because the patient had reported that she was looking for me now in order to, "Punch him in the nose." Turns out she was upset because, "He told me that my tests were all normal and here look at these in red are clearly not."

In a routine complete blood count, comprehensive chemistry panel and urinalysis, there are 48 different values reported and inevitably one or more are a tick or two just outside the normal range and are of no consequence at all. Normal lab value ranges are calculated to be within a 95% confidence interval, so 5% of the time values may fall just outside that range and be inconsequential. That's why I try to never refer to lab tests as 'normal,' only ever saying 'unremarkable' or 'reassuringly good.' "Did the patient want to ask me any questions about her lab test results?" Her nurse responded, "No, she just wanted to punch you in the nose, so I asked security to be sure that she left the ED." I wasn't overly disappointed but would have taken the time to share the above insights. I'm not sure, though, how far into the meaning of confidence intervals I would have gotten before being bopped on the nose.

This is not to imply that mainstream medicine has reached its peak performance and can answer all the questions that are placed in front of it. Hopefully, we have nowhere near reached our peak yet. I particularly like this quote from Susan Sontag in *Illness as Metaphor*:

> *Theories that diseases are caused by mental states and can be cured by will power are always an index of how much is not understood about the physical terrain of a disease.*[56]

I agree with her totally about the 'cured by will power' portion of her comment and the limited understanding of some disease processes or 'physical terrain' such that earlier theories that mental states were causing diseases like cancer and tuberculosis were certainly and flagrantly mistaken. But I think newer studies since Sontag wrote her book, which will be presented as this book progresses, have pretty much confirmed the links between mental states and a range of illness experiences.

I will also be advancing a very strong stance that it is the quality of the patient-physician connection, and the trust that it engenders, that has been getting short shrift in terms of its ability to achieve healing in illnesses, and even diseases in some cases. Here are just two studies in anticipation of that argument, which I will be presenting more thoroughly in later chapters.

1. "Linking Primary Care Performance to Outcomes of Care" by Dana Gelb Safran, ScD, et al. (1998):

   Our results suggest that when discussions occur, adherence to recommended behavior changes is strongly associated with the strength of the physician-patient relationship. Previous studies find adherence to be positively associated with effective physician-patient communication, continuity, and humane interpersonal treatment. Their relative importance in achieving adherence was not examined. Our study reaffirms the strong association of each, but suggests that patients' trust in their physician and the physician's knowledge of the patient supersede all other factors. With all other factors held constant, adherence rates were nearly 3 times higher in primary care relationships characterized by very high levels of trust and whole-person knowledge than in those with very low levels.[57]

2. "Is the Quality of the Patient-Provider Relationship Associated with Better Adherence and Health Outcomes for Patients with HIV?" by Mary Catherine Beach, MD, MPH, et al. (2006):

Our study demonstrates that the essence of patient-centeredness—the patient's perception of being known "as a person"—is significantly and independently associated with receiving HAART (highly active antiretroviral therapy), adhering to HAART, and having undetectable serum HIV RNA. These associations persist even after controlling for multiple potential confounders, and confirms the findings of 2 previous studies that the quality of patient-provider relationship is significantly associated with adherence to HAART.[58]

Tension #2 – Suffering versus diagnosing

Tangentially related to Tension #1 is one that is prominent in emergency medicine 24/7/365. There is nothing more satisfying in the practice of medicine than relieving a patient's suffering, nor conversely anything more satisfying as a patient than having one's suffering alleviated as rapidly as possible. But the degree of interest in arriving at a specific diagnosis for that suffering is not at all comparable in the two roles. We need to know what we're treating as physicians in order to deliver the most appropriate medications, interventions, and subsequent treatment. On the flipside as patients, the fact that the suffering is gone is quite often sufficient. "They didn't do anything for me" and "They didn't tell me anything" are a common pair of phrases we hear from patients who just the prior week were seen for the exact same set of symptoms at another hospital's emergency department. Then the requested and faxed-over records reveal an extensive ED evaluation including x-rays, bloodwork and urine testing, with sometimes admittedly just a speculative diagnosis, but always with a follow-up plan and prescriptions for symptom relief, substantial portions of which the patients may often not have chosen to follow or even fill (e.g., 'you likely have alcohol-related gastritis so therefore reduce your alcohol intake, begin the prescribed medications, and follow up with your own physician.')

As it happened, it was during the five-year hiatus in my emergency medicine career, following my 1992 disabling stroke, that the pain scale was introduced as the 'fifth vital sign.' I was very surprised to see it upon my return to the emergency department in 1997, especially so since this completely subjective number was given pride of place along with the classic, very objectively measurable, vital signs of temperature, respiratory rate, pulse rate, and blood pressure. This was accompanied by very overt pressure placed upon physicians to 'control' patient's pain discomfort as rapidly and completely as possible, with narcotics as needed...because somehow, in the interim, narcotics had been deemed not a danger to patients! I was immediately resistant to this notion, having been trained and seen very early in my career that narcotics had a dangerous inherent tendency to become habit forming.

It is now well-documented how pharmaceutical companies unduly influenced physicians' prescribing decisions regarding narcotic pain medications. This was also greatly facilitated by hospital administrators' simultaneous and continual pressuring of physicians to again *be more productive* and *keep patients more satisfied.*

As an example of how this might have led to unnecessary complications, and completely apart from the accompanying opioid epidemic, in one case I was seeing an elderly woman in her late 70s or early 80s who had fallen and fractured her hip. It was quite straightforward, and she took the information with admirable aplomb when I informed her that she would need to be admitted to the hospital and have surgery on her hip. I added that while her admission was being arranged, we would be relieving most of her pain with narcotic medication.

We commenced giving her doses of intravenous morphine in low doses of just 4 mg to start followed by 2 mg per dose increments as per usual protocol. Her nurse (excellent and clinically astute) came to me several times to be certain that it was okay to continue with the 2 mg doses, while I was in the process of evaluating several other new ED patients. At a certain point, when asked yet again for another dose of morphine for that patient with the fractured hip, it occurred to me to stop further new patient evaluations and go re-evaluate my patient, for whom I had already arranged admission to the hospitalist and had a discussion with the on-call orthopedic surgeon. At that point I confirmed that she had received 10 mg of morphine total intravenously, a not outrageous but fairly generous dose for a woman of her age. When I spoke with her again our conversation went this way:

> Me: "How are you feeling? I understand that you're still having hip pain, which surprises me somewhat because you've gotten a fair amount of pain medication."
>
> Patient: (very matter-of-factly) "Oh yes, I'm still having the hip pain, but I can't feel anything else in my body!"
>
> Me: "Well then, I think you're exactly where you need to be. Remember when I said at first that the job of a broken bone is to be constantly reporting, "I'm broken, I'm broken, I'm broken," and, as I said, we can make that voice less loud, but we shouldn't take it away completely. Your pain, of course, will not be

chronic, because once your broken hip is fixed and healed, then the pain voice will be gone."

Patient: "Oh, okay, I'm fine then."

In the service of reflexively *keeping the patient satisfied* and *being productive*, we had crept up on, but fortunately had avoided, the potential complications of overmedication. This could have included accompanying sedation and respiratory arrest, or sedation to the point of nausea and vomiting with aspiration of vomit into the lungs, either of which could have been life-threatening.

A briefer episode of a similarly aged patient with pain was one in which I saw a patient who had come in with intractable low-back pain as a chronic condition. She was perfectly pleasant when I evaluated her, and we were awaiting results of her urine sample just to be sure that nothing out of the ordinary was going on in addition to her known chronic low-back pain. When I informed her nurse of that plan, she replied that she would be happier when the patient was gone from the ED, so I asked her why. My nurse, who was consistently pleasant and professional in her demeanor, responded, "She may be fine with you now, but she was quite unpleasant with me until I gave her that 4 mg of morphine intravenously, she even called me that CU Next Tuesday word, which always gets to me!"

Pain specifically, and medical suffering in general, certainly does not bring out the best in us as patients, and we can lash out verbally, and even physically at times, with the people trying their best to help us. Nurses often bear the brunt of this by being the first-line troops in the ED and EMS personnel sometimes even more so by being the first responders and seeing patients 'in the wild.' We are left with the challenge in healthcare of constantly trying to call upon the best in ourselves in treating you.

I think the heart of this conflict is captured quite succinctly in the novel by Patrick O'Brian *The Nutmeg of Consolation*. In this passage, the

Napoleonic era British battleship's physician/surgeon Stephen Maturin is recalling this advice to his medical assistant:

> *I remember telling him of the miseries of human life, particularly as they affect medical men. I spoke of that continual, insistent demand for sympathy and personal concern that exhaust all but the most saintly man's supply before the end of the day, leaving him openly hard in a hospital or poor practice, secretly hard in a rich one, and ashamed of his hardness in either case until he comes to what terms he can with the situation.*[59]

I can definitely relate to that sense of shame at my hardness at times. I always find it impressive and gratifying when a nonmedical person so clearly captures a professional medical insight in a meaningful way!

In the same vein, I recall when an EM nurse colleague said to me one day in frustration about trying to accommodate a patient's unreasonable expectations, "You know what bothers me the most about this work? It's that sometimes it makes me just hate people." She was and is a perfectly compassionate and professional nurse, and we knew each other well enough that she wasn't afraid that I would misinterpret what she meant. I understood perfectly what she meant, and then shared the above passage with her.

As a related aside, some eye-opening statistics show:

- In 2010, enough prescription painkillers were prescribed to medicate every American adult around-the-clock for one month. [60]
- Millions of people (12 million in 2010) use prescription painkillers in the United States nonmedically every month. [61]
- The United States is 5% of the world's population but consumes 80% of the world's prescription narcotics.[62]
- According to the CDC as of 3/28/2022, Fentanyl now appears to be the number one cause of death for Americans ages 18 to 45.[63, 64, 65, 66]

Given the current pandemic of opioid use and overdose that we are suffering from, most prominently here in the United States, we are still trying to wrestle this problem back to some balanced position between usefulness and harm reduction in all patients. Again, having a one-on-one trusting relationship with a physician who knows you and your conditions well (and can guide us in the ED on your behalf through a phone consultation if needed) is the most effective way of receiving the pain control methods most appropriate for your condition and to avoid falling on either the undertreated or overtreated side.

Tension #3 – Living fully versus just living

I'll now give just a few preliminary comments here on this third tension, a much larger topic which requires and will receive a chapter of its own in Chapter Twelve. I placed this here because it is one of those tensions that is frequently present between patient and physician, though sadly, more often than not, goes unaddressed, thus causing much misunderstanding and, at times, substantial avoidable suffering. A still memorable case from 1981 during my medical internship (first hospital training year out of medical school) is illustrative.

I was one of the two medical interns assigned to the 'code-team' that night while working on the overnight internal medicine team in the hospital, and periodically catching a brief but much needed catnap in one of the physician call rooms. I was awakened when my pager went off indicating that a code (cardiac or respiratory arrest) on an already admitted patient had been called and the room number was given. The adrenaline surge response was nature's caffeine and so it was easy enough to unthinkingly be up and running in that direction quite promptly. As quick as I was, the other intern had gotten there first and so had been assigned to do chest compressions on the patient, thus leaving me mostly in the background in a learning mode.

The more senior resident doctor running the code was standing in front of me giving orders and delegating responsibilities. In his impatience to resuscitate the patient, he had grabbed an IV line and was in the process of administering a full syringe dose of epinephrine (adrenaline) into it, when I heard the nurse next to him quietly inform him, "Dr. Baker that IV line is not yet in the patient." Looking down at the IV line, and shaking his head, without missing a beat, he just as quietly said back to her, "Tell me, are my pants on?" In another setting it would have been enough to make me laugh out loud, but not then fortunately.

What was actually taking up much of my attention as I glanced around the room was that there were about a half a dozen handmade posters on the wall all proclaiming in very large text 'Happy 100th birthday!'

We dutifully 'coded' the patient since it had not been proscribed, and with every chest compression we could hear another one or two cracks of the fractures occurring in his frail rib cage from the required force. He was unsurprisingly not able to be resuscitated successfully. This was a form of mercy for him, given the pain that he would have been in from all of those rib fractures had he regained consciousness.

Could he really have wanted to spend his 100th birthday in the hospital, or wanted an attempted resuscitation in this fashion? Since he hadn't been my patient, I had never gotten a chance to meet him, speak with him, or even learn why he was in the hospital, so perhaps he had reasons to want to try to live a bit longer, such as a grandchild's upcoming wedding to attend. I couldn't be sure, but one thing I felt somewhat certain about was that the conversation had probably never occurred. I was absolutely sure, though, that I would be certain to have that conversation in advance of my ever being in his position.

CHAPTER FOUR

BELIEF

It should come as no surprise that nearly all of the decisions that we make regarding our healthcare are based on the beliefs and biases that we have acquired throughout our lives. What is less commonly evident to us, though, are the sources and foundations for those beliefs and biases. Michael Shermer's insightful book *Why People Believe Weird Things* focuses on beliefs and how they develop. He writes, "The problem in seeking and finding patterns is knowing which ones are meaningful and which ones are not. Unfortunately, our brains are not always good at determining the difference." [67] His cogent analysis is more complex than can be briefly summarized here, so I highly recommend that readers read his book as well. I will point out now that Shermer and I do part ways when he concludes that this explains why religious belief is simply "magical thinking."

In contrast, I think of myself as both a theist and a medical scientist and find that they can be compatible rather than contradictory philosophies and approaches, further discussion of which will occur at the end of this book. Inevitably, we all have healthcare beliefs and act upon them, with or without conscious aforethought. We therefore need to make a conscious and diligent effort in attempting to verify their accuracy by recognizing and making adjustments for our biases. Belief is also one of the core components of the placebo effect itself that we will take a closer look at in Chapter Seven.

We acquire our healthcare beliefs often unconsciously and readily from a variety of sources: family, friends, community, our healthcare system, the media, and even our sociopolitical alliances. Prior to COVID-19, those beliefs frequently revolved around less dire considerations, such as: What are the health benefits or costs to be derived from a vegan diet, over-the-counter dietary supplements, meditation, yoga, wine, coffee, dark chocolate, alternative medicine, and so forth? In this current political climate, some of us have felt the need to include other concerns, such as: Did the media over-hype the impact and statistics regarding this COVID-19 pandemic in order to undermine the reelection chances of our then President? Should we follow medical advice from our President or other laypersons? Does this support our preferred political party or an over-arching political agenda? And so on....

I firmly believe that none of us should follow any kind of medical advice, whether from professional or unprofessional sources, without questioning that advice rigorously. If that advice is given in a dogmatic fashion, especially from someone who has not benefited from science-based formal medical education, training, and experience, then our mental red flags should be snapping loudly and repeatedly in the wind. However, as outlined in this book's introduction, I believe that even with qualified licensed physicians, the second step of the process in my thesis is so critical that it cannot be left out. We need to question our physicians carefully so that we can understand (to the full extent of our abilities) what is being explained or advised and why it is important. This enables us to then wholeheartedly commit ourselves to a joint treatment plan. I'm drawing a very sharp distinction here between the above and a simplistic blind following of the advice given without submitting it to a critical appraisal process. I neither mean to imply that this is a simple and easy process, nor one that is guaranteed to work, nor that our physicians are an unerring source of wisdom. Despite the maxim that two heads are better than one, it is certainly very much within the realm of possibility that we and our physicians can agree on an erroneous course of action. This may inadvertently leave us blithely skipping down the garden path together towards catastrophe.

There was a period of time in the 1950s when doctors were actively advertising specific brands of cigarettes for their patients to smoke. "MORE DOCTORS SMOKE CAMELS THAN ANY OTHER CIGARETTE"[68] was a popular advertisement. This was an early example of the lure of money influencing healthcare advice. This was also a prime example of healthcare advice running far ahead of scientific justifications.

A second disturbing occurrence was the case of thalidomide, again in the 1950s. Thalidomide was promoted as an insufficiently studied over-the-counter, anti-nausea, and sedative medicine for use during pregnancy. Developed and first marketed in West Germany in 1957, there were ultimately estimated to be over 10,000 cases worldwide[69] of infants born with phocomelia (a malformation of the limbs),[70] with a 40% mortality rate among them. Far more cases occurred in Europe, with only a limited number of cases occurring in the US.

America's fortunate avoidance of widespread phocomelia deformities was entirely due to the efforts of Francis Oldham Kelsey, MD, PhD, who at the time was a relatively new employee at the FDA. Despite continued pressure and repeat applications for approval from the company producing the drug, Dr. Kelsey had the personal courage to consistently refuse to approve thalidomide for use in the United States due to the absence of sufficient evidence to confirm its safety. [71] She ended up receiving the President's Award for Distinguished Federal Civilian Service from President John F. Kennedy in 1962, only the second woman to ever receive this honor.[72]

A third consideration is the tragedy of the Tuskegee Study, carried out in Alabama from 1932 to 1972. The US public health service conceived this as a longitudinal study of the natural history of the disease syphilis which, at the time the study was begun, had no known cure. Tragically and inexplicably, the study continued unchanged for decades, even after effective treatment with penicillin had been developed.[73]

The fourth concern that occurs to me is the phenomenon of lobotomy in the 1940s. This neurosurgical procedure was initially conceived of as a more humane way to treat out of control psychotic patients than the standard treatment of the time of resorting to physical restraints, cold-water hose-downs, confinement, and warehousing. However, ultimately it was used more broadly as a pacifying technique in thousands of patients (Rosemary Kennedy, the younger sister of JFK, was one famous recipient of the procedure[74]).

Lobotomy actually won its inventor, the Portuguese neurologist Egas Moniz, a share of the Nobel Prize in physiology or medicine in 1949.[75] The American physician Walter Freeman came up with his own simplified version of this procedure which involved inserting an ice pick upward under the upper eyelid and through the bone of the eye socket. This 'icepick lobotomy' was designed and carried out as a ten-minute office-based procedure. If you have the stomach for it, have a look at the Freeman references I've included. One image shows an ungloved hand with watch in place, and the obviously not intubated and possibly even unmedicated patient![76] A 10-minute video about the 'Icepick Surgeon' (Freeman) who performed over 2,000 such lobotomies provides even more details on this phase of the then 'modern' medical intervention. [77]

Those are just a few of the things which adhering to our physician's advice might have exposed us to. If your luck had been running full tide against you, by following your doctor's advice, you could have ended up as a lobotomized, syphilitic, armless cancer patient!

The physicians in the aforementioned cases were generally thought to have been proceeding with patients' overall best interests in mind. In contrast, the following are three of the most egregious and more recent cases of demonstrably untrustworthy physicians:

1. Michigan oncologist Dr. Farid Fata was sentenced in 2015 to 45 years in prison for healthcare insurance fraud. He was found guilty of treating multiple patients with chemotherapy drugs for contrived diagnoses of cancers that did not exist.[78]

2. Dr. Larry Nassar was the US women's Olympic gymnastics team physician when he was found guilty of serial sexual assault and sentenced in 2018 to 40 to 175 years in a state prison, which is the equivalent to life in prison, given that this is on top of first serving a 60-year federal sentence for the possession of child pornography. [79]

3. From 2011-2013, neurosurgeon Dr. Christopher Duntsch operated on 38 patients in the Dallas area, leaving 31 paralyzed or seriously injured and two of them dead. He became known as Dr. Death and was sentenced to life in prison in 2017.[80]

Please accept my apologies for having inflicted all of the above distressing events and information on the reader. I wanted to make it crystal clear that I do not have an uninformed or incomplete view of some of the limits and hazards of my profession. However, even acknowledging that, as patients, we may encounter inadvertent, or on rarer occasions even purposeful, inappropriate medical advice and behavior, I see no legitimate alternative to seeking the advice of scientifically trained, trustworthy, honest, and conscientious physicians. Having encountered multiple hundreds of physicians at this point that I've worked with, or have personally sought their advice, I have confidently concluded that those individuals and events mentioned above are the outliers. In fact, I have never personally encountered a single physician whose overriding priority wasn't convincingly 'getting it right' with regard to the care of patients.

I do not personally know the oncologist in the following exchange with his new hospitalized patient, a woman in her 40s with a just-diagnosed, advanced-stage, metastatic cancer. He eloquently portrays the agony of uncertainty in his compassionate attempt to 'get it right':

"Whatever we do," I said, *"you do not have disease that I can cure."*

She cried then, realizing what a horrible situation she was in and that she would no longer go back to her normal life. Indeed, she seemed to grasp that she was probably facing the end of her life and that it could be short.

"My concern is," I continued, *"that treatment could do the exact opposite of what I hope it would do. It could kill you sooner than this cancer will."*

Instead of making a treatment plan, I decided that it would be best to come back another day, so I said my goodbyes and left. Still, I could not stop thinking about her and what I should suggest as her next steps. My heart wanted to try treatment, give her a chance, even if it killed her. But my brain told me that treatment is not likely to work and may make her life even shorter. I asked colleagues what they would suggest. Some recommended hospice care. Others recommended treatment. Clearly there was no one way to proceed.

One might wonder: Why is it so hard to do the right thing?

Ask any clinician and I think you will hear the same answer: because we do not have the luxury of certainty.

Am I certain that this person will not benefit from intubation? Am I certain that she has only weeks to live? Am I sure that there are no treatments that will work?

The answer to these questions is no — I am not certain. It is that uncertainty that always makes me pause because it reminds me of my own humanity.[81]

Not that I don't find myself and my colleagues at times making decisions that can be more self-serving than perhaps they should be. My own decision-making regarding Thomas in Chapter Two is an example of my inappropriately prioritizing my own and externally imposed 'productivity' needs. Similar are the occasions when I'm signing over patients to a colleague at shift change and they comment, "Why don't you just admit her to the hospital?" or "Why don't you just intubate that guy?" These are colleagues whose judgment I trust, but I see them in those moments, like me, falling victim to the pressure of 'productivity' (not wanting to get bogged down in completing the evaluation and treatment of one of my patients, for which the system gives them no recognition or financial credit).

Of course, being fallible human beings, we can at times fall short of our own, and society's, high standards of conduct and certainty. In essence, we all, patients and physicians alike, can jointly acknowledge that human error is inevitable, but when it comes to healthcare, we all find it unacceptable! The difference is that as physicians we can understand how it happens, while as patients we struggle with understanding the difference between foresight and hindsight when it comes to medical diagnosis and treatment. The consequences of this can include physicians feeling suicidally depressed at their own errors,[82] while patients and/or their families may feel vengefully litigious in response to bad outcomes.

So that leaves the difficult dilemma of how to wisely choose a physician and also how to safely choose what advice to follow—definitely no easy tasks! We can best approach this by soliciting recommendations from trusted friends and family about physicians that they have considered competent and trustworthy. But then we would need to make our own assessment after consulting with that physician, preferably more than once, to see whether we find them competent and trustworthy as well. If you cannot bring yourself to that conclusion, then it's time to move on and try the same process with another physician. At this point, you also need to be certain that you're not just 'doctor shopping,' that is, you're simply trying to find a physician who agrees with what you have already concluded, and you don't really want them to bring to bear their own experience and knowledge.

When we are ill, we often believe that the world's most important medical problem is the one that we have right now and the best use of the physician's time is with us personally. Illness quite often makes us self-centered and impatient. Up through the end of my career, I remained surprised by how often patients appear skeptical and almost disappointed to learn that their physical suffering is due to an illness and not an overtly serious disease process, that is, their own (or a loved one's) abdominal pain is just a transient GI bug and not appendicitis, their cough is not pneumonia, their chest pain is not a heart attack, their headache is not a brain tumor, and so forth. This often leads to a very antagonistic interaction along the lines of directly or indirectly conveying:

Patient: "Prove to me that I'm not dangerously sick!"
Medical staff: "We just did!"

Studies also fairly consistently show that as patients we only follow through on about 50% of what we are advised to do. Even the prescriptions we are given either go unfilled (up to one-third of the time) and/or are often not properly adhered to. In addition, as patients we only recall about half or less of what we are told during our interaction with our physician. The important corollary to this is the logical progression that we adhere more closely to medication regimens and treatment plans that we understand, and studies show that this in turn leads to better outcomes. The CDC reported in September 2016 that one in four Medicare participants aged 65 or older—that's 5 million people—do not take their blood pressure medicine as directed. In fact, 20 to 30 percent of prescriptions for chronic health conditions are never filled, and about half are not taken as prescribed, according to the CDC.

Patients' failure to follow their medical treatment regimens is a common and costly problem with potentially dire consequences. A 2012 study in American College of Preventive Medicine found *that nonadherence accounted for an estimated 125,000 deaths annually and at least 10 percent of hospitalizations. The repercussions also cost the U.S. health system as much as $300 billion a year, according to a 2014 study by Johns Hopkins University researchers.*[83]

It makes little sense that we would spend the time and money to consult a doctor, especially in an ED, then not do what we were advised; but it is a humdrum daily occurrence for us in EM. When patients choose to see us in follow-up for a lingering illness, they'll readily confess that they stopped their antibiotics after several days when they noticed a slight improvement, thus not following the standard advice to complete the full course of antibiotics regardless of degree of responsiveness. This also contributes to the global antibiotic resistance problem by not completely eradicating the bacteria under treatment. This very risk was presciently pointed out regarding penicillin misuse by Alexander Fleming in his Nobel prize acceptance speech in 1945 when he stated:

There may be a danger, though, in underdosage. It is not difficult to make microbes resistant to penicillin in the laboratory by exposing them to concentrations not sufficient to kill them, and the same thing has occasionally happened in the body. The time may come when penicillin can be bought by anyone in the shops. Then there is the danger that the ignorant man may easily underdose himself and by exposing his microbes to non-lethal quantities of the drug make them resistant.[84]

You might think that the idea of taking medications as prescribed is far too obvious to merit pointing out, but try the unfinished antibiotic challenge right now. Try looking in all of your home's medicine cabinets and see if you don't find an incompletely finished antibiotic prescription container. To my chagrin, I even found one in my own home, but my wife reassured me that she was advised to stop it and substitute a different one by the pediatrician treating our son.

One of the factors that has made these dilemmas more difficult for us in the United States is a surprisingly widespread 'antiscience' stance.[85] Ironically, the very strengths and utilities of the scientific method appear to be making it more difficult for many of us to understand and believe in it. Good science is constantly subjecting itself to examination and revision, testing and retesting prior conclusions, and then modifying them based on new results, which necessarily results in revised medical recommendations.

As a novel infection, COVID19 has produced a constantly moving target environment for medical scientists, public health experts, and those of us who practice on the front lines of medicine. If you had wanted to design a pandemic to further confuse the unscientific, you could do no better than COVID19!

The degree of confidence in and strength of promotion of daily advice on factors such as the utility and reliability of testing methods, masking, social distancing, and other preventative measures have varied from day to day as new insights have been gained in the scientific studies of this infection and as clinical facts present themselves. Since graduating medical school in 1980, I have never had the experience before where the daily updates we were receiving were ranging from mildly to significantly different from the advice that we had received just the day before. We weren't actually flying by the seat of our pants, but COVID19 was certainly making us feel and appear that we were. In fact, 'building the plane as we were flying it' is probably the most apt metaphor for how the medical community felt in the face of the novelty of the COVID19 pandemic.

As one example, personal protective equipment (PPE), such as N95 masks, that had previously been considered as invariably one use/disposable, were now suddenly either not readily available or considered re-sterilizable/reusable. For another example, we were receiving recommendations on, and experiencing different approaches in, our decisions on intubating patients early or late in their illness, how we should be positioning them, delivering oxygen, and protecting ourselves.

Just one of the truly odd novelties of this disease is that patients who in the past would have been positioned sitting upright or at least on their back, have been feeling and doing better clinically when they are placed face down on the stretcher despite oxygen levels so low that, prior to COVID19, they would have already been placed on a ventilator. One posted stunning image shows a woman facedown, apparently imperturbably using her cell phone screen with her oxygen level in the background being displayed as in the 50s, which is essentially half of normal and generally considered incompatible with continued life, let alone with contented cell phone use.

I want first to state very clearly here that I have never been a member of any political party, nor do I ever plan to be. I believe that partisan politics coming from any corner represents a distinct public health hazard. Therefore, I'm using the following examples for their instructive value regarding our healthcare beliefs and not to cast aspersions in any direction. I will not engage in a full discussion of the COVID19 pandemic along with the strengths and weaknesses of the US responses to it. However, one phenomenon that was dramatically highlighted by COVID19 is deserving of closer attention—that is what I like to call the 'I'm not a doctor, but...' illusion.

Unfortunately, the phrase 'I'm not a doctor, but...' has evolved to mean that whatever comes next should be considered with utmost seriousness, rather than with the complete inattention that any following comments truly deserve. The speaker has, with feigned modesty, already forewarned the listener that the speaker has no formal training in, clinical experience with, or any experience with being able to convey accurate, individualized, medical advice, so therefore is unburdened by any responsibility of trying to make an informed, rational, and well-considered statement. We somehow have come to believe that this false act of integrity increases rather than decreases the speaker's credibility.

Here the US's 45th president was the most prominent and recent serial practitioner of this illusion. One memorable statement went, "I'm not a doctor, but I'm, like, a person that has a good you-know-what." This statement was made while gesturing to his own head and struggling to imagine and convey some process by which disinfectants and sunlight could be safely delivered into the human body to treat coronavirus. He was apparently confident that we would easily recall his previously saying, "Because I have a very good brain and I've said a lot of things," as well as his tweeting, "Sorry losers and haters, but my IQ is one of the highest—and you all know it! Please don't feel so stupid or insecure, it's not your fault."

In fact, that had been the third time that I'd heard him use the phrase "I'm not a doctor, but" with one of the others in reference to the not scientifically supported use of hydroxychloroquine to treat coronavirus, concluding "I'm not a doctor, but I have common sense." Actually, many people with common sense would immediately realize the danger inherent in taking medical advice from a layperson, but unfortunately not all people did; and in several media reports, some individuals came to demonstrable harm from following that layperson's medical advice about using hydroxychloroquine.

The following day he tried to pass off the previous night's statements as a simple act of sarcasm on his part, which I did not find to be a credible explanation. I had yet to see him be able to convey a sense of humor of any kind. I don't want to belabor the point, but I conclude that the 'I'm not a doctor, but' illusion is one that we all need to stand on guard against.

The United States' constitutional protection of free speech is simultaneously one of the most wonderful and frightening aspects of our great democratic experiment, that is, the fact that it protects free speech, no matter how ill-founded or ill-considered it might be. However, this principle does then place us under the consequent obligation to independently investigate the validity of statements that others might make.

The article "The Death of Expertise" by Tom Nichols summarizes this phenomenon succinctly as:

> *Having equal rights does not mean having equal talents, equal abilities, or equal knowledge. It assuredly does not mean that "everyone's opinion about anything is as good as anyone else's." And yet, this is now enshrined as the credo of a fair number of people despite being obvious nonsense.*[86]

In one last example of 45 overstepping the bounds of his expertise regarding COVID, he memorably proclaimed, "We have more cases because we test more." That statement has great appeal to our common sense since we reconfirm it nearly daily; it's only sensible that if you look harder for something, you're more likely to find it! He was apparently not well-informed enough to recognize a more applicable public health statistic. He did, however, have ready access to many public health experts who were well informed, had he chosen to avail himself of their greater knowledge and experience.

To achieve the relevant epidemiological statistic, the proper question to ask was, "What are the test positivity rates?" For example, if you are looking for an uncommon condition of which there is just one in a given population and 100 tests are done, which just happen to include that one case, this gives you a test positivity rate of 1%.

But then if 1,000 tests are done to find the same one case, the case positivity rate plummets to 0.1%. In the COVID pandemic, just the opposite was happening. As more testing was done, the test positivity rates were rising proving that COVID was a widespread, not an uncommon, condition.

Thus, my modest proposal is as follows: Politicians will come and go, but the 'I'm not a doctor, but' illusion is a forever problem! Common sense is a necessary but not a sufficient prerequisite to arriving at appropriate medical conclusions. We should therefore consider promulgating this illusion as equivalent to practicing medicine without a license and sanction it that way...with guilty offenders being at risk for punitive damages for bad outcomes, as in a medical malpractice suit.

In 45's defense, he is certainly not the first or only one to fall into the 'I'm not a doctor, but' logic trap, meaning that being reasonably bright, as he no doubt is, and being able to form what seems like a logical conclusion, justifies expressing that conclusion as a medical fact. If that were true, grandmothers would have never been replaced by trained physicians. It just happened that 45 was in the most powerful position in the world to do historically large amounts of harm, or good, as he saw fit.

Some people took major exception to the fact at that time that Dr. Deborah Birx (White House Coronavirus Response Coordinator) in discussing vaccination effectiveness used the word 'hope' with regard to what was expected of it, with people even commenting that "hope is not science."

Let me point out here that unless you've earned the right to, and have adopted the burden of responsibility for, having to make decisions directly impacting the health of another individual, it is understandable that you might not realize that there is a substantial component of hope involved, along with ideally as much medical science as is currently available. In my 40 years of emergency medical practice, I roughly estimate that I made at minimum close to one million or more direct patient-care decisions (1,000 to 2,000 patients seen per year x 40 years x 10 to 20 decision points per patient on average, with the sickest patients easily requiring 2 to 3 times that, and even the simplest of cases involve at least half a dozen decision points. For example: Infectious or noninfectious illness? Viral or bacterial? Antibiotics or not? Which one? Which dose? What duration? etc., etc.). I didn't make a single one of those decisions without some measure of hope that I was making a wise choice and the ever-present fear that I might be mistaken!

So, to speak of hope does not negate the role and function of science. The way medical science, like all of science, works is that we are constantly questioning, reevaluating, and, when appropriate, revising our conclusions and decisions. Uncertainty is baked into the process, so it is an inherent feature, not a fault of the system. When COVID19 first appeared, it was consistently identified as a "NOVEL" coronavirus. I suppose one could argue now that the very next statement from physicians and public health experts should have been, "So therefore we are trying to figure this out as quickly as we can."

Those of us in healthcare who had previously lived and worked through the novelty of the first days of HIV/AIDS to some degree did realize the implications of the use of the word novel there. However, we had also experienced the other recent coronaviruses—MERS (middle east respiratory syndrome) in 2012 and SARS (severe acute respiratory syndrome) in 2002—two similar coronavirus outbreaks which had quickly burned out. I must admit, therefore, that personally and professionally, I was not particularly concerned about what would come next. Realizing my own limitations, it was not an opinion that I chose to share with anyone except my wife, who was fully aware of my limitations.

As a medical student and resident physician from 1976 to 1983, if I had answered that antibiotics had no role in treating gastric acid problems and that sexual intercourse was not a risk factor for cancer, I would have been congratulated as being correct. Now we know that H. pylori bacteria contribute to the first, and sexually transmitted viruses contribute to the latter (human papilloma virus/HPV and cervical cancer, along with other genital region cancers; hepatitis B virus/HBV and liver cancer; human immunodeficiency virus/HIV and Kaposi's sarcoma, as well as some forms of lymphoma are now all well-known). Both HPV and HBV do have effective vaccines.

So, it is absolutely correct that "hope is not science," but it is definitely heavily embedded within the health sciences. Science is that process by which we divorce our personal and political leanings from the open-minded asking and answering of difficult and often completely novel questions. Science in and of itself does not ask you to, "Trust the science." In fact, it says just the opposite, to "Continuously question the science," that is, subject all of your conclusions to a rigorous critical-thinking process. And yes, science and medicine can at times get it very wrong! See earlier discussion in Chapter Three.

Therefore, we should be on guard against being misled by any partisan political commentary. Instead, choose to rely on your own trusted, personal physician for your medical guidance. Never stop questioning, but ultimately you have to choose a course of action, ideally when guided by medical expertise.

On the topic of false beliefs, and for the sake of balance here, let me relate that I was fully confident enough in my own low-risk profile that I ignored distinct warning symptoms in the weeks preceding my stroke on March 2, 1992 (discussion of that and other case incidents in Chapter Six – Denial).

Mine was arguably the more boneheaded false belief by someone who should have known better, but at least my erroneous conclusion only affected me, rather than millions of other Americans.

CHAPTER FIVE

BIAS

I suggest that it's helpful to think of bias as belief's less well-educated and more dull-witted stepsibling, who enjoys playing hide-and-seek. The human mind does not appear capable of operating without having both belief and bias. In his best-selling book *Thinking, Fast and Slow*,[87] the psychologist Daniel Kahneman writes extensively on heuristics, the shortcuts our minds tend to take when thinking about complicated topics in settings of uncertainty. He does present a few examples of how this applies to the medical field in his book, but the bulk of his examples are economic ones, and in 2002 he won the Nobel Prize in economics for his work.[88, 89]

Kahneman writes extensively about the two systems of thought of the human mind: System 1 which we use for automatic intuitive thinking, and System 2 which is the more conscious, slow, and deliberative portion of our minds. System 1 is prone to multiple biases and to overconfidence. Although we were not overtly trained to be aware of this as physicians during my education, I believe it is something that very early on in our careers all physicians become cognizant of to one degree or another, and particularly more so in emergency medicine, in which we are highly reliant upon System 1. We are also prone to these same biases and false confidences as patients. Developing an awareness of our propensity towards these incompletely considered ways of thinking is critical to the success or failure of the physician-patient interaction. Examples of these biases in medicine include availability bias, confirmation bias, anchoring bias, optimism bias, hindsight bias, and so forth. In her article "List of Common Cognitive Biases," Kendra Cherry goes into greater detail on the variety of biases which the mind is susceptible to and how and why they form.[90] Of these biases, I believe that the several most hazardous in healthcare decision-making are confirmation bias, anchoring bias, optimism bias, and intervention bias.

Confirmation bias is the tendency to notice and more quickly accept information that is most similar to beliefs that we already hold. Anchoring bias is the tendency to not allow new information to move us away from an initial impression or conclusion, despite the initial conclusion having been purely reflexive and possibly erroneous. We all dislike the stressful and fatiguing mental work involved in weighing the pros and cons of alternative theories and tend to gravitate toward what is familiar, comforting, and less challenging to believe. F. Scott Fitzgerald has captured this succinctly, "The test of a first-rate intelligence is the ability to hold two opposed ideas in the mind at the same time, and still retain the ability to function."[91] Fitzgerald was not speaking to the medical context but was making a general life observation, which is relevant here nevertheless.

Optimism bias is the tendency to mistakenly underestimate the likelihood of a bad outcome, which I am aware that I am at risk for (my 1992 decision to not seek objective evaluation for my neurological symptoms is exhibit A there). Intriguingly enough though, studies we'll look at in Chapter Twelve suggest a strong association between optimism and a decreased mortality rate. So, I've chosen to sustain my optimism, albeit now accompanied by greater caution. Intervention bias is the tendency, now very prevalent in American healthcare (on the part of both patients and physicians), to choose some form of action or treatment when the choice of not intervening represents an equally viable alternative.[92]

If we look back now on the opening hemophilia case example, we can recognize that my System 1 was telling me that Thomas could not be seriously ill because he looked so remarkably well. My considerations of multiple common ED categories to try to fit him into was again my System 1 trying to make this into an easy problem to resolve. My System 2 was doing what our System 2 is supposed to do, which is the background cognitive work of trying to logically make System 1's conclusions sit well with us, at which, very fortunately in that case, it clearly wasn't succeeding.

As it turned out, I had allowed selfish considerations to prevail, that is, could I still get out on time and please my emergency department director while still doing right by Thomas. I never fully allowed System 2 to slow me down and take over, as I should have. It was only by sheer luck and the intervening wheeled stool near the door to his room that slowed me down enough to ultimately order the right test, but almost entirely for the wrong reason.

Here again our desire as patients to have quick and convenient medical care along with the healthcare system conspiring with us to keep us 'satisfied' and maximize the profit they can make by 'moving more product' makes our healthcare ultimately much more hazardous to our health. On that day, in that particular interaction, I was very disappointed in myself for transiently becoming part of the problem, rather than part of the solution.

The brilliantly insightful Australian comedian/actor/musician Tim Minchin summarizes this System 1/System 2 battle of ferreting out our biases more succinctly and humorously in the following way:

> *A famous bon mot asserts that opinions are like arse-holes, in that everyone has one. There is great wisdom in this...but I would add*

that opinions differ significantly from arse-holes, in that yours
should be constantly and thoroughly examined. We must think
critically, and not just about the ideas of others. Be hard on your
beliefs. Take them out onto the verandah and beat them with a
cricket bat.... Be intellectually rigorous. Identify your biases, your
prejudices, your privilege. [93]

This quotation is taken from Minchin's graduation address entitled "9 Life Lessons" and can be viewed in full on *YouTube* in a 12-minute video which is well worth the watch.

I was infinitely more disappointed in myself when I lost that battle in a much earlier patient encounter, when I was appropriately sued for malpractice. In that episode, a young man told me he was having eye discomfort because, "I scratched it while putting in my contact lens." Then, when I readily saw the epithelial defect on the surface of his cornea by fluorescein staining, I concluded that he had indeed scratched it. A year or so later, I received notice that I was being sued for malpractice because the patient had required a corneal transplant due to an infection of his cornea. When I reviewed my chart from our encounter, I noticed that I had drawn a sketch of a very discreet circular defect more compatible with a corneal ulcer/infection and unlike the linear and irregular one that would more commonly be produced by the scratch of a fingernail. With a sinking heart, I immediately realized that I had indeed misdiagnosed his condition.

This is an example of what is termed confirmation bias in which one sees what one expects to see; as well, this was assisted by anchoring bias in which even though the defect was round and regular, I was unwilling to think beyond the very first conclusion offered up. I did not make the attorney who'd been assigned to me by my malpractice insurance company very happy when I told him, "This was malpractice, you should settle this case immediately."

Minchin further expounds on confirmation bias in another *YouTube* video (again, worth the time!) with:

*So, if there's this information out in the world here, a bit of data,
or an idea, we're much more likely to notice it in the first place
and subsequently accept it, believe it, you know, integrate it into
our belief system if it confirms what we already think.*[94]

As it turned out from my patient's subsequent medical records that
were provided to me, the patient had done himself no favors either
because he had been admittedly practicing poor contact lens hygiene
(by leaving them in overnight and not placing them in a cleaning solution), which no doubt contributed to his initial corneal ulcer and which
he did not correct, leading to his needing a second corneal transplant.
Regardless, my mistake was the more egregious one because I should
have known better and been more thorough in my evaluation and
decision-making.

Kahneman again writes:

*Overconfidence also appears to be endemic in medicine. A study
of patients who died in the ICU compared autopsy results with
the diagnosis that physicians had provided while the patients
were still alive. Physicians also reported their confidence. The
results: 'clinicians who were "completely certain" of the diagnosis
antemortem were wrong 40% of the time.*[95]

Dr. Pat Croskerry writes extensively on how these two systems and
biases affect our medical decision-making. He states::

*Bias is so widespread that we need to consider it as a normal
operating function of the human brain.*[96]

As patients we might then reasonably ask, "So what am I supposed
to do about that, to try to avoid those kinds of bias errors?" The short
answer would be to ask our physicians the question, "How certain are
you of your conclusions, and is there more that can be done to confirm

that?" Yes, you run the risk of annoying us! But here's a way to convert that annoyance into respectful consideration. You add, "I'm simply trying to become more of an engaged patient and adopt the model of shared decision-making that I've heard about."

I also want to point out that this was not my only medical error. In my first year of emergency medicine residency, I was seeing a wheelchair-seated older woman sent in from a nursing home with a chief complaint listed on her chart as "fell/won't walk." However, when I spoke to the patient, she said her main problem was that she was constipated. When I countered with the information on her chart that she fell and couldn't walk, she immediately jumped up out of her wheelchair and said that she could walk perfectly well, went a step or two, but then sat right back down. So, it was a complete rookie mistake on my part when I did not x-ray her pelvis/hips and just treated her constipation.

A week later one of the orthopedic residents showed me her pelvis x-ray which indeed showed a hip fracture, along with her chart from an intervening ED visit when one of the other EM residents had diagnosed her ankle swelling as due to CHF (congestive heart failure). The hard-won (on her part) learning point was that people who are not in complete control of their mental faculties, as her mild dementia state made her, cannot be relied upon to give an accurate history or necessarily to respond to pain in a typical fashion.

In that case, I was not sued at all, but it was terrible decision-making on my part, and I certainly could have been sued. As perhaps some sort of cosmic balance for that case, I was sued for only my second time ever on the case of a patient for whom I didn't participate in the care of, or even lay eyes on. In this case, my initials were used to place protocol-driven lab preorders for this patient, who ended up with a bad outcome, despite the fact that the nurse practitioner who saw the patient had done a proper workup and given proper advice. I was eventually dismissed from the suit itself by the plaintiff's lawyer, but only after I had traveled to their big-city office to give a lengthy deposition pointing out repeatedly, as had already been done by letter, that I had not seen the patient, had placed no entries in the chart, and, although I was present in the ED when the patient was, I was not involved in her care at all. Unfortunately, there's every good chance that I have made other mistakes that I never became aware of, and so I can only apologize for those here and now.

CHAPTER SIX

DENIAL

As a young and earnest first-year EM resident in 1982 in a large teaching hospital in the South, I was one day hustled into an examination room by one of the nurses to see a supine, stocky, 16-year-old young woman writhing in abdominal pain. As my mentors had trained me in my internal medicine internship, I went immediately to the head of the bed and started peppering her with questions about the onset and quality of her pains and wisely moved quickly on to such questions as, "Are you sexually active?" and "Could you be pregnant?" As she was firmly and confidently answering no to both of those questions between her groans, her nurse tapped me on the shoulder and gestured that I follow her. While I had been interviewing the patient, she and a couple of the other experienced nurses had been down at the other end of the examination table opening up the obstetric pack. In two quick strides in that direction, I was able to follow their attention between the young woman's legs to see the head of her full-term newborn child emerging.

Turns out that in triage she had answered no to both of those questions as well, and so had spent several hours in the waiting room progressing through labor until she had reached an obvious crisis point and started to yell out loudly thus bringing her to the head of the 'Needs Attention Now' line. I was stunned by this turn of events, as any reader who has experienced pregnancy likely would be as well.

Pregnancy denial is commonly seen in emergency medicine. Later in my career I had been on duty, although not personally involved, when several similar cases had presented to my ED. One involved a college woman who delivered onto her kitchen floor while standing at the sink doing dishes. Both came in by ambulance unharmed, although stunned in their own ways. The second was a young woman, working in an office side-by-side with her mother, who apparently excused herself (reportedly with neither woman having acknowledged the pregnancy), came to the ED and delivered her baby, then left it for adoption and returned to work.

Another variation on the pregnancy theme was the time I tried to convince a truly virginal young woman that she was actually pregnant by virtue of a positive urine pregnancy test. She persisted in insisting that she had never been sexually active, and I was bringing her to tears in my reluctance to believe that story. I finally agreed to order a serum pregnancy test, which is more time-consuming, expensive, and usually not needed. In fact, the lab tech said to me, "Come on Doc, you're not actually believing that story, are you? These urine pregnancy tests are super accurate." Nevertheless, at my insistence, he reluctantly ran the serum test, and to my chagrin and the woman's great relief, it was negative…as it should have been.

A second more comical variation on this theme was when some guy came running through the ED's rear EMS entrance all in a lather yelling, "Quick, quick, my wife's in the car having a baby, and I can see the head!" I was sitting at the desk closest to him, and along with the male nurse near me we rather jadedly got up to attend to his situation. I had previously watched a senior EM resident deliver a baby in the back seat of a car in the EMS bay during my EM residency, during which her husband stayed behind the wheel of the car looking back over the seat, with the car still running.

Therefore, I was expecting some version of that, although without the guy behind the wheel, as he was cautiously trailing us at a safe distance at this point. So, imagine my surprise when I opened the car door to find his wife in the back seat but fully dressed in tight blue jeans without any obvious staining of her pants. Where exactly was the alleged head? At any rate, we got her in a wheelchair and sent her up to the labor and delivery suite and were wonderfully entertained by the subsequent news that not only was she not in labor, but she was not even pregnant.

Let me quickly state here that I'm not at all making fun of these women. In fact, as an emergency physician, I've always felt that it is one of God's greater mercies to us that men cannot get pregnant (what was with the husband's report of "Seeing the head"?!). One's mind hesitates to contemplate the heights of absurdity and pathology that men could reach if entrusted with that condition! (Think beer.)

However, what really brought home an understanding of denial to me was the case of a 38-year-old otherwise healthy man without any of the commonly known risk factors for cerebrovascular disease—smoking, hypertension, diabetes, hypercholesterolemia, drug use, obesity, or family history—who denied that episodes of neurological symptoms could possibly indicate that he was at risk for having a stroke...and then went on to clot off one of the major arteries in his brain. That patient, of course, was me, and, in not listening to my own symptoms, I caused my greatest miss and most egregious case of malpractice. I remain grateful that my poor judgment did not inflict this damage on one of my actual patients. But, more pertinent to this discussion is that it brought home to me the reality that in order to pay attention to warning signs or symptoms, we patients have to actually be able to conceive of ourselves and a certain medical condition existing in the same sentence, or more concretely to exist in our same slice of space/time. In my case, other than for possibly a heart attack, a stroke was the most inconceivable of all medical prospects that I could imagine being relevant to me. In the same fashion, I now have no trouble understanding why some young women could not imagine themselves being pregnant, regardless of what was going on within and around them. Without the ability to imagine something being possible, the human mind simply cannot absorb any pertinent information that indicates that such a thing does truly exist. In my own case, just prior to my stroke I had had two warning episodes of transient neurological symptoms which I had managed to deny the significance thereof. I was young, fit, active, and on no medications, so a stroke was the last thing that I thought I was at risk for.

Both of those two distinct episodes of stroke-warning symptoms came after seven straight night shifts in the ED (of the graveyard 11 p.m. to 7 a.m. variety) followed by three hours of playing soccer in a scrimmage setting, which at the time was how I spent every Sunday morning (even indoors in the off season), independent of whether I had spent Saturday night working or sleeping. The first episode consisted of a very transient occurrence of double vision lasting less than a minute, and only noticeable because I was slowly driving up my street coming home after our soccer session. I attributed that first episode to my over-worked, underslept, and overexercised state. My only conclusion was, "Boy, I need to get some sleep." The second episode, which again lasted less than a minute and occurred with similar timing a couple of weeks later, was distinctly odd enough to get my attention. In that instance, I woke up at home after an abbreviated sleep, and while hurriedly wash-ing up saw out of the corner of my eye that my left hand was reaching out seemingly of its own volition as I was not consciously intending to reach for anything. I briefly thought that I was hallucinating.

As it happened, though, when I had those left-arm symptoms, I did speak out loud at the breakfast table, "Now I'm having stroke symp-toms." But in reality, I was saying it as a perverse sort of joke to myself like, "That's so inconceivable, it's actually funny." Although my wife at the time was in the room, I was not really speaking to her, I was just commenting out loud about the absurdity of the idea that I could have a stroke. I was continuing to blithely attribute my symptoms to fatigue and overwork. So, I just chose to go on about my business without bothering to consult a physician for an independent and more objective opinion (at the time I did not even have a personal physician).

Then several weeks later, on the morning of March 2, 1992, I woke up at work having a stroke. I had no idea whatsoever of this in the moment, and I was only looking forward to getting out of the hospital and heading home to my own bed. I had just completed a fairly hectic night shift in the ED, but I had managed to catch an hour of sleep before the end of my shift at 7:00 a.m. After using the john and taking a quick glance in the mirror to make sure I didn't have some crazed bedhead look, I wandered out to the break room area to sign out to the oncoming physician. I was surprised when he and the several nurses there started peppering me with questions like, "Drew, are you feeling okay? Hey, are you awake? Have you ever been sleepwalking before?"

Although I had experienced those odd neurological symptoms in the preceding weeks, I had casually and erroneously chalked it up to my fatigue, or my other idea was maybe low blood sugar. I was unaware of any symptoms at all at the present moment, but with that in mind I said, "Oh, I'm probably just a little low blood sugarish, I probably just need something to drink." When someone put a cup of orange juice on the table for me, I inexplicably reached out with my nondominant left hand to get it and promptly knocked it over spilling juice all over the table. That only struck me as a little bit odd, and I simply asked for another please. However, my colleagues had entirely different plans. Before I knew it, there was a stretcher in the room and they were ushering me on to it. Talk about your abrupt transition. One moment I was the physician still in charge of the entire emergency department, and in the next instant I was literally removing my white coat and becoming a patient!

At that point I was still only minimally concerned and as my physician colleague was doing a quick exam of me concentrating on having me look to the left and do things with my left arm and leg, I recall thinking, "Well this is good, this will at least address those symptoms I was having recently." Within minutes I had undergone a brain CT scan which was reported to me as looking completely normal, no surprise there to me (in the setting of an acute stroke, though, a non-contrast CT scan can show bleeding but not necessarily any signs/changes associated with a blood clot). I was still entirely unaware of any deficits at all on my part. I only learned later that I apparently had a fairly prominent weakness of the left side of my face, in conjunction with some mild unsteadiness on my feet and slow-wittedness. My colleagues later told me that they were at first optimistically trying to chalk it up to a combination of a Bell's palsy accounting for my facial appearance and that I was sleepwalking. Their closer examination, though, showed that I had fairly pronounced weakness of my entire left side as well.

At that point while we were still all in the radiology suite adjacent to the ED, they announced that I was going to need an angiogram. Up until that moment I was busy trying to sell myself and them on the low blood sugar explanation, despite it already having been debunked by a standard finger stick blood sugar test. An angiogram (which was state-of-the-art in those years) is a more invasive procedure involving injecting dye through the carotid artery up into the brain to outline all of the arteries there. The fact that they were proposing proceeding that far definitely caught my attention. I can distinctly recall still feeling very optimistic, though, about my condition being relatively harmless, and that my emergency physician and radiology colleagues were likely overreacting, but I wisely chose to defer to their judgment. Plus, they kindly listened to my protestations without saying, "Stop being an idiot, Drew, this is serious."

Imagine my surprise then when the radiologist announced, "Yes, the right middle cerebral artery is completely occluded at its origin." I had two near simultaneous thoughts, one being, "Oh, that makes perfect sense that there would be a right-sided lesion since they're worried about my left side," along with the competing thought being, "Wait a minute now, that doesn't make any sense at all, we're talking about *my* right middle cerebral artery!"

I was experiencing a classic symptom of a stroke which is termed 'neglect,' which is an entirely separate phenomenon from denial. In 'neglect' the entire consciousness somehow chooses to overlook even severe neurological deficiencies. It is almost as if the brain in a fit of pique says to the affected areas, "Well, if you're not going to send me any sensory input or follow my commands, then I'm not going to pay any attention to you either." For example, a stroke patient may neglect to either shave or apply make up to one entire half of their face.

In time, the motor deficits in my left arm and left leg, which by later that day had left me unable to walk or to even raise my arm off the bed against gravity, would assert themselves vigorously and require great effort to overcome. What was unexpected and more disturbing, though, was the experience of my mental cognition being so slow and unfamiliar, similar to a constant state of having just woken up and not being completely functional yet. That lack of a familiar mental feeling made me wonder at one point if I had actually lost my mind and, if so, would I know it?

To this day I find it surprising that a trained medical mind could simultaneously be aware of the warning symptoms of a stroke and yet still be able to keep them at such arm's length. The natural tendency may be to attribute this to the old adage that 'a little knowledge is a dangerous thing.' In point of fact, I think the more accurate conclusion is that 'too little knowledge is the dangerous thing.' The thing that I was unaware of was that my ulcerative colitis (UC) had put me at a greater risk for clotting abnormalities. Surprisingly, this risk apparently persisted even though my UC had been 'cured' by my general surgeon removing my entire colon ten years before my stroke.

Medical denial is not a rare hazard. Both sexes are guilty of denying cancer with reported cases of women with necrotizing breast masses who have managed to not take in the possibility of this representing breast cancer, and with the men in turn ignoring testicular masses. I've only had one personal case of this, which was a guy with a softball-sized tumor just above his right collar bone. He had presented to the ED with an unrelated complaint and was very blasé in his responses to my questions about how long this obvious mass had been there. It was probably an advanced lymphoma at that point, but I never did learn his outcome. I mention these examples of denial in an effort to convince the reader that our own healthcare is not amenable to being seen as a completely do-it-yourself project. Also, despite the previously acknowledged hazards of engaging with mainstream medicine, it still represents our best avenue for treating disease states.

CHAPTER SEVEN

PLACEBO EFFECT

In researching this book, I have studied 100+ articles and books about the placebo effect hoping to come to a single definitive conclusion. Instead, I have learned that there is a range of strong opinions on either side of the question of the degree to which the placebo effect is powerful or not, and what role it should play in patient care.

For clarity's sake, we'll briefly define a placebo as a sugar pill or some other reliably inert substance or intervention given to a patient for the purpose of, and which succeeds in, producing a positive response (placebo effect) for which no completely understood physiological explanation currently exists.

A very brief historical review of the word placebo dates its first use to the fourteenth century (placebo being from the Latin for 'I shall please'). Its initial use was in reference to hired mourners at funerals, carrying "the connotation of depreciation and substitution, because professional mourners were often stand-ins for members of the family of the deceased." The first appearance in a medical context dates to 1785, with a medical dictionary of the time defining it at first as 'a commonplace method or medicine.' Several decades later, the medical definition took on an even more negative flavor with its description as 'an epithet given to any medicine adapted more to please than to benefit the patient.' The above recap is based on "Placebo and Placebo Effects in Medicine: Historical Overview" by de Craen, et al. from their article in the *Journal of the Royal Society of Medicine*, which states:

> *Until the first half of the 20th century the use of placebos seems to have been widespread in medicine. In 1807 Thomas Jefferson, recording what he called the pious fraud, observed that 'one of the most successful physicians I have ever known has assured me that he used more bread pills, drops of colored water, and powders of hickory ashes, than all the other medicines put together.' About 100 years later, Richard Cabot, of Harvard Medical School, described how he 'was brought up, as I suppose every physician is, to use placebo, bread pills, water subcutaneously, and other devices.' Only a few physicians considered the bread pill a threat to the integrity of medicine, and most ethical codes endorsed 'necessary deception'. A polychromatic assortment of sugar pills was routinely quaffed by patients. However, placebos were thought to bring only comfort to the patient, with no impact on pathophysiology. The value of placebo was thought inversely related to the intelligence of a patient; the use of a medical ritual was more effective and necessary for 'unintelligent, neurotic, or inadequate patients.*[97]

More modern studies have not consistently shown a specific subset of individuals who are 'placebo reactors,' although the latest work in this area is looking at the actual genomic profile of individuals to see if placebo-response tendencies can be identified in that way.

The preceding chapters have focused on the negative effects that our beliefs can have on our healthcare decisions and medical conditions.

Now we will take a look at the positive effects that our beliefs can have as well. In his groundbreaking 1955 article "The Powerful Placebo" in the *Journal of the American Medical Association*, Dr. Henry Beecher made the claim that in some 35+ percent of cases, "placebos have a high degree of therapeutic effectiveness."[98]

The placebo skeptics accurately point out that other factors might be involved in these apparent patient improvements, related predominantly to the natural history of the maladies under study. In other words, the self-limited illnesses being studied were merely resolving spontaneously, that extremes of sensation in either direction will statistically tend to regress to the mean, and other factors. These skeptics also accurately point out the methodological shortcomings in Beecher's seminal article.

However, in the summary of his article Beecher does qualify that, "It is evident that placebos have a high degree of therapeutic effectiveness in treating *subjective responses*...." He then goes on to suggest that in order to draw accurate conclusions from clinical trials, this "requires the use of the 'double blind' technique, where neither the subject nor the observer is aware of what agent was used or indeed when it was used."[99]

Throughout most of the nineteenth and into the mid-twentieth century, it was generally concluded that the placebo effect was something that occurred most prominently in weak-minded or suggestible people, and it was, and still is, mostly perceived by mainstream medicine as more of an annoyance than a tool. So, it was just shunted into the background and seen as useful only as a 'control' when trying to prove that a specific treatment does actually work. Thus, we have arrived at the gold standard of clinical research, the randomized clinical trial (RCT). This is a study in which the treatment of interest is compared to a reliably inert substance or intervention, and neither the recipients nor the researchers know who is getting what during the course of the trial until the random and secret assignments to specific treatments have been revealed at the end of the study.

Placebos have been, and continue to be, used as 'controls' in all respectable scientific studies. More recent and specific studies on placebos themselves have shown the following results:

- Colored pills are more effective than white ones.
- Injections are more effective than tablets for most people.
- Physical interventions are more effective than just pills alone.
- Sham surgery (where anesthesia is delivered, and a surgical incision is made but no procedure is performed) can at times be just as effective as full procedural surgery (as in arthroscopic surgery for osteoarthritis of the knee).[100]
- Emergency department treatments are more effective than office-based treatments.
- Higher-priced remedies are more effective than cheaper ones.
- Branded medications are more effective than generics.
- Two placebos are more effective than one.
- A placebo added to a true medication is more effective than a true medication alone.
- Open treatments are more effective than hidden treatments (in other words, medications for pain, anxiety, cancer-related fatigue, and even Parkinson's disease given within the patient's ability to know that they have been medicated are more effective than the same dosages of the same medicines when their administration into an IV line is hidden behind a curtain!).[101]

These findings do tend to make us sound rather weak-minded and suggestible, don't they? I find that placebo studies do serve to advance a strong case for the conclusion that we are all subject to influence by the placebo effect, which has been demonstrated to be strongly related to our expectations from treatment. These studies repeatedly show that negative expectations can lead to placebo's 'evil twin,' the nocebo effect, meaning reports of negative effects from inert treatments rather than improvement. Thus, even while taking inert sugar pills, a substantial portion of participants in placebo studies will report a wide range of side effects.

In the ED, we see this manifested at times when patients come in and tell us that they are 'allergic to all antibiotics.' This, though lacking credibility, has to be taken at face value and can be an unfortunate barrier to the patient's most effective treatment. The more likely explanation is either a true allergy to one antibiotic class or simply antibiotic side effects, which as a general class of medications are prone to cause quite noticeable gastrointestinal symptoms in many patients. This experience can then cause the patient to generalize to an expectation of having those same effects from all antibiotics, resulting in a self-fulfilling prophecy.

A very balanced overview article addressing the most prominent placebo factors and considerations, which is accessible even to the lay person, is titled "The Placebo Effect: Illness and Interpersonal Healing" by Franklin G. Miller, et al. In an attempt to not try the reader's patience, I will repeat just a number of their findings here:

- "We suggest the hypothesis that the placebo effect operates predominantly by producing symptomatic relief of illness, such as pain, anxiety, and fatigue, rather than by modifying the pathophysiology of disease."
- Placebo analgesia (pain relief from inert treatments) appears to be mediated by release of endogenous opioids (internally produced narcotic equivalents) since some studies show the ability to block this effect with Narcan (naloxone used to reverse narcotic overdose). They say here, "This scientific credibility is particularly important in light of the dismissive and confusing characterization of the placebo phenomenon within biomedicine."
- A large meta-analysis "found no evidence of placebo effects for objective and binary outcomes."

- Studies for conditions such as migraine, tension headaches, chronic low-back pain, and osteoarthritis of the knee showed that no different results were detected between real and sham acupuncture, but patients receiving either of those interventions experienced substantially greater symptom improvement than no treatment or usual care groups.

- "Technological healing is a major focus of the science of medicine – the development and testing of technological interventions to successfully treat disease and symptoms of illness. Interpersonal healing concerns the art of medicine, oriented therapeutically towards relief of suffering – the illness component of disease and injury. A theory of interpersonal healing will need to illuminate why and how the clinical encounter independently contributes to healing, separate from (though often associated with) natural healing and technological healing."

- "As the symptomatic manifestation of disease, illness has subjective and objectively measurable dimensions, both of which may be modified by placebo effects. For example, reduced arthritic pain from a placebo effect may also be associated with improved mobility. Accordingly, the thesis that the placebo effect predominantly operates on illness does not imply that it is 'all in the mind' or that it only involves subjective outcomes, based entirely on patient reports."

- "Although traditional forms of medicine know virtually nothing about disease from a scientific perspective and may have had few treatment interventions with any specific efficacy, much of the success of traditional medicine can be attributed to the placebo effect, operating on illness." They add a quote from JD Frank's book *Persuasion and Healing*, "Scientific medicine......while paying copious lip service to the doctor-patient relationship, in actuality largely ignores it."

- They repeatedly reinforce the primacy of the physician-patient relationship and emphasize this by quoting from Kleinman's

1988 book *The Illness Narratives: Suffering, Healing, and the Human Condition*, "The chief sources of therapeutic efficacy are the development of a successful therapeutic relationship and the rhetorical use of the practitioner's personality and communicative skills to empower the patient and persuade him toward more successful coping." [102]

One of the above article's authors, Ted J. Kaptchuk has demonstrated several other interesting study results, which I'll mention briefly here. He has run comparison studies with the use of open label placebos (OLP) which have shown positive results in treatment of several conditions, including irritable bowel syndrome (IBS), chronic low-back pain, and cancer-related fatigue—in other words, substantial reported improvement, even when the patients in the placebo arm of the study were told that they were taking an inert placebo.

In the IBS study, significant symptom improvement was found in IBS patients randomized to a group fully informed that the pills they would be given were "Placebo pills made of an inert substance, like sugar pills, that have been shown in clinical studies to produce significant improvement in IBS symptoms through mind-body self-healing processes." [103]

In a back pain study, participants were informed that they would participate in "a novel mind–body clinical study of chronic low-back pain." It was further explained that the addition to their usual treatment consisted of a "placebo pill" which "was an inactive substance, like a flour pill, that contained no active medication in it." Despite knowing this, placebo recipients reported significantly greater improvement in their chronic low-back pain. The researchers concluded, "Our data suggest that harnessing placebo effects without deception is possible in the context of a plausible rationale." [104]

A similar OLP study of cancer-related fatigue found that even after medication discontinuation, "The improvement in fatigue was maintained for 4 weeks." [105]

On the concerning side, in his similar study of asthma patients it was shown that study subjects reported subjective improvement to placebo inhalation treatments, even though they manifested no objective measurable improvement in lung function. This is particularly concerning with asthma because a significant delay in initiating effective treatment to improve objective lung function can lead to complete respiratory failure and even death. So, this highlights the danger involved if, as patients, we simply want to feel better, and for business-profit reasons, hospital administrators predominantly want our physicians to focus on keeping us more satisfied. By achieving only those things, we may actually be putting ourselves at greater risk of harm (the danger of prioritizing *patient satisfaction* will be discussed at greater length in Chapter Ten).

The conditions of irritable bowel syndrome, chronic low-back pain, and cancer-related fatigue no doubt engender significant medical suffering. But unless a more serious diagnosis has been missed, they do not pose any immediate risk to your life. However, asthma can follow a more dangerous path even with state-of-the-art treatment, so just making a patient feel subjectively better is an inadequate goal.

One ED patient I was treating had the following course. She was a known asthmatic, in her mid-30s, who reported that she had run out of two of her usual asthma medications leading to feeling badly enough to need emergency department treatment. She denied any recent hospitalizations for that condition, or any prior intubations. She was in moderate distress initially, so I initiated aggressive treatment with two IV medications known to be effective in significant asthmatic wheezing (the steroid Solu-Medrol and magnesium sulfate as well). Since the onset of their effects is known to be delayed, we also initiated treatment with the more immediately effective inhaled bronchodilators nearly continuously.

We did also ultimately have to resort to noninvasive positive-pressure ventilation. This involves placing a very tight-fitting mask around the nose and mouth to enable oxygen to be forced deep into the lungs every time the patient initiates a breath. My goal was to avoid the more invasive process of intubating her and placing her on a ventilator. Both the respiratory technician and I spent a long time at her bedside describing what we were doing while coaching her through this process and the patient confirmed through nods that she was feeling progressively better.

Not knowing what direction her course would take, I had initially examined her thoroughly around the face and neck and in her mouth and throat to make sure that an intubation process would encounter no obvious obstacles. I also had immediately made sure that all of the equipment was in the room to perform an intubation, including that a suction catheter and tubing were attached to the wall behind her bed, that I had a working light on my laryngoscope (the curved metal tool used to elevate the tongue and see the entry to the airway), and that I had even taken out and prepped an endotracheal tube. Her nurse asked me off to the side, "Are we intubating?" To this I gave my equally quiet usual response of, "No, I'm just trying to ward off evil."

That part is pure superstition, but hard experience had taught me that in the midst of the intubation process was not when you wanted to discover that the bulb at the end of the laryngoscope is no longer lighting up, or that the cuff at the end of the endotracheal tube would either not inflate or not hold air! The patient was at first responding quite well to treatment, with reduced wheezing and notably less 'work of breathing' (the effort required to move air). I had also initially explained to her that my hope, as always, was to improve her condition well enough to perhaps allow her to be discharged home for further treatment there. It had become clear at this point that she would not only have to stay in the hospital but now even stay in the intensive care unit, given her need for the positive-pressure breathing setup. I had stepped out of her room several times very briefly to check her lab work results and her chest x-ray, but I had never removed the intubation tools from the roomy pockets of my white coat (another superstition that putting those tools back in their proper place might make their need more likely). I explained to her the need now for hospitalization and reassured myself that she did not appear to be fatiguing from all her work of breathing and also did appear to be substantially improved, with far less wheezing than upon arrival along with less anxiety (which can be worsened by the discomfort and novelty of the tight-fitting mask). I then stepped out of her room one more time to let the ED secretary know to contact the admitting doctor for the ICU to discuss her case and complete the admission process. Within just a couple of minutes I heard the code bell go off and I ran back to the end of the department where I had been treating this patient. I had no suspicion that it would be her room where the code was taking place. When I reentered her room, I found one of my colleagues had already arrived there, but I waved him off saying that she was my patient and I was fully involved with her treatment, gesturing to my intubation equipment. I learned from her nurse that the patient had experienced a sudden need to empty her mouth of accumulated excessive saliva and both she and the patient had understandably taken this as a sign that she was on the verge of nausea and vomiting (highly inadvisable with the mask in place). Promptly after the mask was removed, she had a fainting episode and her breathing rate dropped precipitously. Though the reason for this exact sequence was not fully clear to me, intubation was now mandatory. When the admitting ICU doctor, who happened to be a pulmonologist, called back and pointed out that it was best to avoid intubating asthmatics because treating them on a ventilator could be problematic, I had no hesitation in pointing out to him that I had waited until forced to do so.

I finished my clinical career firmly believing that in healthcare the physician and the patient need to form a trusting partnership with acknowledgment of their different expertise. The patient is the expert in how they are feeling and what they hope to achieve, while the physician is the expert in the advisability of those goals and how they can most safely be achieved. Despite our lack of consciously resorting to placebos in emergency medicine, I also finished my career convinced that we physicians, like healers of all stripes, do function to some degree as 'walking placebos,' even in the ED.

I want to point out immediately that I do not subscribe to the idea that we can think, wish, or expect ourselves into good health. I spent all of my 20s expecting and believing that 'somehow' I would eventually become well and no longer suffer from my UC. As it turned out, not being aware of its importance at the time, I never did make the effort to establish the type of patient-physician connection and relationship that I am endorsing so strongly in this book.

With the persisting naive expectation that my UC was some kind of cosmic mistake that would somehow eventually correct itself, I continued on through my education in college, medical school, and postgraduate training which brought me from New Hampshire to New Jersey to Connecticut and then Florida before ultimately returning to New England to start my first attending EM physician job. I did not have a specific objection to having a personal physician, but I was never in one place long enough to establish a sustained relationship with one. Frankly, at that point I did not even believe it was a necessary or helpful thing.

The 1992-1997 interlude in my EM career, forced upon me by my stroke, allowed me to pursue a Master of Public Health degree. This exposed me to the social determinants of health outlook, the biopsychosocial model that Engel proposed, and eventually to the bold claim that Herbert Benson, MD, made in a 1996 medical journal article (he was at the time a Harvard-trained cardiologist and head of the Mind/Body Institute at Harvard Medical School and Massachusetts General Hospital, so pretty much near the pinnacle of mainstream medicine in the US). Benson's article was titled "Harnessing the Power of the Placebo Effect and Renaming it 'Remembered Wellness'" in the *Annual Review of Medicine* and the content at first blush sounded anti-scientific and too soft-headed to believe.

He begins with:

> *Because almost all treatments prior to 150 years ago were, we now know, without scientifically proven specificity, the history of medicine could be considered the history of the placebo effect.*[106]

Benson then goes on to describe the components of the placebo effect, which he proposes to rename "remembered wellness" in order to shed some of the pejorative connotations attached to the word placebo. I recall thinking that it was quite a clunky name that would not likely catch on, and in fact it did not.

The following is another direct quotation from that article:

> *It is important to emphasize that the administration of a placebo is not necessary to evoke the placebo response. Three components, however, are necessary:*
>
> *(a) positive beliefs and expectations on the part of the patient;*
>
> *(b) positive beliefs and expectations on the part of the physician or health care professional; and*
>
> *(c) a good relationship between the two parties.*
>
> *... Unlike most other forms of therapy, remembered wellness has withstood the test of time and continues to be safe and inexpensive. Furthermore, its use can easily be incorporated into standard pharmacologic and surgical treatments to act synergistically with them.* [107]

He is proposing using placebo effect in conjunction with, rather than in place of, mainstream medical therapies. He is also identifying that the effectiveness is heavily reliant upon a close and trusting relationship being established between the physician and the patient.

I recall reflecting at the time I read this, "Really, just those three things, that sounds very powerful, relatively easy, and wonderfully inexpensive! Why aren't we putting that to better use?"

But if this placebo effect theory is actually true, then there is a potentially extremely dangerous downside to this seemingly simple process. If that's all it takes to get a resultant degree of healing, then any fool thing might work. So, hypothetically you and I could agree that by placing henna tattoos of passages from your preferred religious scripture, or favorite poet/writer/aphorism, over the affected area of your body we would be able to induce healing. That is assuming we could get ourselves to believe strongly enough in the concept and had a good relationship, then you should be able to experience some improvement.

The obvious danger there is that if you choose to rely on some degree of improvement from this 'alternative medicine' for a severe malady such as a dangerous infection or cancer, particularly ones for which more mainstream medicine has very effective and more definitive treatments available, you might deprive yourself from learning about and benefiting from a more effective treatment plan.

Of course, currently there are a whole range of alternative medicine approaches to healthcare, my henna tattoo example above being one that I just made up. Further research though did end up showing me that a form of therapy called 'tattoo therapy' does exist, which involves actual tattooing, but I did not take the time to investigate that further.

There is an unresolved debate among knowledgeable and experienced individuals as to whether or not the effectiveness of alternative medicine is solely due to the placebo effect in action. Although for the sake of study, investigators have been able to come up with a credible version of 'sham acupuncture,' the unique nature of many alternative medicine interventions make it difficult to have a true double-blinded placebo-controlled study. Consider, for example, how to develop sham versions of 'colonic hydrotherapy' and/or 'vaginal steaming,' both of which exist as interventions purported to 'improve energy.' As a third example, these are quotes from an online advice forum for the health benefits of 'exposing genitalia to the sun':

Let me tell you about one of my biohacks I did on my last cold in 2015 in the winter. I spent 15 minutes in AM sunlight naked. 7.5 minutes on my front and then 7.5 min on my back. Then put four ounces of 35 percent hydrogen peroxide (reagent grade) in a gallon of water. I then ran a cold humidifier in my bedroom all night with this mixture. My biohack had cold gone in the AM before I had to go to surgery.[108]

The forum administrator writing then goes on to appropriately point out that women's ovaries/gonads are intrabdominal:

Ladies reading this should stop........and now realize why they need their breasts in the sun too. A woman's gonads...are...hidden from the sun...but their breasts are out in the open awaiting the sun signal.[109]

I'm hoping here to offend the least number of people that I can, but I will confess that I tend to believe that the bulk of what is done in the name of alternative medicine, admittedly along with a sizeable portion of what we do in mainstream medicine as well, is effective by tapping into the potential healing power of the placebo effect for non-specific symptoms of feeling generally unwell. These examples above make it easy, if unpleasant, to visualize why it would be difficult to run double-blinded placebo-controlled studies on these kinds of health recommendations! And no, I'll admit to never having personally tested these recommendations myself—the first two involving organs that I either no longer have, or never did have, and the third presenting a not insurmountable, but nevertheless substantial, modesty barrier.

In my practice of emergency medicine, I have never intentionally used placebo medications, but I expect that I have successfully tapped into the placebo effect on multiple occasions. I have witnessed some version of the placebo effect in my patients on many occasions. In the usual sequence, a patient's nurse will have had the first contact with them before I enter the room. Not uncommonly they will have started an IV and even initiated one or two IV medications, such as for pain and nausea control, via standing, preapproved treatment protocols. In my subsequently obtaining a history of the illness from the patient, they will then often gesture to the IV and say they're "feeling much better now after what the nurse gave me." As often as not when I seek out their nurse, I will learn that no medications had yet been given, nor had a significant volume of IV fluids been infused.

There are a range of reasons why this may be so, the patient having safely arrived in the ED and been attended to kindly by their nurse goes a long way in relieving anxiety, which may be contributing to, or possibly even be the sole reason for, their feeling unwell in the first place. In addition, at that point patients are often accompanied by caring family members and/or friends for whom they are now the center of loving attention. These first two are, in my mind, legitimate reasons for seeking healing attention, but these often can be common ailments that may have been prevented or attended to safely at home. That is not an opinion that I confront patients with, but after a thorough evaluation, I always do try to educate them regarding safe ways to attend to minor symptoms and discomforts, for example minor nausea or diarrhea, at home in the future, should they choose to do so.

As an aside, a third and less healthy reason why people may report feeling improved shortly after arriving in the emergency department often does not become evident until the very end of their evaluation when they ask for a work note, while expressing no interest at all in any health advice that I have to offer! It is a fact of modern life that minor ailments that did not impede one's lifestyle during the weekend will become more pressing on a Monday morning, given the choice of going to work or presenting to the ED. "I was in the emergency department," serves as a valid excuse for not being at work or many other obligations one might prefer to avoid (contributing to the consistent finding that Mondays tend to be the busiest day in emergency departments).

There is definite merit to the placebo revisionist point of view, which although I do not share it, I respect the grounds for it. I will now present four separate modern studies (while sparing you an equivalent number of additional ones) both within and outside the cardiology literature that show a 50% reduction in mortality with consistent placebo use, which may confirm the existence and importance of the placebo effect.

The cardiologists, bless their hearts, are not content to rely upon a patient's subjective report of improvement and have carried out a number of studies, the end point of which is that most objective of all measurements—mortality—with some very eye-catching results!

Here are parts of several studies' conclusions:

- Poor adherers to treatment whether propranolol or placebo "were 2.6 times more likely than good adherers to die within a year of follow-up.... Furthermore, this increased risk of death for poor adherers was not accounted for by measures of the severity of myocardial infarction, sociodemographic features (e.g., race, marital status, education), smoking, or psychological characteristics (high life-stress or social isolation)." (1990)[110]

- "For patients with good adherence to placebo or beneficial drug therapy, the risk of mortality was about half that of participants with poor adherence." (2006)[111]

- "It is surprising that better adherence to placebo should be associated with reduced mortality since placebo by definition has no specific biologic or disease modifying activity. Therefore, placebo adherence must be a marker for some other factors responsible for this extraordinary survival advantage, but what those factors might be remains a mystery." (2010)[112]

- "Total in-study mortality was reduced by nearly 40% among those participants who were at least 75% adherent to their study medication [beta blocker or placebo] relative to those who were less adherent.... Adjustment for numerous baseline risk factors did not substantially attenuate the relationship. There is no clear explanation for why better adherence to an inert pill should be associated with a 39% decrease in one's mortality risk.... While probably not due to publication bias or simple confounding by healthy lifestyle factors, the underlying explanation for the association remains enigmatic." (2012)[113]

So, the question arises, what in the world is going on here? One might conclude that we are seeing the placebo effect phenomenon being proven repeatedly. What could better demonstrate one's expectation of a good result and a reasonably good relationship with one's physician than to actually follow the advice that was given, by taking the recommended medication? An alternative explanation has been proposed called the 'healthy adherer effect.' This theory posits that those patients who are more likely to adhere to advised medications are also more likely to adhere to other general good health recommendations, like following a better diet, exercising, seatbelt use, moderate alcohol use, no smoking, and so forth, thus reducing their mortality rates in those ways. Both the first and fourth studies listed above did control for a number of confounders, but it would take substantially greater study efforts to control for the whole range of health recommendations that patients either adhere to or not.

It strikes me that if a specific drug or medical intervention could claim and prove that it decreased our mortality rate by 50%, it would be hailed as an earth-shaking advancement. A similar therapeutic breakthrough might garner 'Nobel Prize in Medicine'-type prizes and huge investments in and profits from producing. And that in and of itself may be the problem, the fact that this would be a parentless, unpatentable, and therefore unprofitable venture, that is, the placebo effect and/or healthy adherer effect could not be monetized. Therefore this 'mystery' or 'enigma' does not have legions of supporters or investigators currently. I conclude that whether it is placebo affect or healthy adherer effect, or some part of each, there are undeniably consistent results showing a halving of the mortality rate in patients who are following general good health advice; therefore, it is a substantially less effective and riskier proposition to be a passive uncommitted participant in your healthcare.

One last quote from the article opening this chapter is:

Laboratory studies have shown that placebo interventions can elicit quantifiable changes in neurotransmitters, hormones, and immune regulators. During the past decade, numerous studies have investigated the neurobiological mechanisms underlying placebo effects by means of brain imaging techniques. [114]

In other words, actual brain imaging studies such as with functional MRI and PET scans demonstrate the areas of the brain that are active while placebo effects are being observed clinically. The three authors of this article (Miller, Colloca, Kaptchuk) are all prominent investigators into and proponents of the importance of the placebo effect. I find their comments both intriguing and convincing that although placebo effects predominantly influence the subjective experience of illness, they are nevertheless accompanied by measurable bodily changes. The major proviso there is that there is no known way yet to harness and intentionally guide those processes.

This is where it gets really interesting on the science side. Psychoneuroimmunology (PNI) is a relatively new field of science which is identifying all the ways in which the immune system is in communication with and directed by our central nervous system, as well as the psyche. Psychologist-researcher Dr. Robert Ader, PhD, experimented with pairing a sugar solution with an appetite-suppressing chemotherapy drug in rats (1975). In addition to its purposeful suppressing of the appetite, as a chemotherapy agent it also had the effect of suppressing the rats' immune systems. Ader ended up training the rats' immune systems to become suppressed by just the sugar solution alone, even when the chemotherapy drug was withheld. This was something of a stunner to the scientific community because the immune system was previously felt to operate entirely independently of the other organ systems of the body. Ader concluded:

Here we had a conditioning effect that had a major biologic impact on the survival of the animal. That suggests that the placebo effect is a learned response available to anybody under the appropriate circumstances. [115,116]

In 2002, a similarly structured study by another investigator showed that the exact same process of conditioned immunosuppression was demonstrable in humans.[117]

In a 2010 interview, Ader responded at length about the setting for and implications of his study and psychoneuroimmunology:

> *Our research had demonstrated a functional link between the brain and the immune system, which shouldn't happen, because there were no connections between the brain and the immune system. ...As a psychologist, I was unaware that there were no connections between the brain and the immune system so I was free to consider any possibility that might explain this orderly relationship between the magnitude of the conditioned response and the rate of mortality.[118]*

So, the natural questions then are, how is it that the brain developed the ability to communicate with the immune system, what is it trying to accomplish, and how sophisticated can this conversation become? This harkens back to the much earlier Mr. Wright/Krebiozen case in Chapter One, in which both consciously and inadvertently manipulated expectations appeared to exert influences on his survival.

That case has always been scientifically dismissible as simply being anecdotal, with an 'N of 1' (N representing the number of people enrolled in a study, thus indicating a very low level of confidence in its general applicability). However, other well-documented case reports of spontaneous resolution of cancers do exist with suspected mechanisms being the immune system itself ridding the body of the cancer. The credibility of these events is now significantly higher since immunotherapy has been successfully harnessed and applied in treatment of a number of different cancers. Spontaneous resolutions of cancer are considerably rare, with estimates in the 1 for every 100,000 cases of cancer range...so therefore definitely not something one would wish to solely rely upon.[119]

As I am writing now, I am by coincidence awaiting a cancer-screening procedure tomorrow. More specifically, this is an ERCP procedure by way of which my doctors can biopsy a suspicious-appearing area in one of my liver's bile ducts. Annoyingly, this appears to be from the same autoimmune disease process that I've been living with since 1973. Hopefully, this will appear benign under the microscope and simply be an inflammatory stricture related to my diagnosis of primary sclerosing cholangitis (PSC), a condition causing an increased risk of bile duct cancers as well as the risk of progressing to complete liver failure. I'm being seen by GI specialists in a nearby major teaching hospital upon referral by my own local gastroenterologist, whose judgment I've come to trust. My plan is to follow whatever treatment course they recommend. If Dr. P. there advises that I should be treated aggressively by having a portion of my liver surgically removed and then follow this up with chemotherapy and/or radiation therapy (as my own brief research indicates are potential considerations), I will say, "Have at it." Of course, I plan to only concur after asking a series of questions, particularly including if we can use immunotherapy as an effective approach. I'm fully expecting that the biopsy pathology report will indicate harmless inflammation, but I'm pursuing my usual lifelong adaptive approach of hoping for and expecting the best, while preparing for the worst!

I bring up my ERCP procedure here in this context because I ask myself how in the world would an alternative medicine practitioner even diagnose, much less treat, my current condition? The concerning answer is that from my reading and my, granted minimal, direct exposure, it appears that the vast majority of alternative medicine approaches do not actually use objective diagnostic testing or even make a specific diagnosis, defaulting to claims that their approaches 'improve energy' and 'fortify the immune system.' I actually don't even doubt that those claims could be true. But what then to do in cases of an autoimmune disease like my UC, where the immune system seems to be overly energized and fortified, but also confused about where to apply its skills? Is it biologically plausible that the same therapeutic approaches and interventions can be used to both fortify and energize and also to restrain or redirect the immune system?

It does turn out that immunotherapy can be used effectively to treat cancers, but this involves a very specific cellular level biochemical intervention to educate one's immune system cells to target only the cancer cells specific to the individual tumor at hand. I particularly like the idea of the immune system being turned into an effective treatment for a specific condition caused by my immune system's own initial confusion. Having come of age in the 60s, my reflex inclination was to trust the body's natural healing mechanisms, as well as to have a degree of suspicion about large powerful organizations like the American Medical Association (AMA), of which I've never been a member. I was also intrigued and convinced by Walter Cannon's description of 'the wisdom of the body,' along with the elegance of the body's ability to sustain homeostasis. I still respect that way of thinking, but my own health experience has revealed that at times the body can be a self-centered and spiteful ignoramus!

The fact that chronic inflammation of a cell can ultimately lead to cancerous changes is well-known, being demonstrated by lung cancer caused by smoking. Historically, this conjunction of chemical irritation and inflammation leading to cancerous changes was first observed in chimney sweeps having prolonged direct exposure to chimney soot (young boys wriggling up the then broader but still confining chimney flues), who then developed scrotal cancer. In 1775, this was the first identified occupational cancer. A similar sequence now occurs when the inflammation caused by sexually transmitted viral infection leads to cervical and genital cancers, as well as liver cancer (as mentioned in Chapter Four).

I don't mean to come across as being against Complementary and Alternative Medicine (CAM)—I'm all for reducing medical suffering through any manner that is not unhealthy or dangerous in its own right (such as substance abuse). I believe that CAM practitioners are likely achieving healing effects predominantly by having longer and substantially more compassionate interactions with us as patients, all of which is quite valuable in its own right. But I'm very concerned about patients being in the right place at the right time and receiving the right treatment. I do strongly prefer the approach that alternative medicine should openly acknowledge its limitations while being integrated alongside mainstream medicine rather than aspiring to being used as a replacement for it. For example, in support of the dangers of relying exclusively on alternative medicine (AM) in place of conventional cancer treatment (CCT), there are these findings and conclusions from a recent study:

> *After controlling for sociodemographic and clinical factors, the magnitude of difference was largest for breast cancer because women who used AM as initial treatment without CCT had more than a fivefold increased risk of death. Patients with colorectal and lung cancer had a more than fourfold and twofold increase in risk of death, respectively.*
>
> *In conclusion, we found that cancer patients who initially chose treatment with AM without CCT were more likely to die. Improved communication between patients and caregivers and greater scrutiny of the use of AM for the initial treatment of cancer is needed.[120]*

Thus, I believe that the phrase CIM for complementary and integrative medicine is preferable. I will confess to some jealousy, too, that those practitioners of alternative medicine do not have to run a similar risk as we mainstream medicine physicians do with our potential of inadvertently harming our patients by at times necessarily invasive treatment. For very good reasons, we don't ever see CAM/CIM hospitals or emergency departments. Their treatment methods, especially ones involving an unrushed, sustained, and supportive listening environment, accommodate many illness symptoms reasonably well, but are really not appropriate for many disease states. Again, this is summarized quite nicely by Tim Minchin, "You know what they call alternative medicine that's been proved to work? – Medicine."[121] If you have the time and interest, this statement comes at about the midpoint of a nine-minute rant that he has posted on *YouTube* entitled "Storm" on the topic of critical thinking and science (worth the time to my mind, although I should warn you that, like all of his stuff, it is articulate and witty, but also somewhat vulgar, entertainingly so).

I've always found it odd, particularly more so now that I've reached the end of my career, that we medical doctors always refer to our profession as 'practicing' medicine. Obviously, this is not exclusive to medicine, since lawyers and some other professionals also say that they are 'practicing' their professions. The key difference there is that they cannot physically hurt or kill you if they are having an off day in their 'practice.'

Two of the most dismaying concepts that you learn in medical school are the existence of categories of health problems that are either idiopathic or iatrogenic. Idiopathic means 'of unknown cause,' and I had unfortunately already learned of that through my personal UC experience. Iatrogenic refers to medical problems that are caused by the medical treatment itself, and that was a truly daunting prospect to consider, that we could inadvertently hurt our patients. Turns out it's surprisingly easy to do, not only by invasive procedures but even at times by the simple act of ordering a lab test, x-ray, or medication (which can at times lead to a cascade of further interventions involving hospitalizations and procedures with their own attendant risks).

Members of all professions, including teaching and others that have not adopted or sustained this somewhat archaic use of the word practice, would no doubt tell you that there is a constant state of learning and refinement of technique involved as they go about their business. The 'See one, Do one, Teach one' ethic though is one that is deeply embedded within medicine. That is how our education takes place. You first observe a technique being done, then attempt it yourself, ideally under the supervision of an experienced and skilled instructor, and then the next time around you adopt the role of instructor yourself to the next novice. Yes, in other words, we are most definitely 'practicing' on you. Simple things like drawing blood, starting IVs, taking patient histories, and doing physical exams...*these* are daily low-tech repetitive processes. However, the challenge arises when the tasks involved are low-frequency events, for example doing a spinal tap, intubating a patient, putting in a chest tube or an emergency temporary pacemaker wire, and a whole host of progressively more invasive tasks.

In one of these events, I was a third-year medical student on rounds on the internal medicine ward when the medical resident turned to me and said, "Do you want to do a spinal tap?" I had in fact seen the requisite 'one,' and I recall still that it was with a sense of hesitant and nervous obligation that I responded, "Okay." This process involves inserting an extremely long, thin needle into a person's low back between the lumbar vertebrae in order to obtain a sample of cerebrospinal fluid from around the spinal cord, as in this case to rule out a meningitis infection. So, I step up to the plate (the patient lying compliantly on his side with his back exposed), and now I'm hearing things like, "Make sure that the bevel is facing up, start between the spinous processes, stay parallel with the floor, and aim for the navel."

This is a blind technique, as in you're not sure where the tip of your needle is in its journey out of sight into the patient's body. You can't see the spinous processes or the navel either, but at least you can to a limited degree feel the prominence of the spinous processes by palpating the overlying skin (one of several good reasons to keep a lean body mass if you can) and you can reasonably picture where the navel should be, opposite of where you're standing. So, the natural question becomes, "How do I know how far to go in?" To which the response was, "You will feel a popping sensation as you go through the meninges" (thin membranes surrounding the spinal column and brain). Having already seen how thin the meninges are, once in an animal lab (think Saran wrap), I was very skeptical that they could be felt all the way to my fingers through the spinal needle. However, as it developed, I could indeed feel this pop sensation, which was good luck for the patient, along with the fact that he did not have findings suggesting meningitis. Talk about beginner's luck! I never again succeeded in a similar first-pass perfect spinal tap procedure. The more common experience was a hunt-and-peck multiple-pass procedure with the spinal needle at times hitting the bony vertebral spinous processes, or gritty connective tissue giving the false impression that you've experienced that "pop."

The quintessential intervention in medicine in general, and emergency medicine more specifically, is what is termed the endotracheal intubation, the procedure whereby a breathing tube is placed into the airway to take over breathing for the patient. In essence, we are rather presumptuously saying, "You can no longer be trusted to breathe adequately for yourself." In the ideal life experience, you will never be subjected to this other than under the care of a skilled anesthesiologist in the operating room for a scheduled surgical procedure, and at that time you'll be fully sedated and unaware of anything going on.

In those circumstances, if the anesthesiologist has concerns about details such as your body particulars, like obesity, stiff or injured neck, small mouth and/or big tongue, full stomach, oral secretions, bleeding, or other concerns, perhaps making endotracheal intubation a difficult procedure, or your vital signs or other health considerations making this a dangerous case, the anesthesiologist can simply choose the option of 'cancel/postpone this case' before even getting started. This option is not available to us in EM; we just have to take on whatever comes through the door.

At the beginning of my EM career in the early 1980s, none of the very effective medications available to the anesthesia folks were available to us yet in the ED. At that time, we were not considered skilled enough to be trusted to use them properly. These various medications allow for immediate sedation followed by complete paralysis, thus facilitating the passage of the endotracheal tube into the airway itself rather than into the esophagus, which in a distinctly poor anatomical design feature have their entries side-by-side in the back of the throat.

So, lacking those medications, we often relied upon an alternative approach by which we achieved blind nasotracheal intubation (BNTI). In a much more felicitous design, in the human being the nasal passages curve backward and deeply towards the airway itself. So, tubes passed through the nasal cavity will find their way into the vicinity of the airway and esophagus. The trick is preferentially passing the endotracheal tube that you are using into the proper opening. With the spontaneously breathing patient, sometimes fully awake or in various stages of distress and/or derangement, you insert the leading edge of this finger-width wide tube into the narrow nostril opening while holding your ear to the trailing opening of the tube. Then you listen for the near approach of the leading edge to where the breath sounds are originating from. With good timing and a bold confidence, with the next breath in you can advance the endotracheal tube into the airway where it belongs, as opposed to it entering the esophagus. The narrower, more flexible, naso-gastric tube when passed through the nostril will more often than not preferentially go into the esophagus. Endotracheal tubes can at times inadvertently enter the esophagus, which in and of itself is not an error but rather a known complication. The error is not recognizing that it's improperly placed and neglecting to pull it back out and reposition it more accurately. This error risks killing the patient since air is then being delivered into the stomach and not the lungs.

I want to present just one of my more memorable cases as a contrast with what's conceivable and achievable through alternative medicine. This one occurred in my very first year of emergency medicine practice as an independent attending physician after finishing my EM residency, and it has stayed near the forefront of my mind through nearly every work shift thereafter. In this event, I nearly actively killed a woman whom I was sincerely trying to help. A middle-aged woman presented complaining of not particularly alarming sounding chest discomfort, but on her cardiac monitor she began to have PVCs (premature ventricular contractions). PVCs are abnormal beats of the heart that may indicate that one of the ventricles (the two largest chambers of the heart) is not receiving sufficient oxygen. This could possibly represent a coronary artery blockage leading to a heart attack and permanent damage. In my training in those years, we were told that if these PVCs came from two or more different areas of the heart based on their configuration, or if they were occurring at a rate greater than six per minute, then we were obliged to initiate intravenous lidocaine, which is a cardiac drug used to treat malignant ventricular rhythm problems in the heart. The idea was that if we gave the lidocaine preventatively, these irregularities would be suppressed and therefore not lead to a sustained life-threatening heart-rhythm abnormality (arrythmia).

By that point in my career, I had realized that by nature and medical experience, I was a relative noninterventionist (a minimalist), that is, I adhered to the principle of 'Don't just do something, stand there' which can at times be nerve-wracking, but less harmful than the alternative of 'Don't just stand there, do something.' Observing the progression of a patient's condition can be an acceptable and thoughtful alternative to dashing in willy-nilly. So, I was pretty much glued to this patient's bedside for quite some time watching her monitor as the frequency of these PVCs waxed and waned, at times reaching and occasionally even exceeding the six per minute limit, while her subjective and objective condition did not vary at all.

Finally, my internal debate brought me to the conclusion that I could no longer justifiably not intervene and have her go into ventricular tachycardia, or even worse into ventricular fibrillation and die right then and there. So, I then gave the order for intravenous lidocaine, following which she promptly had a seizure (a known potential side effect of lidocaine use, but one that I had never seen before or even heard of, despite having used this medication successfully and without incident in similar settings several dozen times). On this occasion, her postictal (usual post-seizure sedation) nonverbal state then left us incommunicado regarding her subjective condition. That, along with the novelty (to me) of a seizure, accompanied by her persisting PVCs, convinced me that she might be actively deteriorating or suffering heart damage and therefore required intubation. Within our persisting limitations at that time, I did BNTI, which I had developed some facility with and, to my great relief, it went as smooth as silk.

My moment of satisfaction and relief was ephemeral, though. She was experiencing the usual amount of nasal drainage with a very small admixture of blood around the short portion of the endotracheal tube protruding from her nostril. Then in an alarming sequence of events that I had also never witnessed before or since, the hard plastic hub of the endotracheal tube, to which the Ambu-bag for artificial ventilation is attached, became detached from the more flexible tube itself (again something that I'd never seen before or even knew could happen). In the respiratory technician's efforts to reinsert it, the old-fashioned cloth athletic tape that we used in those days to stabilize the tube in place also slipped up and partially off the end of the tube, immediately adhering to itself and completely blocking off the opening of the tube and thus her airway itself. There is an inflatable cuff at the innermost end of the tube designed to keep secretions from passing into the lungs, while also allowing the air being blown through the tube to inflate the lungs fully and not seep back out around the tube itself. But in that process, it necessarily prevents the patient from being able to breath around the tube.

We all immediately tried vigorously to remove the tape, but no amount of pulling the tape was going to separate the now fully adhered surfaces of it. I was now in a position of asphyxiating this unfortunate woman in a far more effective way than if I had been choking her aggressively with both of my hands around her throat or trying to smother her with a pillow over her face.

So, in what I at first thought was a flash of brilliance, I grabbed a pair of scissors and cut off an inch or so from the end of the tube, tape and all. This had the desired effect of reopening the tube and thus her airway, but I was horror-struck again when, in a compensatory deep inspiratory effort, the now foreshortened end of the tube started to disappear down her nostril (a third thing that I'd never seen before). My mind was racing in an effort to not teeter over into complete panic mode, so I called for and took a Kelly clamp to grip onto the end of the tube thus allowing us to reinsert the hub again, and so disaster was averted. It was only later that it occurred to me that she would not have been able to fully inhale the tube because it was secured in place by the pressure in the tube's air cuff on the farther end that was in her main airway. But definitely, the image I had at that moment was this woman completely inhaling her endotracheal tube, thus dying from no longer being able to be ventilated and oxygenated. And what would I do then, or how would I ever explain that sequence to her bereaved family (or my colleagues)?! As is typical for emergency medicine, I admitted her upstairs to the hospital's ICU given her need for a ventilator and I never heard about her again. I took this as good news, because typically we only hear about our patients further on when bad things happen.

So yes, in retrospect, the patient may have benefited from a smoother course had I chosen to continue to just stand there and not do something. However, there's also the possibility that had I not given the lidocaine she might have developed a life-threatening arrhythmia, all of this highlighting the fact that mainstream medicine in general and emergency medicine more particularly are practiced in real time, not in retrospect! Also yes, in any form of an alternative medicine setting, none of those airway complications would have occurred, but in the same breath those potentially life-threatening PVCs would have been completely inapparent as well, at least up until the point where they killed her. But at least any alternative medicine practitioner would have had the consolation of knowing that they had not actively killed her.

Raymond Tallis again, as mentioned in the introduction, and from his same book, offers the following very insightful comment:

> *One of the arguments mobilized by alternative medical practi-*
> *tioners (of whom more later) against orthodox medicine is that*
> *the latter is constantly changing while alternative medicine has*

remained largely unaltered for hundreds, even thousands, of years. Change reflects strengths rather than weaknesses in conventional medicine: it is not a question of replacing one useless drug with another but of replacing a useful drug with one that is more useful. This places the claim that alternative medicine remedies belong to 'an ancient tradition' in an interesting light. The lack of development in 5,000 years can be a good thing only if 5,000 years ago alternative practitioners already knew of entirely satisfactory treatments for conditions that orthodox medicine has only recently started to be able to cure or improve, or cannot yet cure or improve. (If they did, they have kept remarkably quiet about them).[122]

I suspect that many here in the US who espouse the effectiveness of ancient traditional medical customs, particularly Chinese medicine, are unaware of the following facts pointed out to me by my cousin, Dr. David Rutstein. David is a board-certified family practice physician with an extensive public health career, having risen at one point to be the Deputy Surgeon General of the United States. After completing his twenty-four-year career with the US Public Health Service (USPHS), he worked for several years in China in an administrative position with a US-based hospital chain that was building hospitals in Beijing. He shared the following observations:

While Chinese people, in general, respect Traditional Chinese Medicine (TCM) they greatly prefer modern western medicine. Now, many TCM hospitals have built whole wings where western medicine is practiced. As Chinese people have become more educated and prosperous, so has their preference for western medicine. Thus, many of the TCM hospitals are now indistinguishable from hospitals based on western (allopathic) medicine, maintaining only a token TCM department, if any. And, the demand for western medicine is so high, and the numbers of patients so many, that it is difficult for public hospitals to provide high quality care. It is not uncommon for physicians to see 150-200 patients in a morning. Obviously, patients dislike the care they receive under such conditions. Yet, still they come to western medicine physicians over those practicing TCM. Hedging their bets, some may seek care from both TCM practitioners and physicians practicing western medicine. This is facilitated by the fact that there are usually no lines and the waiting time to see a TCM practitioner is short.[123]

My takeaway from all of this is, once again, the primacy of establishing a close and trusting patient-physician relationship within a modern scientific medical approach. If we as patients want to pursue alternative medicine interventions in addition to that, that's a perfectly acceptable option, but only as long as our physician is kept fully informed as well and agrees that this can work in tandem with their own medical advice.

CHAPTER EIGHT

HOW MUCH HEALTHCARE
IS ENOUGH?

Regardless of what schools of thought or theories of disease and illness we adopt for our healthcare choices, we will always be faced with the critical decisions of how much, when, and where to apply these interventions. All of this carries varying degrees of uncertainty, and as we'll see, it's definitely a matter of 'buyer beware' out there. I don't think that many people would disagree with the proposition that some of us are getting too much healthcare while others are getting far too little.

I have grave concerns about the status of mainstream medicine here in the US. We are in the midst of a radical, but mostly silent, transformation in our American healthcare system. Bluntly, it is American healthcare going to hell in a handbasket! That unique connection between those of us who are medically suffering and those of us who are dedicated to healing is being trivialized and commoditized. We need to seize that connection back. Transformation is too benign a word for it. It's more akin to a corruption or a process of decay.

I know it and feel it from the perspective of my 40-year career as an emergency physician, overlapped by a 50-year patient experience with my chronic autoimmune disease. In short, I've had 15 hospitalizations, 7 abdominal surgeries, and a major stroke at age 38, so I feel well educated from both inside and alongside the patient care bed.

Regarding the hell in a handbasket comment, I am referring to the dollar-driven decision-making that is converting the patient-physician relationship into a 'consumer-provider' relationship. This process is nearly complete, leaving a healthy patient-physician relationship almost irrecoverable.

Think I'm being overly pessimistic? Then please consider the following two points of view.

First, have a look at this direct quote from a published interview with the CEO of a $1.5 billion healthcare system, with 30 years of experience (emphasis mine):

> Question: What's one conviction in healthcare that needs to be challenged?
>
> Answer: THAT EVERY PATIENT NEEDS A PRIMARY CARE PHYSICIAN. As we start stratifying our patients into distinct populations based on their health needs and develop that insight further into CONSUMER DRIVEN WANTS, we are finding that a substantial sector of the population does not want or need a primary care physician relationship. PEOPLE NEED PRIMARY CARE BUT NOT NECESSARILY A PHYSICIAN RELATIONSHIP.[124]

As a physician, this is stunningly insulting, disturbing, and downright dangerous to hear, especially coming from someone who is helping to drive the direction of US healthcare. No doubt this is a brilliant business idea, that is, to remove physicians from their role in guiding patients through wise medical decision-making, thus allowing hospitals to sell services directly to us as anxious and incompletely informed 'consumers.' I was actually delighted to come across this interview because here the respondent had said the quiet part out loud, confirming what has been, or should have been, obvious to all of us, that dollar-driven decision-making rather than patient-welfare-centered decision-making is ascendant! In most media interviews, hospital administrators are quoted as insisting that their priority is delivering 'services that are in the best interests of the community,' and yet at times hospitals will close down maternity wards, pediatric wards, and even emergency departments if this is better for their bottom line.

Now consider this viewpoint from the 'Chief Experience Officer' at a several-hundred-physicians group practice in Ohio, "I am really focused on creating a church-like environment here. We want a total cultural transformation. I want that Disney-like experience, the Ritz Carlton experience."[125]

I'm going to take a guess here that most, if not all of us, have spent an overnight in the hospital, or maybe just an unexpectedly long day at our physician's office or even in the ED. Have any of us at any point thought to ourselves, "I wonder what the CEO of this place thinks I need next?" Or, "That's the last time I check into this place, it's definitely not up to my usual Ritz Carlton expectations, or anything like the last time I was at Disney, or at church!"

This way of thinking derives from an unhealthy obsession with *patient satisfaction*. It's not that patient satisfaction is necessarily a bad thing. As a patient myself, I certainly seek out convenience...and satisfaction as well. A study from UC Davis in 2012, however, showed that patients who reported being most satisfied with their care had greater chances of being admitted to the hospital, had higher total healthcare costs, higher prescription drug expenditures, and...wait for it...**higher death rates** than patients who were less satisfied with their care.[126]

Granted, this is just one study and no, logically I don't believe that satisfaction leads to a greater risk of dying. The link is more likely the reverse; we report being satisfied when we get more medications, more healthcare services, and more hospitalizations, and that those things lead to an increased risk of death.

I will confess that I totally resent the fact that an ED experience should be compared to a pleasurable one in order to evaluate its utility. In fact, in my more cynical moments, it has occurred to me that if you leave my ED feeling noticeably less miserable, significantly better informed, and with all of the body parts and most of the bodily fluids that you arrived with, then that's been a success. If, in addition, you are leaving the ED upright and under your own power, then you've had the Ritz Carlton equivalent!

Apparently one woman in Germany had that Ritz Carlton mindset because she was arrested after twice turning off her roommate's ventilator "after feeling disturbed by the noise." The victimized roommate fortunately was able to be revived, so the charge was only attempted manslaughter.[127] There are evidently no laws on the books yet against excessive "consumer-driven wants."

Also, keeping with the "consumer-driven-wants" theme are the profit-driven efforts to further blur the line between hotels and healthcare settings and thus between what is needed and what is just wanted health-wise. A *Becker's Hospital Review* article provides details on this "race to win the wellness war" as such:

> *Luxury hotels are intensifying the "wellness" amenities they offer, with many now veering closer to traditional healthcare services, The Wall Street Journal reports.*
>
> *[The] article details services offered by the Peninsula New York and Four Seasons Resort Maui and the wellness companies high-end hotels have partnered with to expand their offerings.*
>
> *Four Seasons Resort Maui's partnership with Los Angeles-based preventive and diagnostic healthcare center Next Health leaves guests with a menu of IV drips (the 45-minute ozone treatment*

involves fortifying blood with oxygen) and hourlong stem cell therapy sessions for $12,000 per session.

The FDA has issued multiple warnings against unapproved and unproven stem cell therapies. Next Health President Kevin Peake told The Journal, "At Next Health we only utilize these services for the purpose of health optimization and general wellness. We do not claim any benefits. We are able to explain to customers the science of these treatments, but beyond that they must do their own research to decide if the services are right for them.[128]

The verbiage there finesses a neat little sidestep from responsibility for your, the patient's, incompletely informed healthcare decisions! Plus, I doubt that they are truly "able to explain the science."

So, what in the world to do about all the above? I see only one realistic possibility for progress. We doctors are no longer steering the ship of US healthcare! Although we share the incentive that patients also have to make changes, neither of us (the doctor nor the patient) in isolation has the power to do so.

But as allies, we can form a true patient-physician partnership as the first step in abolishing this consumer-provider aberration. As physicians, we are beyond ready for our patients to step up and become more knowledgeable about, engaged in defining, and committed to adherence to their own healthcare plans. In my dual roles as patient and physician, I am equally offended by being referred to as either a 'consumer' or as a 'provider.'

Not surprisingly, it's not limited to mainstream medicine where this process of commoditization has reached out its tentacles. Results from the 2012 National Health Interview Survey conducted by the National Center for Complementary and Integrative Health (NCCIH) show:

Americans spent $30.2 billion out-of-pocket on complementary health approaches—$28.3 billion for adults and $1.9 billion for *children.....representing 1.1 percent of total health care expenditures in the United States ($2.82 trillion) and to 9.2 percent of out-of-pocket health care spending ($328.8 billion).* [129]

So, it's just 'a drop in the bucket' percentages compared to across-the-board total healthcare costs. However, these percentages get much higher when you take out hospital and other ancillary healthcare costs and just look at office visit and medication costs, where:

Americans spent $14.7 billion out-of-pocket on visits to complementary practitioners, which is almost 30 percent of what they spent out-of-pocket on services by conventional physicians ($49.6 billion). Americans spent $12.8 billion out-of-pocket on natural product supplements, which was about one-quarter of what they spent out-of-pocket on prescription drugs ($54.1 billion). [130]

In following through on our preferences to take 'natural remedies' in place of expensive, possibly harmful prescriptions, we run the risk of harming ourselves anyway. I know nothing about turmeric other than what I hear on all of those television commercials, but there are now very recent reports showing an increase in the number of cases where use of this supplement can lead to significant liver damage (an organ I'm admittedly more sensitized to now). In EM we see liver damage from alcohol and acetaminophen overdoses regularly, so the fact that certain other chemicals can damage the liver is unsurprising. Therefore, 'natural remedies' does not necessarily equate with 'non-toxic remedies.' [131]

I'm also understandably sensitized to all those commercials touting the effects of supplements on 'brain health performance.' I can't decide whether my brain damage from my stroke puts me at a greater risk for ultimate cognitive decline, or a lesser risk given that in my recovery I had to recruit other brain cells that I had apparently not been putting to good use yet, thus calling in newer, fresher players from the bench who may now have greater intrinsic longevity.

Regarding the utility of those supplements, the Harvard medical school website states:

> *A recent survey found that about 25% of adults over age 50 take a supplement to improve their brain health with the promise of enhanced memory and sharper attention and focus. The problem? There's no solid proof any of them work. The main issue with all over-the-counter supplements is lack of regulation. The FDA doesn't oversee product testing or ingredient accuracy—they just look out for supplements that make health claims related to the treatment of specific diseases. In terms of brain health, this means a supplement manufacturer can claim a product helps with mental alertness or memory loss—but not that it protects against or improves dementia or Alzheimer's disease. This way manufacturers don't have to back up any claim that their product is effective.*[132]

In contrast to this, a number of studies have shown that modest exercise can slow our cognitive decline. I find it discouraging, but only a bit surprising, that we choose to spend good money on unproven interventions when we have scientific proof of a no-cost, no-harm, easily accessible intervention, like more movement, simply because taking pills is so much easier to do. We are unlikely to ever see definitive scientific studies proving the usefulness of such brain supplement pills. Why would the companies successfully producing and marketing these products bother to spend the time and money to investigate any actual scientifically proven effectiveness, when their study results might undercut their claims? Especially since they already have people willing to buy their products based on no evidence at all, except for anecdotal testimonial reports that may be subject to placebo effect and/or post hoc fallacy.

Pediatrician and public health expert Dr. Paul Offit offers the following observation:

Because the vitamin and supplement industry is not regulated by the US Food and Drug Administration (FDA), negative studies have not precipitated FDA warnings or FDA-mandated changes on labeling; as a consequence, few consumers are aware that many supplements have not delivered on their claims. In 2010, the vitamin and supplement industry grossed $28 billion, up 4.4% from the year before. [133]

Also highlighted is this industry comment:

"The thing to do with [these studies] is just ride them out," said Joseph Fortunato, chief executive of GNC Corp. "We see no impact on our business."[134]

That last line is particularly telling in that it makes good business sense to just make the claims, sell the product with televised anecdotal testimonials devoid of scientific data, and "ride out" the absence of supporting evidence. In addition to the problem of the wasted cost and uselessness of many of these products, there is the additional hazard of unlisted and harmful additional ingredients. Consider the following from an article in the financial and business news website *Business Insider*:

In November, researchers at Harvard Medical School and independent product testing company NSF International identified four unapproved, unlisted stimulants in six supplements currently marketed for weight loss and fitness. Evidence suggests the stimulants could be similar to ephedrine, a compound derived from ephedra, the dangerous and lethal weight-loss supplement that the FDA banned in 2004.[135]

It's critical that we make our healthcare decisions in the most fully informed way possible, and mainstream medicine is most definitely not immune to issues of uncertainty. In fact, in mainstream medicine the issue of uncertainty makes a major contribution to care that is considered 'low value' and/or 'wasteful.'

In one study, researchers estimated that in the US anywhere from $760-$935 billion was wasted annually, amounting to approximately 25% of total of healthcare spending. The reported causes for this waste ranged from administrative complexity to failures of care delivery and coordination, as well as fraud and abuse.[136] A separate study found that administrative costs in the US amounted to 34.2% of all healthcare expenditures, which was over twice the Canadian rate of 16.7%, for comparison.[137]

In 1973, John Wennberg, MD, MPH, published an article identifying what he called "small area variations in healthcare delivery." This paper reported his discovery that the frequency of identical medical interventions and surgical procedures varied widely throughout the state of Vermont in very similar communities. When I came across his ideas and publications during my stroke rehab in 1996, I was dismayed by the data he presented. For example:

> *In one region of Vermont physicians perform 20 hysterectomies for every 10,000 women, while in another area they performed three times as many. In one region 7% of children had their tonsils removed while another had a 70% tonsillectomy rate.*[138]

I still recall how confusing and disturbing I found it, that the necessity of certain healthcare services was apparently not based solely on a consensus within the medical community. Wennberg's follow-up studies also found significant variations in nonsurgical care such as in the frequency of hospitalizations, ICU use, and outpatient follow-up visits, and confirmed that similar findings were evident across the entire country. This was even apparent when he compared treatment-decision differences between academic/teaching hospitals in Boston versus New Haven, so it was not a phenomenon simply attributable to more rural areas lagging behind modern treatment methods.[139]

Wennberg pointed out that in healthcare something very different was being done than the typical "exchange relationship" that exists in all other markets. The doctor-patient relationship was being seen as different in that here there was an "asymmetry of information." So, patients were doing something that was unheard of in other markets, that is, delegating decision-making to the sellers of services, the physicians, who by virtue of their special knowledge and skill could act as their "rational agent" in healthcare-purchasing decisions. He went on to demonstrate that this was not a problem with unethical outlier physicians but was more obviously associated with the availability of services, with more service availability resulting in higher usage, and he attributed this to an attendant lack of a scientific basis for a consensus within the medical community for when certain interventions were inarguably justified.

Not surprisingly, Dr. Wennberg's study at first met with stiff opposition within the medical community. Although his once heretical ideas are now well accepted, there remains a wide range of medical conditions even today where a treatment consensus still does not exist. Dr. Wennberg and his colleagues at the Dartmouth Institute for Health Policy & Clinical Practice were instrumental in initiating a "preference-sensitive" model, to replace the existing "supply-sensitive" paradigm, in which patients would become well-informed and together with their physicians pursue a process of shared decision-making. This transition is unfortunately making very slow progress. In his 2010 book *Tracking Medicine*, Wennberg concludes:

> *If the United States can make this transition to a democratized doctor-patient relationship, it will be the first nation in the world to do so.... After all we are talking about transforming a gargantuan industry whose growth has been driven in part by deeply held, but nonetheless faulty, beliefs about the nature of healthcare markets, the scientific underpinnings of medicine, and the power of more care to heal.* [140]

One of the quotes that Wennberg starts his book with is from Upton Sinclair, "It is difficult to get a man to understand something when his salary depends on him not understanding it."

I definitely agree with Wennberg's description of this as being an iffy proposition to transform our "gargantuan" healthcare industry. As a reflex optimist, I do believe that substantial improvement is still quite possible. However, if I were a betting man, I wouldn't place much of my own money against our continuing to follow our current hell in a handbasket course. I have become convinced that we patients are the ones who can ultimately do the most to alter this.

We cannot change this alone, of course. But we need to take the initiative in a concerted effort in forming a true partnership with our primary care physicians, and as patients working in concert with our doctors, to take the initial necessary steps. As pointed out in Chapter One with the healthcare industry now being the largest employer in the US, decision-makers within the industry itself have little incentive to change policies. Additionally, politicians seem to be more distracted by trying to score political points while inserting themselves into medical care decisions inappropriately. To repeat myself, I consider partisan politics to be a severe public health hazard, rather than a likely avenue to rely on for the initiative of achieving further healthcare reform.

Complicating matters, the Centers for Medicare & Medicaid Services (CMS), hospital administrators, and we patients are all guilty of worshipping at the altar of *patient satisfaction*. CMS holds hospitals to standards of *patient satisfaction* scores such that falling short can lead to a hospital's reimbursement from CMS being withheld to the tune of millions of dollars. So as surely as you know what rolls downhill, hospital administrators lean on emergency department administrators to make us frontline emergency physicians become *more productive*. (In other words, spend less time with individual patients so that more patients can be seen…and more charges generated!)

Just one example that more healthcare is not necessarily always better for us is the universal agreement that the overprescribing of antibiotics has led to the pervasive, costly, and potentially deadly global problem of antibiotic-resistant infectious diseases. In the US, more than two million people every year are affected by antibiotic-resistant infections, with at least 23,000 dying as a result of the infection.[141] This is particularly concerning for that portion of physical symptoms and complaints that are self-limited, for which antibiotics, hospitalization, and extensive healthcare services are not needed. This is a determination which your physician, and not CMS or your hospital's CEO, is in the best position of guiding you through.

In 2006, EM physician Brian J. Zink wrote a book on the history of emergency medicine titled *Anyone, Anything, Anytime*.[142] I was initially reluctant to read it for two reasons—firstly, because I felt like I had essentially already lived a good part of it, and secondly, because I was concerned that the content might not live up to the perfection of the title itself. After recently reading it while researching for this book, I found that my second concern was only partially accurate. Though not as perfect as the title, it was quite thorough in conveying a great deal of information that I was unaware of about the origins of emergency medicine as a specialized practice, as well as providing confirmation of many of my own conclusions.

When we are ill or injured and uncertain about the seriousness of our condition, we naturally want to relieve our discomforts and anxieties as rapidly as possible, as in 'right now.' Additionally, in regard to the question of how much medical care we are willing to receive to address this uncertainty, the answer is typically 'whatever it takes.' Regarding the third question of what we should have to pay for that, the typical answer is, 'I shouldn't have to pay anything.' That's not even very far off from what I think myself. But these are typically moments when our critical thinking skills are not operating at their utmost capacity. So, in EM it still makes sense for patients to engage us as their "rational agents" in situations where they are either incapable of or unwilling to engage in shared decision-making.

Much of what we do in emergency medicine is not conducive to this transition that Wennberg envisions because in EM we are required to initiate life-saving interventions in patients who at times are not even capable of communicating. Nor would we necessarily have reasonable alternatives to offer for their emergency needs if they requested something other than standard emergency medical interventions. In those slower moments like with the ARTI (acute respiratory tract infection) example that we looked at earlier, shared decision-making is more achievable. Other examples do occur, such as what is the advisability of getting a head CT scan in a minor head injury setting, especially in a child? Of obtaining repeat abdominal CT scans in patients with chronic recurrent abdominal pain? Of the utility of advanced x-ray imaging in low-back pain? And then there is the perpetual problem of whether chest-pain symptoms require further inpatient or outpatient workup. All of these are conditions that definitely benefit from a more measured conversation and shared decision-making.

To illustrate this distinction, I want to present my most memorable patient encounter, one which provided no opportunity for measured conversation and shared decision-making. In the early 1990s, I had graduated from medical school 10 years previously, had completed my emergency medicine residency, had earned emergency medicine board certification, and felt like I'd seen a little bit of everything. On this particular winter night shift as I headed into the ED call room to try to take a little catnap, like we could still do on occasion in those days, I heard the emergency services radio begin to squawk. I tried to convince myself that it was either random interference or a routine radio check from a neighboring town. But instead of getting comfortable in the call room bed, I reversed course back out to the ED proper to listen in.

Sure enough, it was a real trauma case. Generally, emergency medical technicians (EMTs) are pretty stolid and reliable, but this one sounded just a little bit rattled. She reported that she was at the scene of a single-car motor vehicle accident (MVA) with a young male who had a neck laceration from ear to ear that was—get this—"possibly self-inflicted." This made no sense. First, how could you bring yourself to draw a knife across the entire width of your own neck? Second, why at an MVA and why just "possibly"? Why not just ask the guy how it happened? Anyway, the EMT described the patient as stable but breathing through his neck and reported that their estimated time of arrival (ETA) was eight minutes.

The nurses and I moved into the resuscitation room to prepare for whatever. Again, I had seen the requisite 'one' trach tube placement through the neck in my emergency medicine residency. In that case, an assailant had stabbed a young woman once deeply front and center in her neck and left her for dead. I had watched the senior resident place a trach tube relatively easily through this narrow opening. However, he had not mentioned, nor had I asked, how one chooses the proper trach tube to use (in fact, I didn't even know there were different sizes). I was therefore sorting through various-sized tracheostomy tubes with my back to the door when I heard them coming in. I turned and saw this guy on his back on a gurney with his head thrown back. His neck lay open like the Grand Canyon. It was, as described, truly sliced from ear to ear. His lower neck had sagged down toward his chest so that the wound was open in all directions. The EMTs were appropriately holding an oxygen mask loosely over the opening as the patient breathed on his own.

I had never seen anything like it before. Everyone turned to me for professional words of guidance. "Holy sh#t!" was all I could manage. Then I said it again for good measure. The tracheostomy tubes were obviously useless, so I tossed them aside and grabbed a laryngoscope and an endotracheal (ET) tube. The worst thing was that this guy was fully alert; his eyes were bugged out and darting rapidly around the room. The neck wound had obviously bled extensively, but by then had all but completely clotted up, thank God. As I examined the wound to determine the status of his airway, this unfortunate soul was swallowing reflexively. With each swallow, his lower neck took on a life of its own, heaving chinward in a vain effort to meet its mate. The epiglottis, the guardian of the entry to the trachea, was visible as his neck muscles relaxed and the gap again fell open.

I considered passing the ET tube through the wound into his airway but discarded this idea when I realized the tube would get in the way of repairing the wound. Intubation via the usual oral route seemed preferable, so I moved to insert the laryngoscope into the patient's mouth. But his eyes bored through me as he gritted his teeth tightly. He was beyond reasoning with, and in fact he tried to get off the stretcher. It was frightening to see a man in his condition needing to be restrained by four people, each holding a limb.

"Valium, five milligrams, IV," I ordered. After a repeat dose, he was much calmer. I then opted for a nasal approach. As described earlier, under ideal circumstances an endotracheal tube passed through the nose will follow the natural curve of the throat and, with a minimal amount of head positioning, will find its way smoothly past the epiglottis and into the trachea where it belongs. In this case, however, the tube began by following its expected course but then rose like a cobra up through the patient's gaping neck wound. I grabbed the tube with Magill forceps and redirected it past the epiglottis into its proper position. Once the integrity of the patient's airway was ensured, I could finally take a few deep breaths of my own.

In the meantime, the nurses, skilled professionals that they were, had been following standard procedures without direction from me. In fact, the only other thing I had managed to say until ordering the Valium was "Call in the general surgeon and the ENT surgeon." By then the patient had two IVs in place, was on oxygen and a cardiac monitor, and was having his vital signs monitored. I noticed that he was both hypotensive, the blood pressure gauge showing an abnormally low reading of less than 90, and hypothermic, with a body temperature of only 86 degrees. We were resuscitating him with warmed intravenous saline solution and heated oxygen mist via the ET tube. His heart was racing, not surprisingly. But as we hydrated and warmed him up, all the severed blood vessels that had been clotted off began to bleed again.

For the first time, I looked closely at the wound. I could see that he had positioned the blade so it was too far up on his neck to sever his carotid arteries. In fact, the blade had passed so high that part of his mandible, or jawbone, had been shaved off on the right. Most of the bleeding was coming from the right submandibular salivary gland just below that shaved bone. I had to use more than a dozen small vascular clamps on the little vessels before the flow of blood was reasonably stanched.

On the left side of his neck, there was less bleeding. As I was using a gauze pad to soak up the pooled blood, I came across the entirely exposed carotid artery. It had been bluntly dissected from the surrounding tissue and was standing free like a large pipe. Reflexively, I yanked my hand away from it, not wishing to disturb any clots. Had the blade reached this vessel, the patient would have bled out instantly. As I was completing the task of clamping off the final bleeders, I became aware of the general surgeon looking over my right shoulder. After a long silence he said, "This guy has to go to the OR." It wasn't a hugely helpful observation, but it was a whole sight better than "Holy sh#t." Soon we were done packaging the patient for transport, and he was on his way to the OR.

I could finally relax, although my adrenaline was still pumping. I joined the EMTs and the police, who gave me a more complete story. A cop had been making routine rounds in a remote parking lot when he came across a car that had crashed headfirst into a tree. Its windows were frosted over. As he approached the vehicle, he noticed several large areas of deeply blood-stained snow. He opened the driver's door and found this guy sitting there, covered with blood. "Are you okay?" the cop asked. The guy turned silently and looked right through him. Later the cop told his partner, "I'm sure that if he had come toward me, I would have shot him."

Further investigation revealed the following items on the floor of the car: a piece of two-by-four, the blade from a large butcher's cleaver, a ruler, and several C-clamps. As per history obtained much later, after a disagreement with his girlfriend, the guy had clamped the blade to the two-by-four, which he placed across the steering wheel. Then he accelerated into the tree, apparently in an effort to cut off his head.

He nearly succeeded. I shudder to imagine his shock when he found himself still alive. The blood in the snow and the backseat of the car made it clear that he had moved around quite a bit, no doubt trying to find a comfortable way to breathe while awaiting death. But the cold weather, which slowed his bleeding, and his unacknowledged will to live conspired against him. The next day I went to the ICU to look in on the guy. I felt more than a little trepidation about seeing him again because, frankly, he scared me. He was obviously a person who was capable of carrying out a plan, and I wasn't sure I wanted him knowing who I was in case he decided he was dissatisfied with his care.

Over the years, I had successfully erected a self-preserving wall between my patients and me. My emotions and I are on one side, and patients and their problems stay on the other side. But the night before, this guy had come barreling through my wall, and, before I knew it, he was right there next to me. I found him in the ICU with his neck wound nicely sewn together. He was medically stable and sleeping, thank goodness. I learned that someone had nicknamed him 'Pezhead.' Although outrageously insensitive, this image was visually perfect. Such black humor is another defense mechanism—like my wall—that medical personnel use to cope with the sometimes grim nature of our work.

Well, that had certainly been my most uniquely challenging case to date. In some ways, though, the obvious directly visible nature of the problem and the also obvious need for immediate OR repair by the surgeon had made my job easier. Other cases, in which the full extent of the problem and the most appropriate care for it are less certain, can be more challenging and nerve-wracking.

Both types of cases are why emergency medicine was approved as a separate specialty in 1979. Zink reports in his book that in the 1950s emergency departments tended to be staffed by the least qualified physicians, typically interns right out of medical school or even medical students themselves, writing, "Some of the sickest and most emergent patients were being attended to by the least qualified physicians." He continues:

Since emergency practice was not considered a real occupation for a physician, only those without a regular job were available to be hired. Hospitals sometimes resorted to hiring troubled, transient, or aged doctors to work in the ER. Some were alleged to have alcoholism, drug abuse, or criminal records. Emergency practice was not something that any self-respecting physician would do for a living – it might be part of a physician's career journey, but it was never a destination.[143]

Starting in the 1960s, and continuing throughout that decade, there was a small cadre of more qualified physicians who gravitated towards the emergency department with emergency medicine as their area of full-time interest. Gradually it became a more professional setting, with the ultimate development of dedicated, hospital-based, emergency medicine residency training programs starting in 1970. But the New England states lagged far behind the rest of the country in this regard. In those years, the Massachusetts General Hospital did offer an emergency medicine fellowship for interested physicians, but this fellowship did not immediately develop into a full-fledged EM residency training program.

As I was completing my emergency medicine residency in 1983, five of my fellow residents and I had the novel idea of forming a group of our own in order to return to the Northeast where we all had family ties. Our own faculty was frankly discouraging this idea since the Northeast was considered a backwater for emergency medicine and not professionally developed or challenging enough for an emergency medicine career, plus the salaries were far less than elsewhere in the country. When he heard of our idea, the physician director of the large emergency department at a New England major teaching hospital said to us, "Gee, if you succeed in that, you should write a book."

This book is not about that, but this passage is, because we pursued the idea fairly vigorously and ultimately succeeded in being awarded the contract to fully staff the emergency department at what I'll call MFH, a small community hospital in New England. As a result, in 1983, MFH became the first New England hospital to have an emergency department fully staffed by EM residency-trained and EM board-certified emergency physicians. Zink includes this quote from one of EM's most eminent 'founding fathers':

> *The solution to the mega group dilemma and exploitation of emergency physicians, as Peter Rosen noted, would have been for well-trained emergency physicians to form small, democratic emergency medicine groups to compete favorably against the PPMs [physician practice management] for hospital ED contracts at all US hospitals. In the 1980s and even to the present, this has turned out to be a pipe dream.[144]*

This quote was not directly about us, but we certainly embodied it at that exact time.

When we first started working at MFH, one of the older ED nurses pointed out to us the doorbell on the outside of the building's ED entrance where the ambulances and any other vehicles pulled up. In earlier days, you rang the doorbell after hours, the charge nurse would come to the door and evaluate what type of problem you had, and then she had to get on the phone and call whichever physician she thought might be able to treat your problem, without any guarantee that they would be willing to come in and see you. By the time we had arrived there, at least that system was no longer in use, but the hospital was staffed full-time by physicians provided by a multi-hospital contract management group (CMG/PPM).

Contract management groups and private equity investments were and still are, to my mind, one of the major shortcomings within the emergency medicine profession. In the 1970s, entrepreneurial-minded emergency physicians quickly realized that by guaranteeing a supply of more qualified EM trained physicians, they could sign contracts with dozens to hundreds of hospitals at the same time and then rotate their stable of physicians throughout those various hospitals as needed. The advantage for the entrepreneurial physician-organizers of these contract management groups is that they would skim a portion of the pay for all of their hired physicians and essentially could therefore earn bucket loads of money without ever actually having to see patients themselves, if that was their preference. These contracts were relatively ripe for the picking because as Zink also points out:

> *John Knowles, MD who had witnessed the changes in the Massachusetts General Hospital emergency ward between 1951 and 1965 noted in a 1966 article in Atlantic monthly: "the chief reason for the ever-expanding use of the emergency ward is simply that it is the best possible place in which to solve a medical problem quickly and accurately. The public knows it and so does the doctor."*[145]

So, we EM doctors have in essence ended up filling our roles too successfully by making it far more convenient and effective for both patients and staff physicians to meet their urgent needs. This has resulted in some unexpected, but in retrospect unsurprising, developments. The definition of what is appropriately considered an emergency has become progressively more diluted leading to a reliably increasing number of emergency department visits annually ever since. The accompanying increase in revenues caught the attention of private equity investment firms who began aggressively buying up EM physician practices. When this happens, costs for medical care reliably go up, and some studies show that patient outcomes deteriorate (see Chapter Ten).

Unfortunately, there was a philosophical split at the outset in this newly forming EM physician community between those doctors who were purely dedicated to improving the quality of emergency care and those who wanted to do that, too, but also wanted to benefit from the opportunity for making serious business profits. The difference in outlook was a disagreement over whether it was professionally ethical for one physician to make money off the patient care efforts of another physician.

I don't want to make the same mistake that I criticized earlier by saying, 'I'm not a businessman or economist, but....' I realize that the economic issues involved here are "gargantuan" and multifaceted enough that there are no panaceas or simple fixes. I've often thought and even said out loud to colleagues that, "I'm a pretty bright boy, but if you gave me all the money and all the power in the world, I don't believe that I could solve our US healthcare problems!"

Some people would like to believe that simply instituting 'Medicare for all' would solve all of our problems, but I believe that wouldn't be sufficient or even the right place to start. This would not come close to addressing the bigger problem of the fact that some people get far more medical care than they need, while others have trouble even accessing the healthcare system equitably.

In fact, studies show that there are so-called superutilizers/superusers who typically visit the hospital at minimum five times a year—usually in the ED. They are often, but not always, uninsured, or on Medicare or Medicaid, and the cost to treat these chronically ill patients is particularly high. In fact, this group comprises just 5 percent of all patients but accounts for half of the country's healthcare spending, with 1 percent accounting for 22 percent of total healthcare spending, and the bottom 50 percent of the population representing just 2.9 percent of total healthcare spending in 2017.[146]

These patients accumulate large numbers of ED visits and hospital admissions that might have been prevented by inexpensive early intervention, better primary care access, and the concept of a team-based approach of providing the additional social supports of a "medical home without walls," as this reference describes as a way of providing effective outpatient medical and psychosocial treatment.[147]

This next reference addresses the same problem and proposed solution with regard to the Medicaid portion of this risk group, with CMS providing the data as follows:

- Five percent of Medicaid beneficiaries account for 54 percent of the program's total expenditures.

- One percent account for 25 percent of the program's total expenditures.

- Eighty-three percent of the top 1 percent of users has at least three chronic conditions.

- More than 60 percent of the top 1 percent has five or more chronic conditions.[148]

In fact, even above and beyond the Medicaid population, statistical reviews show that nearly half of all hospital-associated medical care in the US now takes place in emergency departments. [149] The current default solution of, "just send them all to the ED" is clearly not working well. Unsurprisingly, it is exacerbating ED overcrowding to the point where ED patients are oftentimes receiving the totality of their emergency care while fully clothed and sitting in the waiting room. This is a make-do survival adaptation to ED overcrowding, in which ED rooms and staff are occupied by already-admitted-to-the-hospital patients who have no assigned hospital bed available yet, and so they are "boarding" or "holding" in the ED hallways! This "waiting room medicine" is accompanied by the guidance to "churn patients" (or more colloquially throughout EM to 'move the meat' or 'treat-em and street-em'). It is a sure-fire recipe for minimizing the chance for any meaningful patient-physician 'connection,' while magnifying the chance for a serious misdiagnosis.[150]

I certainly don't mean to imply by the seriousness of my neck-wound case presented earlier that those are the only types of cases we should be seeing in our EDs. However, it's clear that hospitals are spending time, money, and effort to encourage people to come to the ED for their care, regardless of the level of seriousness of their concerns—thus, the billboards advertising the ready availability of their EM services and the estimated wait times to be seen within the ED!

If patients are lucky enough to make it back into the emergency department itself and get a private examination area of their own, there seems to be a conspiracy between them and their nurse to not bother to get out of their street clothes and into a patient examination gown. The nurses often reassure me that they have requested that the patients get undressed. This is believable because I often find the patient fully dressed sitting on a stretcher but with a folded patient gown ignored at the end of the stretcher, which they apparently did not feel the need to get into. We are all, physicians and patients alike, simultaneously victims of and participants in this sinister yet nearly imperceptible conversion to 'high tech, but low-touch' medical care which is happening because it is just so damn time-efficient and revenue-generating.

Alarmingly, we are on the very verge of the physical examination and the touching of the patient becoming an anachronism. I don't believe that I am the last of the Mohicans in this regard, but I am certainly among the last of the Mohicans...in other words, those of us still believing in and staunchly advocating for the power of high-tech, but also high-touch medical practice. Physician, author, and medical teacher Abraham Verghese addresses precisely this when he reinforces the importance of examining patients thoroughly:

"Very often, at the end of a physical exam, I am told two things," Dr Verghese says. *"One: 'I've not been examined this way before'– which, if that's true, is a real condemnation of our system.*

And then, surprisingly, I find that I can tell [patients] exactly what they heard elsewhere: 'This is not in your head. This is real, but the good news is that it's not cancer or tuberculosis, or whatever. The bad news is that we don't know exactly what's causing this, but here's what we should try to do.'

And I always feel that, if I get the buy-in, it's because something happened in the exam."[151]

Elsewhere, Verghese describes and deplores the almost ascendant concept of the "iPatient," where more time is spent in front of and touching computers than in front of and touching patients. His 2011 TED talk "A doctor's touch" is 18 minutes that richly rewards watching.[152]

Verghese describes the example of a critically ill 40-year-old breast cancer patient being diagnosed in an advanced metastatic stage only by way of a CAT scan, done after she had become an unstable patient. Review of her recent medical records then 'tragically' revealed that on "four to five" prior medical evaluations, there had been no examination of her chest and breasts, where bilateral "visible and palpable" masses would have been readily detectable.

Though lacking the same implication for the patient's long-term welfare, I recall two cases I had in which cutting corners on the physical examination would have ended up as missed diagnoses. In the first case, a 70ish woman had presented with family members, all of them reporting to me that she had unfortunately inflicted a burn on her right abdomen area by falling asleep with a heating pad applied to treat an inexplicable ache in that area. That sounded credible, and cursory examination of the abdomen area that was available when she lifted up her blouse in front did show a broad area of redness compatible with a first-degree burn. However, I also noticed that there were some incipient blisters in that region indicating possibly second-degree burning, which seemed less credible to be able to sleep through. By ingrained habit I lifted her top further up and did an examination of her back area as well. That area displayed the classic advanced blisters in a linear dermatomal pattern (one which follows the course of the underlying nerve) which confirmed a now more obvious diagnosis of shingles. This then allowed for more appropriate treatment of her condition than the more cursory examination would have suggested.

In the second case, at shift change a young woman's situation was described to me as her having a miscarriage. My younger, faster, and more proficient colleague had performed her own thorough bedside ultrasound examination and, despite a positive pregnancy test in this patient, could not locate a pregnancy within the uterus or the fallopian tubes. I had agreed that this suggested that she had more than likely already completely miscarried this early pregnancy at home. We were still awaiting the results of her Rh factor testing in order to confirm that there was not a possible Rh incompatibility there, thus requiring a specific medication to be administered. My colleague had also recommended a brief period of ED observation because the patient had remained anxious still about her, admittedly light but persistent, vaginal bleeding and cramping.

I was somewhat surprised to learn that she had not taken the time to perform a pelvic examination on this patient, basing this decision upon the fact that the patient's abdominal examination and ultrasound evaluation had appeared so completely benign. Being more old-school myself, while lacking similar proficiency with bedside ultrasound, I ultimately chose to proceed with the pelvic examination by dint of ingrained habit. Lo and behold, there was the fetus, no larger than a thumb, still firmly wedged within the cervical opening, thus not readily detectable by ultrasound but easily visible. The on-call OB-GYN resident then came down to help this patient to complete that miscarriage of a clearly no longer viable pregnancy.

No significant harm would likely have come to either of these patients had both diagnoses been totally missed. However, in each case more appropriate management could now be initiated, anxiety relieved, and in the second case the ever-present possibility of subsequent infection due to prolonged incomplete miscarriage could be avoided—all arguing for the fact that newer is not necessarily better (see next chapter), and that a physician's eyes, hands, and insight are irreplaceable.

An additional development increasing the risk of missed diagnoses is the fact that, again for financial reasons, hospitals are choosing to replace, rather than supplement, more experienced emergency physicians with less experienced and less expensive to hire "mid-level practitioners." This has also been shown to lead to increased cost of care and length of stay in the ED.[153]

All of the above reinforces my strong belief that step number one needs to be forming my proposed physician-patient partnerships in which we at least first try to get it right with what we are doing together. Step one would be identifying the source of our suffering as patients and then determining the possible need for hospital-level care.

Then there is the additional troubling comparison between rising hospital CEO pay, at the same time that there are substantial rates of American 'medical bankruptcy,' as summarized in this 2017 Healthline article:

> *One in five Americans of working age with health insurance struggled to pay their medical bills in the past year, according to a survey by the Kaiser Family Foundation and* The New York Times.
>
> *Among the uninsured, medical debt is an even bigger problem, with more than half reporting difficulty paying off what they owe.*
>
> *But while millions of people face serious financial troubles due to the high cost of healthcare, some hospital CEOs are raking in millions each year in salaries and other benefits.*[154]

I find it disturbing in the extreme that a phenomenon like 'medical bankruptcy' (estimated as contributing to 62% of all US bankruptcies) can even exist in the US, especially at the same time that healthcare company administrator's pay is at unconscionable levels (ranging from the hundreds of thousands to the hundreds of millions of dollars annually).

Paralleling, and no doubt contributing to that gross inequity, is the following phenomenon, "The number of physicians in the United States grew 150% between 1975 and 2010, roughly in keeping with the population growth, while the number of healthcare administrators increased 3200% for the same time period."[155]

The two most salient facts that most patients in the US are aware of are that doctors earn a very good income and our American healthcare costs are outrageously expensive. Both of these facts are undeniable. Many then naturally conclude that it is the first that leads to the second. But medical journalist and author Elisabeth Rosenthal, MD, puts this in perspective in her 2014 *New York Times* article "Medicine's Top Earners Are Not the M.D.s," when she reports:

> *The base pay of insurance executives, hospital executives and even hospital administrators often far outstrips doctors' salaries, according to analysis performed for* The New York Times *by Compdata Surveys: $584,000 on average for an insurance chief executive officer, $386,000 for a hospital CEO and $237,000 for a hospital administrator, compared with $306,000 for a surgeon and $185,000 for a general doctor. And those numbers almost certainly understate the payment gap, since top executives frequently earn the bulk of their income in nonsalary compensation. In a deal that is not unusual in the industry, Mark T. Bertolini, the chief executive of Aetna, earned a salary of about $977,000 in 2012 but a total compensation package of over $36 million, the bulk of it from stocks vested and options he exercised that year. Likewise, Ronald J. Del Mauro, a former president of Barnabas Health, a midsize health system in New Jersey, earned a salary of just $28,000 in 2012, the year he retired, but total compensation of $21.7 million.[156]*

Elsewhere, in an NPR interview about her book *An American Sickness*, Rosenthal comments:

We've trusted a lot of our health care to for-profit businesses and it's their job, frankly, to make profit," Rosenthal says. "You can't expect them to act like Mother Teresas. ... One expert in the book joked to me ... that if we relied on the current medical market to deal with polio, we would never have a polio vaccine," Rosenthal says. "Instead we would have iron lungs in seven colors with iPhone apps.[157]

The most eye-catching headline on this topic that I encountered was the following from 2016, "Aetna CEO (Mark Bertolini) could make $500 million from CVS merger." This was in regard to the merger between Aetna and CVS which did end up happening in 2018 to the tune of $69 billion involved, but I couldn't find details to confirm the ultimate CEO compensation in that merger deal.[158]

Half a billion dollars for negotiating a healthcare business merger is not a bad payday. I'm honestly not at all jealous of Mr. Bertolini, and I'm absolutely certain that I would have neither the patience nor the financial know-how to have done such a thing myself. As it is, I'm an adherent of this philosophy attributed to Bob Marley, "Money is numbers and numbers never end. If it takes money to be happy, your search for happiness will never end."

More importantly, these kinds of numbers point to the fact that we somehow have come to an understanding or accepted as an inevitability that patients' welfare can be placed secondary to profits. The following commentary is very pertinent here and I find myself in total agreement with this content, except for the second sentence.

The article "Why Doctors Make the Best Healthcare CEOs" by Shakeel Ahmed, MD, CEO, Atlas Surgical Group, the largest private ambulatory surgery center (ASC) group in the US, states:

In medicine, there is no greater philosophical challenge than that of managing a healthcare facility and caring for those for whom that health care facility operates. The principles of economics dictate that profitability supersedes everything else. Put crudely, how far does the CEO of a medical entity cut corners before care suffers? At some point on the Venn Diagram of business ledgers, profits and patients have to diverge. Managing that divergence through a delicate balance of business and humanity is only possible if that CEO is attuned to the sufferings of his clients, and does not merely see them through the prism of money. The only person with that skill has always been, and always will be, a doctor…. But given the sheer amount of profits involved, businesspeople have justified their takeover of medical businesses from the true medical leaders: doctors.[159]

It's that second sentence there that I consider the root of the problem, "The principles of economics dictate that profitability supersedes everything else." I'm no socialist, but why in the world can't we change what we seem to have silently agreed upon when it comes to our healthcare here in the US? Can't we choose to agree that the inverse is mandatory, that patient welfare supersedes profitability!

Yes, it would take a major reimagining of how business principles work within the healthcare sector. Yes, it would mean redefining what it means to be a 'winner' or a 'success' as a healthcare businessperson, but that shouldn't be either unimaginable, or unachievable!

We can choose to overtly and publicly redefine success here as obligatorily observing that the new principles of healthcare economics dictate that patient welfare "supersedes everything else." It seems to me that is what Dr. Ahmed means to say, as the article proceeds, but perhaps his position and the current rules of the economics game may be preventing him from saying so as bluntly and concretely as I'm free to do. Apologies to Dr. Ahmed if I'm misreading him here, but I am hoping that I am not. It will take physicians willing to make the points that he does above, along with the insistence of the rest of us as patients, to initiate and complete this healthier transformation of our American healthcare system.

CHAPTER NINE

SLOW VERSUS
MORE MEDICINE

In 2002, cardiologist Alberto Dolara published a paper in the *Italian Heart Journal* titled "Invitation to Slow Medicine," suggesting that "In clinical practice, hyperactivity is often unnecessary."[160] He proposed that medical personnel take a sufficiently long time in which to address all the psychosocial issues involved in patient care. This Slow Medicine movement in Italy subsequently received attention in the Netherlands, Brazil, and also in a limited fashion the United States.

This philosophical movement calls for treatment of patients that is "measured, respectful, and equitable." In the US this strategy is not synonymous with, but is philosophically similar to, the approach to healthcare at the end of life reflected in the specialty of palliative care medicine. Along with the idea of a slower pace to the interaction is the concept of using medical interventions when appropriately considered, understood, and chosen, instead of defaulting to a 'do everything' paradigm.

As Peter Ubel, MD (physician and behavioral scientist at Duke University) has commented:

> *Quite often the need for hope and the desire for action cause doctors and patients to pursue what are essentially futile measures. As a result, close to 40% of Medicare spending in the United States occurs in the last six months of people's lives. Few experts think that all of the spending and all of these medical interventions are promoting patient's best interests.*[161]

Bernard Lown, MD, put it more succinctly, "Do as much as possible for the patient, and as little as possible to the patient."[162] The natural conflict here is a three-way one between the healthcare system trying to maintain profitability, patients at times mis-prioritizing convenience and satisfaction, and physicians attempting to deliver the care that we feel is most appropriate for our patients. We will go on to look more closely at how everything we have discussed up to this point can be applied to end-of-life issues in Chapter Twelve.

A terrific book, written by H. Gilbert Welch, MD, also associated with the Dartmouth Institute titled *Less Medicine More Health* (2015) makes a very well-reasoned and articulate argument for why more medicine is not necessarily conducive to greater health. Welch has chapters based on what he calls the "seven erroneous assumptions." They are:

> *Assumption #1 ALL RISKS CAN BE LOWERED*
> *Disturbing truth: risks can't always be lowered—and trying creates risks of its own.*
>
> *Assumption #2 IT'S ALWAYS BETTER TO FIX THE PROBLEM*
> *Disturbing truth: trying to eliminate a problem can be more dangerous than managing one.*

Assumption #3 SOONER IS ALWAYS BETTER
Disturbing truth: early diagnosis can needlessly turn people into
patients.

Assumption #4 IT NEVER HURTS TO GET MORE
INFORMATION
Disturbing truth: Data overload can scare patients and distract
your doctor from what's important.

Assumption #5 ACTION IS ALWAYS BETTER THAN
INACTION
Disturbing truth: action is not reliably the "right" choice.

Assumption #6 NEWER IS ALWAYS BETTER
Disturbing truth: new interventions are typically not well tested
and often wind up being judged ineffective (even harmful).

Assumption #7 IT'S ALL ABOUT AVOIDING DEATH
Disturbing truth: a fixation on preventing death diminishes
life. [163]

Though all of these assumptions at first sound perfectly logical, Welch very convincingly articulates why they can all be misleading. His concepts dovetail quite nicely with conclusions that I had been coming to from my own professional experiences, although mine are far from being developed to the level of sophistication demonstrated in his presentation. I don't read his as an argument for therapeutic nihilism, where we let everything run its course and handcuff or unreasonably restrain screening and treatment interventions…but rather more of an endeavor to find an agreeable midpoint between that and overtreatment. The reader should not take my very brief summary above as anywhere near equivalent to reading Welch's book yourself, which I highly recommend.

Neither should the reader conclude that Dr. Welch might agree with all that I've written here. I read him as not being against screening but to be saying that screening needs to be done in a well-considered and rational fashion, after a process of shared decision-making. Additionally, at the end of his book, he does go on to point out that screening measures are not really prevention, they're simply early diagnosis, and sometimes potentially too early for benefits to be gained. He also points out that it is the social determinants of health dimensions where interventions can lead to true prevention, with the admittedly difficult, but most approachable by us, being those things we choose to do with our bodies in terms of eating and exercise.

My key takeaway here is that common sense is a necessary but not a sufficient guide to making medical decisions. Plus, this is yet another point in support of my overriding thesis of our having the type of relationship with our primary care doctor where we can have a frank and honest discussion about the risks and benefits of any forms of action under consideration. This would include guidance given regarding either interventions we may be requesting as patients, or what our doctors may be advising.

In my own case when my primary care doctor wanted to refer me onwards to my gastroenterologist because my liver function tests had persistently been elevated, I initially felt that this advice was likely over-cautiousness on his part. Then in turn, when my GI doctor wanted me to have an in office fibroscan test (specialized ultrasound evaluation of the liver), I'll admit that I briefly entertained the thought that perhaps they were just making money off of me, since it was their own office machine. The results of that test were compatible with significant fibrotic thickening of my liver. The next piece of advice was for me to have a liver biopsy, the more invasive nature of that getting even more of my attention. I was in the fortunate position of knowing and trusting both of my doctors, and so it was easy and reassuring enough to ask a few questions and then follow through with their advice. In addition, I thought, "Oh good, that'll be normal and that'll be the end of that road."

As it turned out, there were several more bends in the road. The biopsy showed inflammation of the liver, actually stage 3 out of 4 chronic active hepatitis (WTF?)! This then necessitated bi-annual follow-up MRI scans of the abdomen to monitor progressive liver abnormalities, which led to my previously described ERCP procedure. Oh, by the way, that result came back showing no malignancy. So, in terms of screening for a disease, mine has been a success story so far. But Welch elaborates upon several not-so-successful ones where well-intentioned testing, screening, or treatment has led to a cascade of complications, as I have experienced myself, but from the physician side, as described earlier in Chapter Seven regarding my ET tube misadventure.

Trying to slow down the medical care juggernaut in the service of safely optimizing our medical care will be a constant test of our ability to balance what we want with what we truly need. As mentioned earlier, when we are ill or injured and dealing with that associated uncertainty, we are impatient for solutions. That physical discomfort, accompanied by the discomfort of uncertainty contributes to the estimated $935 billion being wasted annually in US healthcare.

This raises what I like to call the problem of the zeros. As patients we appear to want most or all of the following:

1. Zero cost

2. Zero risk

3. Zero wait time

4. Zero pain or discomfort

5. Zero responsibility

6. Zero restriction on personal freedoms

Without shame, I'll admit myself to wanting numbers 1 through 4. It's even perfectly reasonable to want those things, but it's not at all reasonable to *expect* them. And the closer you bring numbers 2 through 6 to zero, the more zeros you add to or inflate number 1 (cost). In fact, numbers 4, 5, and 6 are in direct conflict with numbers 1, 2, and 3.

Please recall the earlier statistics related to these points, especially that in 2010 enough prescription painkillers were prescribed to medicate every single American adult around-the-clock for an entire month.[164] We here in the US represent just 5% of the world's population, yet we consume by one estimate 80% of the world's prescription narcotics.[165]

I don't mean to be oversimplifying, or stigmatizing, the serious problem of substance use disorder, but I do find myself intrigued by the following comments from Don Winslow in his article regarding the trial of Mexican drug-trafficking kingpin El Chapo in *Vanity Fair* March 2019:

> *Maybe this is the truth that we can't handle. Corruption is not the sole property of traffickers and their enablers. We own it, too. We have to ask the question: What is the corruption of the American soul that makes us want the drugs in the first place? Opioids – which are killing more Americans now than either car crashes or guns – are a response to pain. We have to ask the question: What is the pain? Until we ask and answer that question, the drug problem will always be with us.*[166]

I've become convinced that the pain we experience as humans is often not just biomedical, but is psychosocial and even spiritual as well. Therefore, any effective solution to this problem has to also involve those parameters. Drs. Stephen Trzeciak and Anthony Mazzarelli in their 2019 book *Compassionomics* convincingly argue in support of the notion that effective treatment of patients, whether for pain or other medical matters, has to involve a person-to-person interaction with compassion. I can't briefly summarize their 300-plus page book with over 430 references, but I will mention that I am entirely convinced by their detailed and unequivocal argument for their following contention:

> *Specifically, the hypothesis is that providing healthcare in a compassionate manner is more effective than providing healthcare*

*without compassion by virtue of the fact that human connection
can confer distinct and measurable benefits.*[167]

Therefore, I will limit myself to just mentioning a handful of their references. Early in their book, they quote from an intermediate source from one man's suicide note: "I'm going to walk to the bridge. If one person smiles at me on the way, I will not jump."[168]

The first of three of their pain-related reference studies showed that a simple empathic intervention, consisting of an additional preoperative visit by surgical nurses who were specifically trained to give compassionate responses to patient's emotions, doubled the pain relief in the experimental group compared to a control group.[169]

The second study showed functional MRI findings of specific brain area activations similar to those seen in previous studies of positive long-term romantic relationships conferring health benefits. These similar MRI findings are accompanied by the patient's report of significant improvement of pain after a simple patient-centered interview process. Thus, even short-term interactions of a professional nature appear to be able to call upon the same brain area neurobiological processes associated with health benefits in long-term relationships.[170]

In the third study, patients who reported higher quality interactions with their physical therapists also reported better pain control for their chronic low-back pain.[171]

They also quote a study in which just a 40-second, scripted, compassion intervention in an oncology consultation substantially reduced patients' anxiety,[172] a factor previously shown to influence outcomes in cancer patients.[173]

Additionally, in another study of residents in training, the researchers concluded that a brief empathy training protocol can improve physicians' empathic interactions with patients, and they report:

*Empathic communication skills are associated with increased
patient satisfaction,[8] improved adherence to therapy,[9] decreased*

medical errors,[10] fewer malpractice claims,[8] better outcomes,[11-14] decreased burn-out[15] and increased physician well-being[15]......
At baseline, 53% of physicians reported that their empathy for patients had declined over the past several years; whereas only 33% reported an increase in empathy (13% reported no change). At baseline, 56% said they lacked the time to be empathic, and 29% reported burnout as the primary reason for their difficulty in being empathic. [174]

I will be addressing the problem of burnout at greater length in the next chapter, but what I considered most eye-catching in this paper was the statistic of how early in their medical careers more than half of the residents already felt that they did not have enough time to express empathy with patients. So then, how can the residents' perceptions that they do not have enough time to be empathic be reconciled with the small amount of time actually required to effectively demonstrate compassion in the 40-second study?

To my mind, this conundrum is clarified by a study entitled "From Jerusalem To Jericho': A Study Of Situational And Dispositional Variables In Helping Behavior." The experimenters contrived to tell seminarian students that they had only a short amount of time to get to another location in order to give a presentation on the story of the good Samaritan. The experimenters then deviously contrived to have a co-conspirator lie helplessly on the ground, along the route the seminarian students had to take, who was coached to appear in need while declining assistance. Their results showed that those students who were most in a hurry were least likely to stop to offer assistance, despite their calling and commitment to enter a helping profession. The authors concluded:

In other words, he was in conflict between stopping to help the victim and continuing on his way to help the experimenter. And this is often true of people in a hurry; they hurry because somebody

*depends on their being somewhere. Conflict, rather than callous-
ness, can explain their failure to stop.*[175]

As I see it, physicians both during and after their training periods
are basically the secular equivalent of those seminarian students. At that
stage, and really throughout our entire careers, we are hyper-responsible
while trying to meet the simultaneous demands placed upon us from
many different directions. Ultimately, and especially in EM, we need to
reach a stage of confidence in our own judgment regarding who needs us
the most and when and where. Left to our own devices, we can usually
succeed quite nicely in learning our patients needs and trying to meet
them in a compassionate manner. But allow in the 'devious experimenters' who then put artificial, externally imposed limitations on our time
(productivity metrics), and we can at times reach conflict stasis, or default
to decisions that we know are wrong, even as we are making them.

I find this disturbing to the utmost whether I am on the patient or
the physician side of our interactions. We need to recognize societally
that this time is sacrosanct when we are trying to accomplish the often
challenging, shared decision-making that circumstances impose upon us.
In those moments, I want administrative faces to be kept out of our faces!

The family medicine physician Douglas Farrago, MD, who is a long-
time proponent of the Direct Primary Care model, puts it this way:

> *It's a funny thing but I could not find anyone using "time with
> patients" as a quality metric. … It is my belief that the more time
> you spend with the patient, the better job you will do. … The
> money train via insurers and hospitals do not want doctors even
> in the equation. They want us gone…. Also, time with patients,
> which I will abbreviate (TWP) goes against the industrialized
> medicine model…. The truth is you cannot bend reality and
> pretend rushing through the patients is still giving great care….
> It wasn't for me. Now that I live in a different model/world,
> TWP is important. And I am a better doctor than I was. That*

metric, TWP, cannot and will not be ever measured by the insurers or the government because it would shatter the myth of how they define quality.[176]

If we can't come to a joint agreement within society and the health-care system itself that these priorities are paramount, we may have to default to involving the legal system in imposing definitions and sanctions for 'healthcare malpractice.'

In the following unique and challenging case, we had only a several-minutes-in-advance radio report from EMTs of a youngish man involved in a motor vehicle crash into a bridge abutment whose entire shirt and anterior torso were described as covered in blood, but with decent vital signs at the moment. That day theirs was more of a scoop-and-run approach, and so the EMTs only raised his shirt upon arrival in the ED which revealed a veritable sheet of clotted blood covering some 18 stab wounds (as I recall it was about a dozen in the abdomen and another six in the chest region). The patient appeared neurologically uninjured and intact but was refusing to converse in much detail.

It developed that he was suicidal and had attempted to kill himself with a knife, obviously repeatedly. Then apparently when this had not succeeded, he drove his car into the bridge abutment, which also did not do the trick. Initial typical ED workup and treatment with two large bore IVs, cardiac monitoring, EKG, chest x-ray, and blood work was reassuring and did not add anything useful to his management.

In 1983 at our small community hospital, we only had access to a mobile CAT scan machine intermittently, bedside ultrasonography was not available at the moment, and EM physician-wielded bedside ultrasonography was nonexistent. So, no additional, more sophisticated imaging could be done to evaluate the extent of his internal injuries. This patient was brought into the ED at the very end of my shift, and I'd only just managed to complete a call to the general surgeon requesting his immediate presence in the ED. Knowing him and trusting that he would arrive shortly, I signed out my otherwise stable patient to the oncoming emergency physician, who was a new part-time physician in our department but with whom I had not yet worked. Neither of us was happy about the situation, but it appeared that, at that moment, a second emergency physician remaining was not required, and so off I went home.

I was not home for very long, though, when the same EM physician from sign-out called me requesting that I return in order to accompany the patient in his transfer out to a higher-level trauma care hospital, in this case in a neighboring state rather than one of the closer metropolitan hospitals. A physician accompanying a patient in transfer was not standard, in fact it was quite unusual (I'd never done it before). But given the severity of his injuries and my initial involvement in his care, I did not think it was an unreasonable request. So, in due course I found myself in the back of an ambulance with my patient again. By this point, he had been seen in the ED by the general surgeon who declared that there was nothing more that could be done for him at our institution, and he required a higher level of care, which also sounded perfectly appropriate to me.

He seemed no worse off than when I had left him about an hour previously, except that now he was more verbal and was repeatedly requesting, "Just let me die." I had been reassured by my colleague that he had been accepted in transfer by, and was expected at, a higher-level trauma care hospital, somewhat nearby but in a neighboring state. I had therefore armed myself with a couple of units of blood to transfuse him if his blood pressure bottomed out, plus a chest tube and associated materials.

The bulk of the 45-minute ride went uneventfully. However, just as we were within shouting distance of the hospital, the patient became more agitated and louder in his same requests to die. I was in the process of trying to make a rational explanation as to why I could not comply with his request when his passing out ended that conversation. So now we are literally pulling into the hospital as I'm just starting chest compressions on him because he is pulseless. To top matters off in bouncing into the ambulance bay, one of our ambulance cabinet doors drops open as I'm lowering my head, and I gash my forehead against the edge. So now I'm doing one-handed chest compressions, with my other hand pressed to my forehead to stanch my own blood flow, while indicating to my two EMTs that no, let's not intubate him here, let's just race inside because there will be a team expecting us, and they can tube him and crack his chest (emergency thoracotomy surgery to get at his heart and address any sources of bleeding) at the same time.

It was definitely amongst the top five disheartening moments in my medical career when we came crashing through the doors only to find not a soul there to meet us! We raced down what seemed like an unnecessarily long hall yelling loudly that we needed help. We finally encountered some staff, and what appeared to be the most senior physician/surgical resident in scrubs who began grilling us about who were we and what were we doing there? It quickly evolved that, yes, she had spoken with my colleague, but she was under the impression that the transfer was going to a different major trauma hospital, which would have been a shorter transport time for us. She concluded her semi-harangue with, "Anyway he's dead now."

He was sure enough pretty much dead at that point, pulseless and not breathing, but with a normal tracing on his cardiac monitor. The trauma literature stipulates that someone who is freshly dead, with vital signs very recently present, in the setting of penetrating chest trauma, which his six stab wounds to the chest qualified him for, mandates an emergency thoracotomy with heroic resuscitative efforts. Also, in the emergency medicine literature and the law, one cannot just let a suicidal patient die, especially if they're not thinking clearly, which his multiple stab wounds, low blood pressure, and passing out also definitively qualified him for.

I was quite vehemently pointing out how recently he and I had been vigorously debating his care, and that if she wasn't going to open his chest then I would (I was indeed angry about all of the details of the event, and particularly that my patient would have the nerve to not hold out for another one to two minutes, thus making me look and feel like a complete incompetent). His stretcher had at least been continuing to move while attracting a small crowd of their emergency staff. We were all now in the resuscitation room, and I started stalking about the room looking for their thoracotomy tray, at which point she called for hospital security to escort me out of the hospital. This I complied with as I saw her reaching for the thoracotomy tray.

I still have some sympathy for that surgeon's position in that here I was a complete stranger claiming to be an out-of-state emergency physician with an obvious and inexplicable forehead wound myself and a dead but still warm body in tow, which body had neither endotracheal tube nor chest tube in place! She ultimately did the right thing with an emergency thoracotomy and got his blood pressure back up and him to the OR, but to no avail as he ultimately got his wish granted, since he did die later that evening.

I only learned those additional details a little later on when the trauma hospital sent a formal letter of complaint to our emergency department director about my behavior. This was annoying, but perfectly understandable to some degree, as I had in point of fact been engaged in loudly insisting on practicing medicine 'in their house,' without credentials in their hospital or even a medical license in their state.

From this perspective now, I can't help but wonder how many opportunities for one person to make even a brief connection with him had been missed. I also wonder how much narcotic use and medical suffering could be avoided if even nonmedical people took the time, and we medical folks slowed down the medical interaction just long enough, to make a compassionate and therapeutic connection.

CHAPTER TEN

IT'S A LOVE-HATE THING

Physicians are very aware of the widespread dissatisfaction with the US healthcare system. We have truly mixed feelings as well not only towards 'the system,' but also towards our patients and towards our profession itself. I have no doubt that this contributes to the fact that doctors have the highest suicide rate of any profession, nearly twice that of the general population. This is supported by my own career-long observation that patient-care demands, and the accompanying lifestyle and work schedule, can at times be overwhelming and downright depressing.

What follows are several, but by no means all, of the factors contributing to why physicians across the board might be experiencing depression and burnout, along with references to supportive documentation and studies.

This first study concluded that primary care physicians needed 26.7 hours per day in order to meet all of the guideline-recommended preventative care along with chronic and acute care and the associated documentation that those interventions required.

1. "Revisiting the Time Needed to Provide Adult Primary Care" by Justin Porter MD, et al. (2022):

Given the large gap between the time required to provide guideline-based care and the limits of a clinic day, many clinicians are likely not completing specific services, not completing them according to the guidelines, or working overtime. If time pressures are driving a gap between guideline-based and clinical medicine, it might explain why national health outcomes are worse than expected.[177]

This second study was done by direct observation of 57 physicians in family medicine, internal medicine, cardiology, and orthopedics for over 430 hours with the following conclusion.

2. "Allocation of Physician Time in Ambulatory Practice: A Time and Motion Study in 4 Specialties" by Christine Sinsky, MD, et al. (2016):

During office hours, physicians in our sample spent nearly half their time on EHR (electronic health record) and desk work activities and less than one third on direct clinical face time with patients; in other words, for every hour of direct clinical face time with patients, physicians spent almost 2 hours on EHR and desk work. In addition, for physicians who completed after-hours diaries, EHR and desk work regularly extended 1 to 2 hours beyond office hours into personal time.[178]

In case you're wondering why these considerations might be important to us as patients, studies in this area, while not totally conclusive, suggest that physician burnout is associated with decreased patient safety and less professionalism on the part of physicians, thus leading to a less effective patient-physician relationship, with the following conclusion from this third study.

3. "Burnout and Medical Errors Among American Surgeons" by Tait D. Shanafelt, MD, et al. (2009):

In conclusion, recent self-perceived major medical errors were reported by 9% of American surgeons. These errors are strongly related to a surgeon's degree of burnout and mental QOL (Quality of Life).[179]

Contributing even more to physician burnout and to jeopardizing patient safety are the shockingly frequent and totally unjustifiable moments in which a physician is literally forced to appeal to either an insufficiently qualified physician, or even a nonmedical person, in order to be certain that what they've ordered for their patients for diagnostic purposes, and even sometimes for treatment purposes, actually gets done and is covered by their health insurance!

This first quotation, and I recommend strongly that you read the article in full, is from an oncologist describing all the hoops she had to jump through in order to actually speak to a qualified oncologist at the insurance company to get approval for the medication that her cancer patient required.

1. "AITA for Pointing Out to the Insurance Company That I'm the Expert on My Patient? (A parody, except happening everywhere.)" by Jennifer L. Lycette, MD (2022):

From the start of the conversation, tons of red flags. First of all, he won't tell me what specialty he is. And I'm like, "Okay, that's kind of weird, but can you at least tell me if you're an oncologist?" Then he asks, "Why does that matter?" So I say, "It matters a lot because I'm an oncologist and this is about a person with cancer. It's literally a matter of life and death because your insurance company denied their cancer treatment."[180]

Out of the loop as I am, I had to look up AITA to learn that it stands for, 'Am I The Asshole.'

This second article also needs to be read in full to appreciate it, representing as it does even more elaborate hoop jumping imposed upon an infectious disease specialist this time, who was trying to obtain approval for the correct HIV medication for his ill patient.

2. "HIV and ID Observations: How to Induce Rage in a Doctor" by Paul E. Sax, MD (2022):

> *If you're wondering how to make a doctor angry — really, really angry — read on. Because asking us to justify treatment decisions to insurance companies and their pharmacy benefit managers must rank right up there with the greatest tortures of practicing medicine in this country.*
>
> *Mind you, this isn't just about my patient, or about me — such infuriating events take place innumerable times in countless offices, hospitals, and clinics around the country every day, wasting everyone's valuable time with no evidence whatsoever that they improve the quality of care.*
>
> *Such struggles are an inevitable part of a healthcare system that values profits over people. The debates require a veritable army of staff on both sides to navigate what should often be very straightforward treatment issues.[181]*

The above HIV example has the added attraction at the end of having a link to a video by the comic genius Dr. Glaucomflecken (aka ophthalmologist Will Flanary, MD). In this brief video (which rewards the effort to watch) regarding the abomination of "prior authorizations," he debates and commiserates with himself, which debate ends as:

> *"Either way the insurance company is making medical decisions that directly impact the health of the patient."*
>
> *"Yeah"*
>
> *"which is also known as..."*
>
> *"practicing medicine."[182]*

Another must see video by Dr. Glaucomflecken, again brilliantly self-debating on the future of medicine/private equity, includes the following 'not so humorous' dialogue:

"There's no way our physicians will work under those conditions."

"What are they going to do quit? Doctors have student loans. Doctors have no transferable skills. They have no choice."

"So, they'll just leave and work somewhere else."

"Oh, you mean one of the other dozens of EDs in the area that we also own? Face it, this is the future of medicine a handful of ultra-rich individuals exploiting the altruistic tendencies of healthcare professionals in order to extract an ungodly amount of wealth from the most vulnerable members of society."[183]

Which brings us to what I consider likely the most prominent factor contributing to physician burnout, as well as posing a threat to our patient safety, and that is the **dollar-driven decision-making** that is happening in healthcare constantly, despite what we physicians think is best for our patients!

Following are salient quotes from articles which support my above contention.

1. "Buy and Bust: When Private Equity Comes for Rural Hospitals" (2022):

    Private equity investors, with their focus on buying cheap and reaping quick returns, are moving voraciously into the U.S. health care system; investments increased twentyfold from 2000 to 2018, and have only accelerated since.[184]

These concerns are seconded by the following article to which question, presented in the title, the answer is a definite NO!!

2. "Private Equity Firms Now Control Many Hospitals, ERs and Nursing Homes. Is it Good for Health Care?" (2020):

Over the past decade, private equity firms like Blackstone, Apollo Global Management, The Carlyle Group, KKR & Co. and Warburg Pincus have deployed more than $340 billion to buy health care-related operations around the world. In 2019, private equity's health care acquisitions reached $79 billion, a record, according to Bain & Co., a consulting firm.

Private equity's purchases have included rural hospitals, physicians' practices, nursing homes and hospice centers, air ambulance companies and health care billing management and debt collection systems. Partly as a result of private equity purchases, many formerly doctor-owned practices no longer are. The American Medical Association recently reported that 2018 was the first year in which more physicians were employees — 47.4 percent — than owners of their practices — 45.9 percent. In 1988, 72.1 percent of medical practices were owned by physicians.

In some parts of the health care industry, private equity firms dominate. For example, TeamHealth, owned by Blackstone, and Envision Healthcare, owned by KKR, provide staffing for about a third of the country's emergency rooms. This has been a seismic shift. During the 1900s, most hospitals were owned either by nonprofit entities with religious affiliations or by states and cities, with ties to medical schools. For-profit hospitals existed, but it wasn't until recently that they became nearly ubiquitous.[185]

Further in support of my aforementioned editorial pronouncement of 'NO' are the following two eye-opening statements.

1. "The Deadly Combination of Private Equity and Nursing Homes During a Pandemic: New Jersey Case Study of Coronavirus at Private Equity Nursing Homes" (2020):

Nearly three-fifths (58.8 percent) of private equity nursing home residents contracted Coronavirus (based on resident cases and average number of residents). This infection rate was 24.5 percent higher than the statewide nursing home average and 57.0 percent higher than at public facilities. The Coronavirus fatality rate (the number of resident deaths divided by the number of cases) was 10.2 percent higher at private equity facilities than the statewide average and higher than at non-profit and for-profit facilities.[186]

2. "Patients for Profit: How Private Equity Hijacked Health Care: Death Is Anything but a Dying Business as Private Equity Cashes In" (2022):

Private equity firms are investing in health care from cradle to grave, and in that latter category quite literally. A small but growing percentage of the funeral home industry — and the broader death care market — is being gobbled up by private equity-backed firms attracted by high profit margins, predictable income, and the eventual deaths of tens of millions of baby boomers.[187]

Okay, I have to admit it, that's a genius business model. I certainly wouldn't bet against us boomers eventually getting sick, hospitalized, some of us needing nursing home placement, and all of us eventually dying! If you can't make all of the money that you feel you need to make off of us as patients in the ED, then maybe you will when we end up in the nursing home (possibly as a result of compromised ED care), and for the perfect trifecta, then you'll get us again when we die (possibly as a result of compromised nursing home care). So then, how motivated can private equity actually be to invest the time, effort, or money to ensure that anything good happens at any of those settings?

I was heartened though to just this week come across this following faint ray of hope. EM physicians are trying to take advantage of the fact that more than half of the US (33 states, plus DC) have laws against the 'corporate practice of medicine.' So, they are now suing on that basis to try to limit private equity's distorted influence over healthcare. Success starting in EM may hopefully progress from there to the rest of healthcare. I think this would only be fitting justice, since EM was one of the areas in which private equity made some of its first major inroads! Have a look at this KHN news article entitled "ER Doctors Call Private Equity Staffing Practices Illegal and Seek to Ban Them" (2022):

> *Now, physicians and consumer advocates around the country are anticipating a California lawsuit against Envision, scheduled to start in January 2024 in federal court. The plaintiff in the case, Milwaukee-based American Academy of Emergency Medicine Physician Group, alleges that Envision uses shell business structures to retain de facto ownership of ER staffing groups, and it is asking the court to declare them illegal. We're not asking them to pay money, and we will not accept being paid to drop the case," said David Millstein, lead attorney for the plaintiff. "We are simply asking the court to ban this practice model."[188]*

All of the above contributes to the reported burnout rate among physicians in 2022 reaching near 50% or greater almost across the board (though with some specialties still remaining in the 26-50% range), with emergency medicine leading the league at the top of a recent list of specialties at 60%. A 2002 article entitled "Physician Burnout Is Up, Gender Inequality Is Making It Worse" also addresses some of the gender inequities that place women physicians at even greater risk for burnout.[189]

An even earlier study in 2016 showed:

> *Compared to 2011, burn out rates were higher for all specialties in 2014. In fact, nearly a dozen specialties experienced more than a 10% increase in burnout over those three years.[190]*

I specifically mention this to point out that these figures are well in advance of the COVID pandemic.

Burnout was first described in Maslach and Jackson's seminal 1981 article as:

> *Burnout is a syndrome of emotional exhaustion and cynicism that occurs frequently among individuals who do 'people-work' of some kind. A key aspect of the burnout syndrome is increased feelings of emotional exhaustion. As their emotional resources are depleted, workers feel they are no longer able to give of themselves at a psychological level. Another aspect is the development of negative, cynical attitudes and feelings about one's clients.... A third aspect of the burnout syndrome is the tendency to evaluate oneself negatively, particularly with regard to one's work with clients. Workers feel unhappy about themselves and dissatisfied with their accomplishments on the job.[191]*

I find this alternative description of the phenomenon even more pertinent:

> *A negative working environment, especially work overload, and the belief that they are not able to deliver the high standards of care expected, bring about feelings of permanent nervous strain, irritability and anxiety. This in turn leads to emotional and physical lassitude. To avoid becoming more personally involved, a doctor suffering burnout distances himself even further from the patient, treating him superficially, in a formal way, indifferently or with a negative attitude (depersonalization).[192]*

I can definitely relate to beginning to feel that way towards the last six years of my 40-year career. I would never have described myself as burnt-out, but jokingly, I thought to myself, I wouldn't be surprised if somebody working alongside me for too long might comment, "Who's making toast around here?" I mention the six-year mark as a measure because that is when I chose a date for my planned retirement at the end of April 2020 (2020 because that would mark 40 years from my medical school graduation in 1980, and April because it is my birthday month).

The retirement idea had come to mind because in 2014, I had just passed my required every-ten-years board certification exam in emergency medicine for the fourth time (this is a daylong, computer-based, 300+ question test that costs $1,000). I decided then that I did not want to take the exam one more time in 2024, at which point I'd be 71 years old and possibly a hazard to my EM patients! I did then experience an immediate distinct feeling of relief at having an end date in sight, even though it was just a faint light at the end of a long six-year tunnel at that point.

Alarmingly, many of my much younger colleagues are already talking about how to exit the medical field, even when just in their first several years out of EM residency. Yet more disquieting are the heartbreaking events of young physicians in their training, and even medical students ("three times more likely than their peers to kill themselves"), committing suicide (please note that this data is all pre-COVID).[193]

Statistics show that doctors are at the top of a list of the 11 professions most likely to commit suicide, coming in at approximately 1.87 times more likely to commit suicide than those working in other occupations. I don't see executives of any stripe on that list, though I'm sure they are not immune to stress, depression, and suicide.

I recall that as a medical student I came across the statistic that dentists were the most suicidal of all professions, but at this point we physicians have passed them by and they're now number two at 1.67 times as likely. Plus, in statistics examining all causes of death as a doctor, nearly 4% of all physician deaths result from suicide. Within this data, male and female physicians are equally as likely to commit suicide, but in comparison to other occupations, female doctors are 2.78 times as likely to commit suicide. This works out to a doctor dying by suicide every day in the United States.[194]

Regarding suicide, physician or otherwise, I feel unqualified to offer much personal comment here as to why it happens and how to prevent it. I can't relate personally to feeling suicidal. At worst I'm misanthropic at times when I consider the mindsets that have become obstacles to improvement in our healthcare system.

I am very grateful for the fact that I have never once in my life considered suicide. It feels next to impossible for me to conceive of going down that path, or to fathom the despondency that makes some people feel compelled to travel it. I am too curious about what might happen next on the world stage to not wait around and see what develops. It came as no great surprise to me, or my family and physicians, though, that I entered a phase of depression following my stroke. Beyond the obvious psychosocial changes, there are suspected neurochemical factors at work in poststroke depression.

Throughout that period of transition, and even now, I have considered my transient depression a relatively minor bump in the road, and so I was surprised recently while reading through my old medical records to encounter my neurologist's reference to it as a "major depression." It certainly involved psychotherapy and the use of antidepressant medications. But during that period, I had taken the time to read William Styron's excellent book *Darkness Visible*[195] about his battle with oppressive depression, which in comparison made my experience seem far less disruptive.

My first reflexive visual image of my stroke experience was that of a cartoon character in the aftermath of a cartoon explosion with the pieces of myself wafting down in a back-and-forth zigzag fashion before they reconnected, leaving me dumbfounded on the ground (bewildering is the most apt word). The actual fallout from my stroke would include losing my job, losing my ability to play soccer with any degree of satisfaction, losing my self-confidence, being divorced by my wife, and most enduringly painful, suffering a significant degree of estrangement from my three children Kirk, Ben, and Laine, who were ten, eight, and four at the time of my stroke. Prior to my stroke, if you had said to me that those five things (six counting the stroke itself) would have happened simultaneously, I would have thought, "No way can I survive that…just shoot me now."

A later image that occurred to me was feeling like Kafka's main character in *The Metamorphosis*[196] who wakes up one morning in bed having turned into a large cockroach. When I reread the book, besides the feeling of physical awkwardness in one's changed body, there was also the parallel tragicomic sense of shortsightedly visualizing a quick return to work and normality despite the new disability. I found the ending in which his family chooses to distance themselves from him at once unimaginably cruel and perfectly understandable; they did have their own lives to lead and he had become a cockroach, after all.

It also did seem to me to be particularly cruel that what would in essence be a second form of chronic illness for me would choose to attack my brain. This was my major organ of coping, having allowed me to outlast most of my UC experience, at least feeling, if not truly being, completely whole. I can't argue with this insight from my old medical records as well, this time from my therapist who wrote, "It was extraordinarily clear today how dependent he is on intellectualization and analytic assessment to protect himself from touching his affect." I can realize and confess now that it was both a strength and a weakness on my part. But I still can't see any other way around it, given how much more damaging and permanent the suffering that I've seen in my patients appears, which again makes my experiences feel like 'small potatoes.'

At any rate, by nature, and subsequently by choice, being an optimistic and a stubborn individual who enjoys a challenge, I chose to set about trying to figure out what to do next. I did have the great good fortune to have the support of my friends and family, both extended, and to some degree my children and first wife. My transition was also immensely assisted by an excellent disability insurance policy, which allowed me to continue to receive benefits while I worked as a physician, since I was insured as an Emergency Physician specifically.

A stroke allows you to see that we never truly multitask—what we are actually doing is rapid task switching, at which we all have varying skill levels. Following my stroke, I discovered that I now had a glacially paced capacity for switching tasks, a speed deficit and personal limit that previously I had never felt particularly restricted by. This manifested itself comically on the soccer field one day, once I was up and running again, when I lifted my foot to trap the approaching soccer ball while scanning upfield to choose from the variety of options for my next maneuver, and I completely neglected to put my foot down to actually stop the ball. When my brain finally clicked in to say it was time to move off, I looked down only to see that the ball had passed completely under my foot and was gone.

By this point, I had also returned to a very closely supervised trial of work limited to just simple cases in my own emergency department. I felt almost childlike in my need to process things slowly and carefully and was somewhat in awe of my colleagues' and my own previous ability to deal with multiple simultaneous patient demands. This had previously seemed like no big deal and was just part and parcel of the job. At any rate, it quickly became clear to my department's director, and somewhat more reluctantly to me as well, that much more recovery work needed to be done on my part.

In compromise, I chose to work in my hospital's occupational health setting while simultaneously pursuing an online Master of Public Health degree. This seemed like a logical, and frankly a much easier, course to follow, with a decision that I would just become an occupational medicine physician. However, after a brief period, I facetiously concluded that such relatively undemanding work was possibly more brain-damaging than the stroke itself—at least in the limited capacity made available to me. I do not mean to disparage occupational medicine physicians in general.

In my limited setting I was seeing only completely healthy people who wanted to work and needed a physical exam for clearance, as well as reasonably healthy people who had experienced an injury or illness which made them feel like they should no longer have to work. Given my own struggles to get back to work, I was not a good match for working with those patients, and I continued to feel that my identity was as an emergency physician.

One of the things that I have always loved about my work in emergency medicine is the opportunity it affords to treat every patient equally without regard to their station in life, or how they may treat me. This includes everyone from those who insult me to even the President of the United States, should I ever have to care for them. At one point in my career, the latter end of that spectrum was marginally less than a one-in-a-million possibility for me.

During his presidency, President George H. W. Bush would occasionally fly to his coastal summer home in Kennebunkport, Maine. The routine was to have Air Force One land at the air force base, which was close to the small city hospital ED where I was working. In anticipation of his arrival, a small table was set up with a dedicated phone line in the central station of our ED for the Secret Service to use if needed, since we were the designated spot for him to be brought in case of an emergency as he passed through our region. It never did happen, but I did enjoy speculating about how the Secret Service would react when I asked them to leave the room so that I could obtain a history and physical on the President, in private, for whatever hopefully only minor thing that was bothering him.

The front end of that spectrum is a regular, not theoretical, encounter with our patients cursing at, sometimes spitting at, and even attempting to hit or kick us occasionally. In one case, I was suturing a laceration on the forehead of a rather large, intoxicated gentleman who was in the process of wordlessly but rather loudly humming out what struck me as some kind of a martial football fight song, and our subsequent exchange went down as follows:

Me: "What is that, Army?"

Patient: "No, it's Notre Dame you dumb-f#ck!"

Me: "That's Dr. Dumb-f#ck to you."

This last was said *sotto voce*, and more for the entertainment of the two security guards who had been standing nearby, just in case. In the event, it did not pierce the alcoholic-haze and self-satisfaction my intoxicated patient was probably feeling for having properly put me in my place. The next day my security guard friends had mocked up a smallish desktop nameplate for me with the name, of course, 'Dr. Dumb-f#ck.'

Some several years after that episode, I found myself in the midst of the bewildering days following my stroke. When I was finally ensconced in a regular bed, after starting in my hospital's ICU, my primary care doctor specifically asked me one day if I had any questions or concerns. I recall that my only question was, "Will I be able to play soccer again?" That was indeed my only expressed and pressing concern. I don't recall the details of his response, but my guess is that he likely hedged his comments into the area of uncertainty, while expressing some open-minded optimism, because that's the kind of physician that he was.

Notably, I did not ask whether I'd be able to practice medicine again. I believed at the time that would be the easier of the two challenges, which ultimately turned out to be partially true. My only voiced concern was partly due to the fact that, as most of us likely envision it, a stroke predominantly raises the prospect of, and concerns about, one's weakness/physical limitations. More subtle and more challenging are the significant cognitive limitations that ensue.

I frankly at this point can't recall the exact details of the timing, but a discussion about my possible cognitive limitations did arise at some early point.

What I do distinctly recall is that I thought I would probably be out of work for at least two weeks. Once I was actually discharged from the rehab hospital six weeks from the day of my stroke, I did also then say out loud to my soccer-playing friends that I would be back out playing soccer with them "in another two weeks." I believe my "two-weeks fixation" arose because that was the lengthiest period of time that I'd had off in a row since finishing medical school 12 years earlier, so I couldn't even picture being out of work or soccer for longer than that. As it developed, I did not practice emergency medicine independently again until five years later. I did play soccer again by that summer but was never able to regain my prior skills at or full sense of pleasure in and satisfaction from that activity.

While still an inpatient in my own hospital in that first week, I remember thinking of the practical details that I would probably have to address which might include having somebody reviewing my charting for possible errors or deficiencies. In retrospect, this is alarming, as I did not appear to be worried about my patient-care decisions themselves! At any rate, at some point my neurologist did feel the need to address that I might not be able to return to the practice of emergency medicine ever again. This was likely in response to my having expressed some of the above thoughts openly.

Subsequent to that discussion, I did talk with my good friend Don over the phone. Don was one of the group of six residents with whom I began our EM practice. For family considerations I had moved on to a new position in 1989. At any rate, having spent eight very trying and challenging years in emergency medicine together, our exchange went as follows:

Me: "So, Don, my neurologist tells me that I might not ever get back into emergency medicine."

Don: "That's great news! ...... No, no, no, I didn't mean it that way."

Me: "Don't worry, Don, I know exactly what you meant."

What he meant was that I now had my 'get out of jail free' pass out of EM, and possibly medicine altogether. It is the holy grail for us practicing clinical physicians to envision some form of work in which we don't have to constantly listen to complaints while simultaneously worrying about failing our patients in some way. We ideally all want to apply our medical knowledge and get paid equally well. In that mix of the pool of complainants are patients, their families, our staff, hospital administrators, insurers/third-party payers, and more or less the entirety of society itself. Although there may only be two live individuals at the bedside (patient and physician), there are a whole host of other visible and invisible, animate and inanimate, forces at play.

The entire practice of medicine is based around the concept of the 'chief complaint'—that is, the precise discomfort or sense of 'dis-ease' which caused the patient to seek you out at this moment. The word chief had to be thrown in there because in nearly every patient-physician interaction, the patient has a not-insignificant number of complaints or concerns, and oftentimes wants to mention them all at once in the same breath and first sentence.

In the ED, I frequently find myself having to ask the patient directly, or through the interpreter with my Spanish-speaking patients, to slow down, pause, and choose just one of their laundry list of complaints as the most important or urgent, and to advise that we will address the others in time. That the patient can get so many words out all at once is a reassuring sign in emergency medicine. Of course, as a premedical student I didn't have the faintest idea that my career would be spent listening to people complain.

If I had known that, I might have opted out immediately, knowing that my nature is one of wanting to help people solve problems and that I am put off by an endless rehashing of problems without seeking a way forward. What turns out to be true for a surprisingly substantial portion of people is that the very process of verbally sharing their symptoms, problems, and concerns is the underlying reason that they are seeking you out, and it can be therapeutic for them as well.

In a 2012 survey of 5,000 physicians, 9 out of 10 said that they would not recommend a career in healthcare.[197] More often than not, I think I'm still in that minority of the one out of ten that would. I've found that trying to provide insight into what it means to become a physician is analogous to trying to explain to someone who doesn't have children what the transition from that state to becoming a parent is like. In other words, it cannot be accurately conveyed.

The transition into being a physician is less abrupt, but possibly even more disorienting. There comes that day when you take on a similar, but even greater, responsibility for a human life, but without a co-parent or extended family to directly assist you. Additionally, unlike your own well-cared-for, trained, well-behaved, and well-educated child, a substantial percentage of our emergency department patients share few, and possibly none, of those attributes, while simultaneously being imbued with an inordinate share of impulsivity and can appear to be in the midst of actively trying to die on you! If that doesn't give you pause, then yes, medicine, and emergency medicine in particular, might be your cup of tea.

Of course, nobody said anything remotely like that to me when I was first at that 'Should I do this or not?' stage. But I did know all of that in great detail when I chose to reenter emergency medicine for the second time in 1997 (we all effectively choose to reenter it every day that we walk in the door for work). Truth be told, in the six months or so prior to my stroke, I had been in the process of trying to develop a health-related video education series directed at improving basic health literacy for patients, as a way of possibly facilitating my exit from clinical day-to-day patient-care medicine.

The love part comes from the unceasing opportunities to relieve pain and suffering, and otherwise have a positive impact on the health, life, and happiness of others. If we find it intuitively appealing to define love as the willingness to place the welfare of another person above and beyond one's own welfare, then as physicians we show a form of love to our patients every single day, and the nurses demonstrate this love even more so as they have the first contact with and spend more time with patients. The fact that those of us in healthcare do this every single day, time after time, with strangers, and despite how we are treated in return, elevates those interactions to the near sacred in my mind (the deaths of over 3,600 US healthcare workers from COVID-19 just during this pandemic's first year acts as an exclamation point here).[198] I sincerely believe that as physicians (and for other healthcare workers as well), we experience not only the obvious immediate satisfaction following a good outcome, but benefit from those interactions within our own souls as well. Additionally, I believe that any thoughtful and caring interaction between the patient and physician (above and beyond outcome considerations) can have an uplifting effect on both of their souls.

This, of course, brings us back to Dr. Benson's formulation and my opening thesis. In order to satisfy Benson's triad of requirements for placebo healing, and follow my own recommended three steps, the patient has to reach a point of an expectation of getting well, which is unreachable if they have not had the opportunity to air their concerns and have their questions and anxieties addressed. Secondly, the physician would have to perform a thorough assessment in order to, in good conscience, feel and convey a logical justification for a sense of optimism in the expectation of the patient getting well. There then has to be a good relationship between the two for any of that to even come close to happening, and for the patient to feel confident about adopting and following through with the decided-upon plan.

Nearly all of the most powerful forces within the practice of medicine today appear to be actively conspiring against the above exchange ever having a possibility of occurring. These forces are attempting to, and are succeeding in, narrowing the window of time in which the patient and the physician can actually be face-to-face exchanging this necessary information and creating the sort of relationship that can truly be healing.

Those forces represent that relatively new and rapidly accelerating phenomenon in healthcare, which is in essence the commoditization of healthcare. For the 'bean counters' it takes no great insight to see that the more patient-care encounters that occur, the more dollars that can be charged. We are all guilty, patients and physicians alike, in allowing this transition to occur, that is, allowing nonmedical people to position us as widgets on an assembly line or as cogs in a machine, and to call the shots in regard to how we physicians and patients spend our time together. I have never once heard a person say that they were unhappy because their physician spent too much time with them, or a physician complain that they had an excessive amount of time to spend with patients.

In fact, the feedback that I get on a regular basis from my emergency department directors, and that they get from the administrators above them, is to please get in line with the following mandate:

1. See more patients

2. See them faster

3. Keep them happier

4. Never ever make a mistake

My response to this, which I don't often articulate out loud, is that my only concern is number 4.

We physicians live and work in a world in which everybody realizes that as human beings, expecting us to never make any mistakes is unreasonable. Nevertheless, anything short of that is considered unacceptable. "Physicians aren't 'burning out.' They're suffering from moral injury," so wrote Simon G. Talbot, MD, and Wendy Dean, MD, in 2018. They continued:

> In an increasingly business-oriented and profit-driven healthcare environment, physicians must consider a multitude of factors other than their patients' best interest when deciding on treatment.... These routine, incessant betrayals of patient care and

trust are examples of 'death by a thousand cuts.' Any one of them, delivered alone, might heal. But repeated on a daily basis, they coalesce into the moral injury of healthcare. Physicians are smart, tough, durable, resourceful people. If there was a way to Mac-Gyver themselves out of the situation by working harder, smarter, or differently, they would have done it already.[199]

They elaborate:

The term 'moral injury' was first used to describe soldiers' responses to their actions in war. It represents, "perpetrating, failing to prevent, bearing witness to, or learning about acts that transgress deeply held moral beliefs and expectations…a deep soul wound that pierces a person's identity, sense of morality, and relationships to society.[200]

For more on the specifics of how these dollar-driven decisions impact those of us who work in emergency medicine, there is this very apt description from a recent *New York Times* article "The Moral Crisis of America's Doctors":

E.R. doctors have found themselves at the forefront of these trends as more and more hospitals have outsourced the staffing in emergency departments in order to cut costs. A 2013 study by Robert McNamara, the chairman of the emergency-medicine department at Temple University in Philadelphia, found that 62 percent of emergency physicians in the United States could be fired without due process. Nearly 20 percent of the 389 E.R. doctors surveyed said they had been threatened for raising quality-of-care concerns, and pressured to make decisions based on financial considerations that could be detrimental to the people in their care, like being pushed to discharge Medicare and Medicaid patients or being encouraged to order more testing than necessary.

In another study, more than 70 percent of emergency physicians agreed that the corporatization of their field has had a negative or strongly negative impact on the quality of care and on their own job satisfaction. [201]

As one small but persistent example of this phenomenon, in the northeastern part of the United States where I spent my work career, even when it is snow-covered and cold outside, as EM physicians we are routinely called upon to discharge our patients back to their homeless predicament on the street, to fend for themselves. In the more ideal situation, we can arrange placement into one of the local homeless shelters that are set up for just this purpose, or perhaps convince the hospitalist to admit them to the hospital for achieving better control over one or several of their chronic medical conditions.

These patients, though, are often their own worst enemies in this predicament in that they may have already burned their bridges at many of the local homeless shelters because of prior on-site alcohol or drug use, which is appropriately prohibited there, and so they are persona non grata. The hospitalists are left with the predicament of the patient 'not meeting any criteria' for hospitalization, given no 'emergency medical reason' at the moment (the fact that you wouldn't even put your own dog outside for fear of hypothermia and death is apparently societally considered insufficient reason for doing more for these individuals). I don't believe that anyone should be absolved of developing and exercising a sense of personal responsibility, but it seems to me that any advanced civilization should have a fail-safe for when people are unable to meet those responsibilities, for whatever reason.

Then for what I feel as a twist of the knife into the hearts of us EM physicians, the EHR makes us document that we have discharged the patient 'home.' The only other alternative being 'admission to the hospital.' The option of 'I sent this unfortunate soul back out onto the freezing- cold snow-covered streets to fend for themself' is just not listed as an option even though it would be the honest truth!

What our current healthcare system effectively ends up saying to medical students, medical residents, and even experienced practicing physicians is, "So, do you have all that stuff down now about the pathophysiology of disease processes; along with the difficulty of communicating with patients and hearing what it exactly is that they are trying to say to you; as well as sussing out the differences between psychosocial processes that are masquerading as biomedical disease and/or biomedical diseases masquerading as psychosocial processes? Okay then, let's proceed. Here's the kicker! We are now NOT going to allow you anywhere near sufficient time or resources to apply all of that learning in a compassionate and just plain humane way with your patients! Why would we even consider doing such an inhumane thing, you might rightly ask? Don't be obtuse...for the obvious reason that 'time is money,' which has been known for ages. Get with the program already! You may point to the fact that 'time is also health,' which is being proven now by modern studies, day in and day out. Granted that is so, but until it is forced upon us by an overwhelming consensus, we are just gonna stick with the program as is, because the financial benefits are just so damn enticing."

Think I'm being excessively harsh in my imagined monologue there, then please consider the following from 2018:

> *Goldman Sachs analysts attempted to address a touchy subject for biotech companies, especially those involved in the pioneering "gene therapy" treatment: cures could be bad for business in the long run. "Is curing patients a sustainable business model?" analysts ask in an April 10 report entitled "The Genome Revolution."*
>
> *"The potential to deliver 'one shot cures' is one of the most attractive aspects of gene therapy, genetically-engineered cell therapy and gene editing. However, such treatments offer a very different outlook with regard to recurring revenue versus chronic therapies," analyst Salveen Richter wrote in the note to clients Tuesday. "While this proposition carries tremendous value for patients and*

society, it could represent a challenge for genome medicine developers looking for sustained cash flow."

"GILD is a case in point, where the success of its hepatitis C franchise has gradually exhausted the available pool of treatable patients," the analyst wrote. "In the case of infectious diseases such as hepatitis C, curing existing patients also decreases the number of carriers able to transmit the virus to new patients, thus the incident pool also declines ... Where an incident pool remains stable (e.g., in cancer) the potential for a cure poses less risk to the sustainability of a franchise."[202]

A 'touchy subject' representing 'a challenge for...sustained cash flow.' Has it really gotten that bad? It's obviously reached the point now where we can talk out loud about purposefully not curing medical conditions because that might "reduce the ability to transmit the virus to new patients, thus the incident pool" thereby affecting the bottom line! I'm not judging any particular individuals here; these are obviously intelligent and forward-looking individuals intent on figuring out how to win in an economic game whose rules they didn't come up with, and in their private moments might not even agree with. The article does point out that GILD's sales on their hepatitis C medication (with a cure rate greater than 90%) went from a peak of $12.5 billion in 2015 down to less than $4 billion in 2018, leading the analysts to ask "Is curing patients a sustainable business model?" Compare this to the question Jonas Salk asked in an interview about any plans to patent his very successful polio vaccine in 1952, to which he replied, "Could you patent the sun?"[203]

As an alternative to the above priority of 'sustained cash flow,' the following is from "Capitalism with A Conscience?" by Tanita Sandhu:

Increasingly, successful companies in the 21ˢᵗ century are those that not only sell and deliver a service or a product, but also contribute to society ... organizations with a conscience that goes beyond the bottom line. This 'do good' principle should evolve out of a corporate credo that encompasses commercial strategies that maximize improvements in human and environmental well-being, as well as profits for shareholders.[204]

That definitely sounds like at least the beginning of thinking differently. But, with business and capitalism rules being as rigid and long-standing as they appear to be in the US, I fear that these ideas will be dismissed as naïve. I think then that in order to obtain and sustain serious widespread changes in dollar-driven decision-making, more dramatic interventions may be required. I tend to think that the only way that we (as thinking and feeling human beings) can default to making purely business and financial decisions about how and what to do regarding medication development and pricing issues is because we are able to stay at a very long arm's length away from the actual suffering endured by patients with the conditions that we are attempting to treat or prevent.

I would propose that any company working in the healthcare field should be legally required to have its upper management have direct contact with a spectrum of the ill individuals affected by the conditions in which they are investing and for which they are pricing treatments. In other words, a field trip to a hospital setting where the company's entire C-suite, from CEO on down, would be required to volunteer on a hospital ward assisting nurse's aides in helping to clean and do bedding changes for patients with advanced liver failure, for example, preferably those with hepatic encephalopathy and incontinence as well. Apologies, there's my impatience showing through again. But I believe that might work to give a different point of view and succeed in re-orienting the priorities of some powerful financial decision-makers.

One of the oddities of experiencing a stroke is that your recovery resembles a compressed version of a second childhood. One of the primary objectives of your rehabilitation staff (your occupational and physical therapists) is to assist you in becoming independent again in what they term the ADLs (activities of daily living). This includes such basic things as safely moving about your room and being competent to wash and clean yourself (yes, your fully clothed female therapist is right there by the bathtub with handheld showerhead with the stark naked you). I was considerably chagrined one day to find myself bound by Posey restraints (like a mini straight jacket) into my wheelchair. Not yet recognizing the limits of my abilities, and given my profound left-sided weakness, I ended up down on my hospital room floor on my butt while trying to get something out of my bureau.

My independent transfer from bed to wheelchair had gone flawlessly, so I was impatient to get some fresh clothes to put on and did not want to wait for staff to help me. No head impact or any other serious injury occurred, which was important since I was, and still am, on the powerful blood thinner Coumadin. I was scolded quite sternly by the rehab facility staff, though, and had to bear up with a brief period of 'involuntary' restraint until I could demonstrate better judgment. My first scolding had occurred on rehab hospital day one when I was asked in my very first session to raise my left arm. When my conscious command to my left arm to move went unheeded, I reflexively reached over with my right hand to raise my left arm. "Never, never do that" was my physical therapist's immediate response.

Not to give the wrong impression here, because the rehabilitation facility staff are infinitely patient, which they have to be in their efforts to reteach you such mundane tasks as how to wash your body, button your shirt, and tie your shoelaces (those last two are tougher than you might think). They also have to find a way to accommodate and negotiate through dealing with a patient's disinhibition. In the common stroke phenomenon termed disinhibition, your conscious awareness of and monitoring of your baser emotions and desires are stripped away. It's a fascinating and disturbing experience to realize how thin the veneer of civilization is over our lower selves. The tendency to lash out in anger, burst into tears, or express lust are suddenly right there on the surface.

I did manage to restrain myself from groping any of my attractive young female therapists…but was far less successful on other fronts. Conversing about, or even just thinking about, my children could, and still can, bring me to tears in an instant, which can be unnerving for a reserved person. Even now 30 years later, I still find myself unpredictably susceptible to maudlin scenes on TV, in movies, or in real life exchanges. I was, and remain, least successful in restraining my anger. This no doubt made a major contribution to the breakup of my first marriage and family, causing estrangement from my children, although only I knew how much angrier I really was and had succeeded in restraining myself from showing the extent of that anger.

On the positive side, I now completely understand the delirious grin that toddlers get when they take their first steps. In rehab, your first efforts to walk again are either between parallel bars or by way of the major bodily support of your physical therapists, and your initial weak efforts are truly discouraging. I can still recall my skepticism when the very first therapist I met on entering the rehab hospital on an ambulance stretcher said to me, "Don't worry, you'll walk out of here." So, several weeks poststroke when the moment came when I finally took my first steps completely free of any supports, I felt like I was literally floating on clouds and experienced childlike glee unreservedly.

An even weirder experience was when I went to watch the Fourth of July fireworks four months poststroke. With every burst of color in the sky, I experienced an accompanying burst of euphoria deep in my brain. I speculate it was some kind of a pop of endorphin release, but I hate to even try to demystify it since it was so pleasurable. Disappointingly, I did not have the same experience the following Fourth of July…experience subdued innocence once again, I guess.

So, even though in certain ways I was disappointed to grow up again, this was offset by the compressed adolescent rediscoveries of the independence of learning to drive again and to develop a confident sense of self, culminating five years later in resuming my work as an emergency physician. I did get to skip high school, college, and medical school the second time around, while studying for and easily passing again in 1994 the required every-10-year American Board of Emergency Medicine (ABEM) recertification exam, just two years following my stroke.

Nevertheless, I did reexperience the anguish of, 'What do I want to be when I grow up?' My neurologist was performing the balancing act of neither discouraging nor falsely encouraging me about my work prospects, and I am eternally grateful that Dr. B perfectly threaded the needle there of giving me a realistic view of my limitations and challenges while not discouraging me. The following was entered into my medical records as a quote from my disability insurance representative's status report on October 24, 1995:

> *With regard to prognosis for continued improvement to the point that he might be able to return to emergency room work, Dr. B felt that this was unlikely although she noted that one would not have anticipated Dr. Remignanti's returning to his current level of function considering the type of stroke that he had sustained.*

In any case, I was considering alternatives to resuming emergency medicine work, which included possibly retraining as a psychiatrist or radiologist (while not undemanding work, at least more controlled and sequential in demands, and not as likely to involve the rapid task-switching required in emergency medicine). As well, there was the aforementioned foray into occupational and then community health center primary care medicine, while getting my MPH degree. I also considered leaving the medical field entirely, possibly training as a teacher. I recall a colleague saying about my predicament at the time, "After going through your stroke and all that, you should not have to work ever again." That thought did have some intrinsic appeal, though on some level I was aware that not working again would be an unhealthy course for me.

Unfortunately (in the long run I think actually more 'fortunately'), my disability insurance had a five-year limit on benefits, which had been imposed on the basis of the risk profile of my prior lengthy UC illness. Therefore, I did not have the option of permanent retirement on disability pay. Given that my disability insurance company was supporting me at over half of my original pay rate during my recovery, I did feel the obligation to make my most sincere effort to rehabilitate sufficiently to reenter my EM career. My international medical volunteer experiences made trying to put my MPH degree to work in that kind of setting a persisting and enticing consideration.

However, I was not willing to take the time away from my family life, or to subject all of us to the rigors of prolonged living in the developing world (I was relatively quickly and happily remarried following my divorce, along with adopting our now 18-year-old son when he was one week old). All of that, along with my stubbornness (have I mentioned that yet?), made me want to be able to leave emergency medicine on my own terms. So, I have ended up in the somewhat unique position of having twice chosen both medicine, and emergency medicine specifically, as career choices.

When presented with a critical or near critically ill or injured individual in EM, we have to quickly establish a compressed 'just the facts ma'am' type of exchange with our patients which rapidly gathers the relevant facts while conveying an expertise that they may rely upon. Often, in these pressured situations, we don't have the time to entertain questions about our interventions. If the patient is in a condition to be able to take in information, we may tell them what we're doing and why, quite frequently not before we begin but as we are doing it. Then when we give medication, if we don't promptly get the result that we want, we oftentimes immediately repeat the medication at double the prior dose given. So, there is no way in which we are looking to create much of a patient-physician relationship yet or waiting for a placebo response.

Here is an illustrative motor vehicle accident (MVA) case to demonstrate this speed of decision-making. On a Halloween evening, EMTs brought in a 30ish-year-old man who had been the driver in a significant impact between his small MGB sports car and a telephone pole. Being in the late 1980s, there were no airbags yet, and it was unclear whether he had been wearing his seatbelt. That turned out to be an unnecessary bit of information because his complaint of significant chest pain along with his low blood pressure told me that a significant internal injury had likely occurred when his chest met the steering wheel. As in my earlier stabbing/MVA case, we were still devoid of readily available CT scan or bedside ultrasound capabilities. He appeared uninjured elsewhere and his chest X-ray and EKG were unremarkable.

I wanted to determine if his low blood pressure in the setting of chest impact might be caused by cardiac tamponade (when chest trauma causes blood to collect between the heart muscle and its surrounding sac compromising its functional ability to circulate blood). Therefore, I chose to put in a central line (large bore IV catheter through either the large subclavian or internal jugular veins) in order to monitor his central venous pressure as well as to give IV fluids.

He had apparently been coming back from a party, as he was in the expected alcohol-intoxicated state with the memorable detail of a perfect red lipstick kiss mark on his left cheek. This I at first thought was maybe a goodnight kiss from his girlfriend before realizing that the perfection of it indicated that it was more likely applied as part of his 'costume' for the evening.

I chose to access the right internal jugular vein, which in those days was again a blind technique. First, you palpate for the carotid artery in the neck. Then starting lateral to the carotid artery in the neck, in a partially visible and partially imagined valley that begins in a V-shape between the anterolateral neck muscles, you methodically insert a moderately long and extremely large bore needle and aim for the right nipple location. While then pulling back on the attached syringe, you hope for a flash of blood that indicates that you are in the correct vessel. If the blood is too bright red, it might be a sign that you are in the nearby carotid artery rather than the vein. Sometimes this is a bit of a hunt-and-peck process in which you have to make multiple passes changing the direction or depth of angle of your approach by a fraction.

I was immediately relieved, in this case, to encounter the appropriate dusky-colored blood quite promptly. However, when I then removed the syringe from the needle in order to insert the catheter itself, I was stunned to see a column of blood shoot over my right shoulder. In immediate alarm and concluding that I was somehow in the carotid artery by mistake, I yanked out the needle and applied gauze pressure to the puncture site. Rechecking the carotid pulse, which clearly seemed to be well to the midline of my puncture site, it slowly dawned on me that the column of blood had been continuous rather than pulsing. This was a relief because I must not have been in the carotid artery and my technique had been correct. The blood spurt was alarming though because it therefore indicated that the pressure in the venous system had to be sky high in order to shoot a column of blood in such a continuous arc over my right shoulder. So, I repeated the process in the exact same spot and angle and confirmed, when I removed the syringe the second time, that the flow of blood was truly not bright red and also was obviously not pulsatile. I didn't even bother to get an actual central venous pressure measurement, choosing to rely on my initial visual measurement of, 'Way too high!' So, this meant that something was obstructing the outflow of blood from the heart causing a backup into the veins, thus causing the patient's low blood pressure.

The next correct step in this situation is to perform a pericardiocentesis procedure (needle drainage of the blood from around the heart). So, I re-positioned myself down just above his waist on his right side and I was again methodically inserting a much longer but somewhat narrower bore needle beneath his sternum, in this case aiming for his left shoulder. This is yet again a blind technique but is assisted somewhat by the fact that you can attach an EKG wire to the metal needle which will show you what's called an 'injury pattern' on the EKG machine when you touch the cardiac muscle, which you are trying to stop short of.

In this case, I hadn't even seen the requisite 'one' of these procedures, but it had been described to me and I'd reviewed the steps from time to time. I did have the advantage of having punctured the heart on purpose with needles on multiple occasions but never in a truly live person (in my 1980-1981 internship days it was not unusual in the last stages of a cardiac resuscitation effort to inject an ampule of epinephrine directly into the heart to try to restart it, before declaring the patient dead, which was the only result I'd ever seen following that technique). The difference here was that this unfortunate guy was fully awake although subdued to some degree by his elevated alcohol level and by staff who were holding him down by the shoulders. But at this exact moment with the needle already inserted about halfway down its length, he raised his head to look down at what I was doing, and yelled his first and only question of the night, "Are you f#%king enjoying yourself?"

I restrained myself from the response that I wanted to yell back which was, "Hell no, I'm not enjoying myself, I've never done this before." So no, we did not have the opportunity to form a cordial relationship! Long story short, I did manage to withdraw a large syringe full of blood from what I presumed to be the pericardial space, since his blood pressure then improved following that, and I had not seen any injury pattern on the EKG lead. He did survive his transport to a downtown trauma hospital where I subsequently learned that indeed he had blood in his pericardial space as well as an unusual form of dissection of his superior vena cava (separation of the layers of the blood vessel wall of the largest vein in the body), just above the heart which was blocking the return of blood flow. Both injuries thus compromised his cardiac output and caused the sky-high central venous pressure.

This patient's life was truly saved by the cardiothoracic surgeons who took care of him in the trauma hospital, but I feel that our care of him kept him alive long enough to get there. I say our care because in the ED we are, of course, reliant upon the continual assistance of our nursing, EMS, and ancillary staff colleagues, as we all consider emergency medicine to be more or less a 'team sport.'

Throughout my work career I have been a JAFERD (just another f#cking emergency room doctor) as we in EM call ourselves. We do this in a mostly faux self-deprecating, proud, and partially bitter way to acknowledge that's how we were thought of when we first entered the house of medicine as a specialty back in the late 1970s and early 1980s. At that time, to our colleagues in other specialties, we were mostly just a source of annoyance with phone calls for consultations in the middle of the night, the wee hours of the morning, or in the middle of busy office hours.

We have also been described as seeing 'the most interesting fifteen minutes of all specialties.' It shouldn't be too hard then to imagine that we are often on tenuous novel grounds, sometimes seeing things for the very first time with patients 'trying to die on us.' The hardest times are when those threats are of clearly premature deaths. So yes, there is a steady process of inurement to the reality that we can't always succeed in staving off death or suffering, and we learn to settle on seeking satisfaction in doing what we can to the best of our abilities and limitations and setting aside our emotions in order to function. When we succeed in managing a difficult case or successfully finishing an extremely busy shift without incident, we temporarily reach the more elevated status of BAFERD (bad ass f#cking emergency room doctor). This MVA case on Halloween was one of several moments in my career where I felt that I had briefly reached that BAFERD status.

After all was said and done, I had indeed 'kind of enjoyed' the whole process. I could only more fully relive the pleasure of the challenge in retrospect, once I knew of his positive outcome. So yes, I guess you could say I 'kinda loved' emergency medicine, especially those moments when I could relieve a patient's suffering or sustain their health.

CHAPTER ELEVEN

THE POWER
OF CONNECTION

There is an extensive amount of information to cover in this chapter, so let's start with the easiest. Correction, make that not necessarily the easiest but the most straightforward and undeniable in its implications. Here I'll be quoting from many of the several dozen studies I found in support of the critical importance of the power of connection for human beings.

As a preliminary comment, let me point out that studies show that loneliness and social isolation are not identical concepts but are more clearly viewed as the subjective and objective versions of the same phenomenon, similar to the way that we spoke earlier of illness and disease being subjective/objective relatives. In the same way that someone can feel ill without a disease, or have a disease and not feel ill, one can feel lonely when in the company of others, or not feel lonely even in their absence. So, it's not simply a factor, as I had initially considered, that people who are living alone have a greater mortality risk because no one is around to take note of and act upon their accidents or worsening illnesses. Following are excerpts from a select several of the many studies addressing just this issue.

1. "Loneliness and Social Isolation as Risk Factors for Mortality: A Meta-Analytic Review" by Julianne Holt-Lunstad, et al. (2015):

   Actual and perceived social isolation are both associated with increased risk for early mortality....... Cumulative data from 70 independent prospective studies, with 3,407,134 participants followed for an average of 7 years, revealed a significant effect of social isolation, loneliness, and living alone on odds of mortality. After accounting for multiple covariates, the increased likelihood of death was 26% for reported loneliness, 29% for social isolation, and 32% for living alone. These data indicated essentially no difference between objective and subjective measures of social isolation when predicting mortality.[205]

2. "Characteristics of Socially Isolated Patients with Coronary Artery Disease Who Are at Elevated Risk for Mortality" by Beverly Brummett, et al. (2001):

   Results: The mortality rate was higher among isolated individuals. Those with three or fewer people in their social support network had a relative risk of 2.43 (p = .001) for cardiac mortality and 2.11 (p = .001) for all-cause mortality, controlling for age and disease severity.[206]

(Author's note: A relative risk of 1.0 would indicate an identical risk, whereas a relative risk of 2.0 would be double the risk, plus any p value < .05 indicates a statistically higher chance of your finding being very significant and not just random.)

3. "The Growing Problem of Loneliness" by John T Cacioppo and Stephanie Cacioppo (2018):

Imagine a condition that makes a person irritable, depressed, and self-centred, and is associated with a 26% increase in the risk of premature mortality. Imagine too that in industrialised countries around a third of people are affected by this condition.... Loneliness is a public health problem that can be largely solved in our lifetime but doing so will require the full engagement and support of the medical community.[207]

4. "Social Relationships and Mortality Risk: A Meta-analytic Review" by Julianne Holt-Lunstad, et al. (2010):

Conclusion: Data across 308,849 individuals, followed for an average of 7.5 years, indicate that individuals with adequate social relationships have a 50% greater likelihood of survival compared to those with poor or insufficient social relationships. The magnitude of this effect is comparable with quitting smoking, and it exceeds many well-known risk factors for mortality (e.g., obesity, physical inactivity).... The overall effect remained consistent across a number of factors, including age, sex, initial health status, follow-up period, and cause of death, suggesting that the association between social relationships and mortality may be general, and efforts to reduce risk should not be isolated to subgroups such as the elderly. To draw a parallel, many decades ago high mortality rates were observed among infants in custodial care (i.e., orphanages), even when controlling for pre-existing health conditions and medical treatment [201–204]. Lack of human contact predicted mortality. The medical profession was stunned to learn that infants would die without social interaction. This single finding, so simplistic in hindsight, was responsible for changes in practice and policy that markedly decreased mortality rates in custodial care settings. Contemporary medicine could similarly benefit from acknowledging the data: Social relationships influence the health outcomes of adults. Physicians, health professionals, educators, and the public media take risk factors such as smoking, diet, and exercise seriously; the data presented here make a compelling case for social relationship factors to be added to that list.[208]

In addition to wanting to highlight the startling and insightful conclusions from these first four studies, I also find myself in agreement with the following concerns voiced in correspondence in *The Lancet* article "Beware the Medicalisation of Loneliness" by Amy K McLennan and Stanley J Ulijaszek (2018):

The medicalisation of social issues has not worked in the past. From obesity to HIV/AIDS, health researchers and practitioners are fighting—with limited success—to convince society that public health problems require integrated and holistic approaches. Medicalisation of loneliness will discourage the collaboration needed, and medicine probably has no effective instruments with which to single-handedly address the absence of human connection.[209]

It would be a grave mistake to try to conclude that this problem should fall solely under the aegis of the healthcare system; this is not a problem amenable to solutions by physicians, nurses, other providers, or public health workers in isolation. This requires an 'all hands-on deck' society-wide awareness and approach, with combined efforts toward resolution. Here is some of what we're up against in this attempt. This observation is from an Op-ed in Brookings "Social spending, not medical spending, is key to health" by Stuart M. Butler (2016):

The US is very much the outlier on spending devoted to social services compared with medical care. The major (OECD) countries *on average spend about $1.70 on social services for each $1 on health services. But the US spends just 56 cents per health dollar.*[210]

In fact, loneliness is a global modern phenomenon (notable even pre-COVID), with the US falling somewhere near the middle of the pack of some comparisons to other nations' reported rates of loneliness. However, addressing it by investing less than a third of what the other OECD nations invest in their social services threatens our chances of success. I believe it also contributes to our impressively outspending them on the balance of the nation's healthcare costs (in an effort to try to provide a purely biomedical solution for this biopsychosocial problem.)[211]

While the above quoted commentary is all based on studies published relatively recently, I was surprised to learn that the seminal article on this topic, a nine-year follow-up study of Alameda County, California, residents, was actually published way back in 1979! That study's concluding statistics demonstrated that the most isolated group of men had a mortality rate 2.3 times higher than the men with the most social connections, while for women the mortality rate was 2.8 times higher for the isolated women than the women with the most social connections in every age group examined. One would think that a readily identifiable risk factor that more than doubled our citizens' mortality rate, especially one whose existence was then reconfirmed on multiple occasions, would have received more immediate attention, but alas no.[212]

While there is no doubt about the clarity of the above data and the severity of the challenge in addressing it, there is little to no consensus on the mechanisms by which social support contributes a survival benefit. I believe that it is this lack of a clear biomedical, or really any completely satisfying explanation at all, that has allowed this problem to languish for over 40 years now. These next two studies address potential biomedical mechanisms for these data.

Bert N. Uchino, PhD, speculates in a 2006 research article that "Social support may also be beneficial because it is associated with lower blood pressure during everyday life." Alternate mechanisms mentioned are "the stress buffering effects of support," as well as possible effects of social support on cortisol and oxytocin levels, with more definitive evidence for "a link between social support and better immune function, especially in older adults."[213]

In this study, "The Neurobiology of Giving Versus Receiving Support" by Tristen K. Inagaki, et al. (2016), which involved only experimentally contrived stressful situations and the self-report of subjective results by the participants while they underwent functional MRI studies, there did appear to be some support of the old adage that, 'It is better to give than to receive.' The authors concluded:

> *To date, our understanding of the association between social ties and health has been incomplete insofar as there is a fair amount known about the benefits of receiving support, but less is known about the benefits that may come from giving to others. The current study examined the associations between questionnaire measures of receiving and giving support to others, self-reported negative psychological outcomes, and neural activity to stressful and socially rewarding tasks. Although both receiving and giving social support were related to lower reported negative psychological outcomes, **at the level of the brain, only support giving was associated with beneficial outcomes**.* [214]
> (emphasis by author)

Let's now move on to some animal studies. Although they also do not give us a completely satisfying biomedical explanation for what we are seeing, they at least provide additional biomedical insight for the connection-loneliness dyad itself.

In a study that was dubbed the 'rabbit effect,' two groups of rabbits were fed the identical diet, while the experimental group was "individually petted, held, talked to, and played with on a regular basis." In contrast to the rabbits that were treated in the more typical lab fashion, the experimental group showed a "60% reduction (in) the percentage of aortic surface exhibiting" (atherosclerotic changes).[215]

Adding to the biological plausibility, similar results were demonstrated in a separate study in an inverse setting involving mice placed under population pressures. The authors concluded, "We show that when a mouse has spent a large fraction of its life-span in a population cage where there is social disorder, cardiovascular disease ensues. At first the changes are reversible, but, as in the human condition, after a long time, the measured blood pressures remain elevated, and arteriosclerosis ensues."[216]

Higher up the evolutionary chain, Harry Harlow's famous studies using surrogate wire mothers with infant rhesus monkeys showed the importance of connection, the lack of which resulted in intense "psychosocial disturbances" and "some even died after refusing to eat." Of course, in these animal studies we cannot determine what the 'beliefs' of these creatures would have been, but they do allow us to suspect that there are biological processes underlying these kinds of connections, or lack of connection.[217]

Now moving back to looking at us humans, the power of connection, or in this case the lack of a positive connection, is again startlingly but definitively demonstrated. In a 1998 landmark study that has come to be known as the ACE (Adverse Childhood Experiences) study, the authors carried out a retrospective study done by way of a questionnaire administered to over 13,000 primary care patients in a large HMO. Briefly, the seven questions asked about their childhood exposures to abuse of either a psychological, physical, or a contact sexual nature and also regarding household dysfunction involving exposure to household substance abuse, mental illness, domestic violence, or criminal behavior. Their findings were:

Persons who had experienced four or more categories of childhood exposure, compared to those who experienced none, had 4- to

12-fold increased health risks for alcoholism, drug abuse, depression, and suicide attempts; a 2- to 4-fold increase in smoking, poor self-rated health, >= 50 sexual intercourse partners, and sexually transmitted disease; and a 1.4- to 1.6-fold increase in physical inactivity and severe obesity.... We found a strong dose response relationship between the breadth of exposure to abuse or household dysfunction during childhood and multiple risk factors for several of the leading causes of death in adults. Disease conditions including ischemic heart disease, cancer, chronic lung disease, skeletal fractures, and liver disease, as well as poor self-rated health also showed a graded relationship to the breadth of childhood exposures. The findings suggest that the impact of these adverse childhood experiences on adult health status is strong and cumulative.[218]

In a follow up 2002 article "The Relationship of Adverse Childhood Experiences to Adult Health," one of the two primary lead authors, Vincent J. Felitti, MD, made the additional comments:

One doesn't 'just get over' some things.... How often are public health problems personal solutions? Is drug abuse self-destructive, or is it a desperate attempt at self-healing, albeit at a significant future risk?... Most physicians would far rather deal with traditional organic disease. Certainly, it is easier to do so, but that approach also leads to troubling treatment failure and to the frustration of expensive diagnostic quandaries where everything is ruled out, but nothing is ruled in. ... If the treatment implications of what we found in the ACE study are far-reaching, the prevention aspects are positively daunting. The very nature of the material is such as to make one uncomfortable. Why would one want to leave the relative comfort of traditional organic disease and enter this area of threatening uncertainty that none of us has been trained to deal with?[219]

After reading this study, I was left with the question of whether the adverse childhood experiences themselves might have a direct influence on health and the mortality rate, rather than solely an indirect one through all of the risk factors that the children developed as adults. My reflex suspicion that there likely was a direct effect as well was reinforced when Dr. Robert Anda, one of the two primary lead authors on the study, very kindly provided me with two additional study results. Each of their conclusions follows:

Adverse childhood experiences may be associated with an increased risk of lung cancer, particularly premature death from lung cancer. The increase in risk may only be partly explained by smoking suggesting other possible mechanisms by which ACEs may contribute to the occurrence of lung cancer. [220]

The increase in [premature all-cause mortality] risk was only partly explained by documented ACE-related health and social problems, suggesting other possible mechanisms by which ACEs may contribute to premature death. [221]

What does all of this have to do with the patient-physician relationship you might legitimately ask? In brief, I believe that the patient-physician relationship provides benefits by virtue of the same semi-mysterious mechanisms that appear to be active in other social connectedness, as related in the aforementioned studies. I also believe that those health benefits can be derived between each and all of us, whether we are in a medical or nonmedical setting. The authors of *Compassionomics* appear to have come to a similar conclusion when they stated:

Of all the things that can impact one's psychological health, there is something that rises to the top as one of the most, if not the most powerful thing: human connection. [222]

They continue:

> *There's simply no reason — neither moral nor scientific — whether you're considering the art or the science of compassion, to ignore the profound benefits it confers.*[223]

I would hate to think that our American culture is incapable of bringing all of ourselves to benefit from this well-documented phenomenon. In fact, I refuse to believe that we are incapable of demonstrating greater compassion, but then again, I'm a stubborn optimist.

The difference here is that the physician-patient relationship is the only one that is, or at least can be, solely dedicated to you, the patient's health. Again, in EM, I am routinely deprived of the opportunity or adequate time to make this kind of connection with my patients. I do recognize about myself, and admit, that I am by nature not much of a 'touchy-feely' type and I fall into more of a Dragnet 'Just the facts ma'am' type of approach, which is one of the reasons why emergency medicine is right up my alley. I do on occasion manage to present myself in such a way that a patient or family member might ask me, "Can I have your office number?" After letting them know that I only work in the ED and don't have an office, my joking response then often is, "A pleasure to have met you, but if you're really lucky, you'll never meet me again!" Or a staff colleague might ask me to preferentially see a family member of theirs who had just checked into the ED.

On one 'anything but routine' occasion, I did feel that kind of connection with a patient, and I think it very well might have been reciprocated. This particular 50ish woman came in upon the insistence of her husband, a role reversal from the usual dynamic. She reported having been intermittently and progressively short of breath over the past two weeks, to which he simply but emphatically said, "Oh yeah!"

More commonly it is the husband who is coming in under the insistence of his wife. In fact, that is so common that I've taken to telling men, "When the woman in your life, whether it be your wife, girlfriend, partner, mother, sister, or daughter, tells you that it is time to see the doctor, there is only one proper response which is, 'Okay.'" I usually go on to clarify that, "No, women aren't always correct, but they are usually more cautious, and often more sensible, when it comes to health issues than we men are. When we are all done here today and if nothing serious has arisen and then you want to turn around and say to her, 'I told you so,' that can be your choice…but I wouldn't advise it."

This may be a cross-cultural phenomenon as well. When I was in Ghana in 2002 working with the CDC/WHO polio eradication campaign, that country was just experiencing the completion of what they termed 'meningitis season' and was going into 'cholera season.' We were visiting the cholera ward at the public hospital one day where a woman had corralled her husband into seeking medical care. He had just become ill with cholera symptoms that morning but had refused to seek medical care. When he ultimately became too weak to object, she called a taxi and forced him inside it. Unfortunately, it had taken too long to convince him to seek medical care and by the time they had arrived he had passed away.

I was in immediate agreement with my current patient's husband's concerns because she had a very rapid pulse, borderline low blood pressure, and a low pulse oximetry reading (that thing we put on your fingertip that gives us an immediate indication of your blood oxygen level), all of which were just screaming pulmonary embolism (blood clot in the lungs). To cut to the chase, the CAT scan of her lungs showed that she had what is called a saddle embolism. This is when an extremely large blood clot straddles the bifurcation of the pulmonary artery as it leaves the right side of the heart to deliver blood to both lungs. To clarify, this is a point where every single drop of blood in the body has to pass by during the course of normal circulation. I had received an immediate phone call back from the radiologist after her scan reporting the embolism and adding, "Is this patient stable? Because it's a pretty massive clot and I'm not sure how much blood is getting past it at this point." I reported that I had been in there a second time already, and a small amount of IV fluids had improved her blood pressure, but not her heart rate, though at least her oxygen level was improved on supplemental oxygen. The radiologist comes back with, "Well, let me know if she becomes unstable because I might have to try something interventional." Again, to clarify, at that particular time we did not have any interventional protocol, or even the use of clot dissolving drugs, set up for a large life-threatening pulmonary embolism, as we subsequently did a few years later.

So, I understood the radiologist to mean that if push came to shove, she would try something that she doesn't do regularly. I asked her to hold a minute while I checked on the patient a third time. She, stoical individual as she was, said she was feeling somewhat better. The radiologist then confirmed my own conclusion that the best plan was to transfer her to a nearby, larger, better-equipped hospital that was set up for specific emergency intervention in just this setting.

I was then left with the dilemma of how much change for the worse constituted unstable. I stuck my head in briefly to see her cardiac monitor and vitals and say, "How are you doing?" on my way to the secretary's desk to have them place a call for me to arrange for a transfer. When I was confident that was in progress, along with at least having her nurse initiate intravenous heparin to slow any further clotting, I was back in her room for a fifth time. I hadn't wanted to get into any details with her until there was a distinct plan in place, so as not to worry her prematurely. The husband had gone to deal with some pressing home matters, so that had made it easier to not yet engage in any detailed conversation. After yet one more, "How are you feeling?" on my part, this selfless and compassionate soul, in the midst of her suffering, says to me with obvious concern, "Oh, I'm okay, but how are you?"

I don't know what I looked like at that point, but my immediate thought was, "Damn it, Drew, you've failed this woman by letting her see how worried you are about her." I felt like I was going to be standing next to this woman's stretcher at the exact moment when she died in front of me and there was nothing further that I could do to change that. Apologies to my family and friends, but at that moment there was no person in the world who was more important to me. I would have jumped into a raging river to save her if given the opportunity just then. Instead, I could only try to adopt a calm that I did not feel, while explaining to her what was going on at that point, and what was going to happen next. I tried to put the gloss on it that quite soon she would be under the care of specialist doctors who had dealt with this exact problem multiple times before, as we had not, and that the IV fluids and heparin that we were giving her would get her there safely.

She was one of only two patients in my entire career for whom I made the effort to look up their medical records to see if they had survived my care and had made another visit to my ED after I took care of them. Thomas, my severe neck laceration gentleman, was the other. As in that first case, a month or so later, I was able to reassure myself that she had indeed survived that day and had been able to visit us again. However, I was unable to learn any details of her further care of that day and beyond, and, unfortunately, we never met each other again. I sometimes wonder if her caring about my welfare, seemingly as much as I cared about hers, somehow had helped her to pull through that awful experience.

What I find fascinating is the large number of studies that show dramatic reductions in mortality based on psychosocial issues, many of which seem to revolve around connectedness (love?), a better patient-physician relationship, or even just nonprofessional social connections, inspiring positive beliefs, and expectations. I've gravitated mostly towards studies that measure mortality since it is the most objective of all measures and cannot be criticized for being 'soft-headed and mushy' or 'too subjective' as many people do who criticize placebo effect and social science-based trial results. The totality of the above and the following effects on mortality rates, in conjunction with the previously mentioned halving of mortality rates by placebo adherence, sure sounds like a whole lot of low-tech mortality rate reduction to me!

The more obvious and reliably effective place to take advantage of the inherent power of the patient-physician relationship is in the field of primary care, where a more sustained, familiar, and knowledgeable connection can be established. This has been borne out by dozens of studies, but I will select just a few to present here.

1. "Contribution of Primary Care to Health Systems and Health" by Barbara Starfield, Leiyu Shi, and James Macinko:

   Studies in the early 1990s (Shi 1992, 1994) showed that those U.S. states with higher ratios of primary care physicians to population had better health outcomes, including lower rates of all causes of mortality: mortality from heart disease, cancer, or stroke; infant mortality; low birth weight; and poor self-reported health, even after controlling for sociodemographic measures (percentages of elderly, urban, and minority; education; income; unemployment; pollution) and lifestyle factors (seatbelt use, obesity, and smoking). Vogel and Ackerman (1998) subsequently showed that the supply of primary care physicians was associated with an increase in life span and with reduced low birth-weight rates.[224]

2. "Primary care physicians and specialists as personal physicians: healthcare expenditures and mortality experience" by Peter Franks and Kevin Fiscella (1998). This study, involving over 13,000 adult respondents, had results showing:

   Respondents with a primary care physician rather than a specialist as a personal physician had lower annual healthcare expenditures (mean: $2029 versus $3100) and lower mortality with a hazard ratio = 0.76.[225]

   (Author's note: This hazard ratio indicates a 24% lower risk of death.)

3. "Is General Practice Effective?" by Sven Engstrom, et al. (2001). Following is this systematic literature review's comment on the value of continuity of care with the same primary care provider (I read some but not all of their included 54 reference articles):

Personal continuity increased patient satisfaction and compliance with therapeutic regimens, reduced hospital admissions, and saved time and laboratory tests in primary care (29). Accumulated knowledge of patients meant time saved in the consultation, reduced use of laboratory tests and more use of expectant management (30). Higher personal provider continuity was associated with a lower likelihood of hospitalization. In the group with high physician continuity the hospitalization rate was 10% compared to 14% in the group with high site continuity but low physician continuity (31). Previous knowledge of the patient increased the odds of the doctor recognizing psychosocial problems influencing the patient's health (32). Continuity of care was associated with a reduction in resource utilization and costs (33). Patients older than 65 years who consulted predominantly one single physician, rather than several, were much less likely to use the emergency department (34).[226]

Hearkening back to the placebo effect associated with 50% mortality rate reductions presented in Chapter Seven, there is another observed 'halving of the mortality rate' described in Atul Gawande's article titled "Overkill" from the May 11, 2015, issue of *The New Yorker* (discussing the medical group Wellmed):

The medical group was founded 25 years ago, in San Antonio, by a geriatrician who believed that what the oldest and sickest most needed in our hyper-specialized medical system was slower, more dedicated primary care.... An independent 2011 analysis of the

company's Texas clinics found that, although the patient popula-
tion they drew tended to be less healthy than the overall Medicare
population (being older and having higher rates of diabetes and
chronic lung disease, for instance) their death rates were half of
the Texas average.[227]

In his article, Gawande referenced a case study, "Case Study of a Primary Care–Based Accountable Care System Approach to Medical Home Transformation" by Robert L. Phillips, Jr, MD, MSPH, et al. (2011), on which he based his comment about the halving of the mortality rate with more dedicated primary care. This study notes that "each patient has a primary care clinician who coordinates all care and refers to specialists as needed. The goal for each physician is a panel of 650 patients for those who also do inpatient care, and 750 for those who do not…" with the additional inclusion of health coaches who "are much more present in the clinics, often attending clinician visits with patients, taking time afterward to clarify care plans, provide counseling, and evaluate for need of other services. Health coaches come from a variety of professional disciplines." [228]

To my mind what appears to be key here to achieving the WellMed mortality reduction results is the relatively small patient panels that each physician takes responsibility for and spends time with (assisted no doubt by the addition of the "health coaches" who "clarify care plans.") For example, a more average patient panel for a US primary care physician is in the range of 1,000 to 2,500 patients. [229]

This is all occurring in the setting of predictions such that, "the United States could see an estimated shortage of between 37,800 and 124,000 physicians by 2034, including shortfalls in both primary and specialty care."[230]

A fuller discussion of what the ideal primary care physician-patient panel size should be, and how to achieve a better balance between patient needs and physician availability, is beyond the scope of this book and beyond my training and experience. However, my own experience and research convinces me that the indispensable first step is for us as patients to become far better informed and actively engaged in our healthcare. There is substantial evidence showing that more beneficial and cost-effective health outcomes can result from forming that patient-physician partnership to guide our healthcare decisions.

I believe that establishing connections with and showing love to other humans has a greater effect, but here we see in the following studies that even showing love on a subhuman level such as to dogs, or to living things on an even lower level such as plants, may lead to an effect as well. The American Heart Association's 2019 article "Dog Ownership and Survival: A Systematic Review and Meta-Analysis" states:

> *Dog ownership was associated with a 24% risk reduction for all-cause mortality as compared to non-ownership (relative risk, 0.76; 95% CI, 0.67–0.86) with 6 studies demonstrating significant reduction in the risk of death. Notably, in individuals with prior coronary events, living in a home with a dog was associated with an even more pronounced risk reduction for all-cause mortality (relative risk, 0.35; 95% CI, 0.17–0.69; I^2, 0%)* [author's note: thus a 65% reduction in all-cause mortality risk]. *Moreover, when we restricted the analyses to studies evaluating cardiovascular mortality, dog ownership conferred a 31% risk reduction for cardiovascular death (relative risk, 0.69; 95% CI, 0.67–0.71; I^2, 5.1%).*[231]

It should be pointed out again that this meta-analysis review article, along with a portion of the others that I've mentioned, are observational studies and, therefore, are not able to confirm a definite cause-and-effect relationship. Plus, it may not be the direct result of a relationship with dogs, but rather the exercise involved with walking dogs, or that only the more exercise-capable and committed people would consider owning and walking a dog (my bias here is to believe that it is due to the love and affection between dog and person). A confirmatory study for these results, along with some of the other studies that I've mentioned, would involve the impossible- to-achieve gold standard of a prospective randomized clinical trial (RCT) with randomly assigned double-blind protocols. To review, in an RCT study, participants don't get to choose which group in the study they want to be in but are randomly assigned to either the intervention group under study versus the comparison group not receiving that intervention. The random assignments would prevent all the dog lovers from choosing to be in the dog-owning group (which would introduce bias if they were allowed to, because they may be more physically fit, have a greater love for dogs, etc.) Also, how would you, for example, blind somebody to the concept that they actually owned a dog? And earlier on, how could you randomly assign somebody to live alone and be and feel lonely, and then blind them to these facts and feelings?

It should be noted that observational studies can be quite useful. One very famous observational study is the classic 1950 Doll and Hill study on smoking cigarettes which identified a very convincing association between smoking and lung cancer.[232] This again is a type of study that would be difficult to do well in an RCT fashion with the impossibility of double-blinding, as well as the unethical nature of randomizing some people to heavy smoking! For readers wanting an easier-on-the-eyes and even more informative, yet brief, overview of the historical setting, structure, and implications of the 1950 Doll and Hill study, I recommend reading "The British Doctors' Study (1951–2001)" by Phil Gaetano.[233]

Let's consider another study by Carl J. Charnetski, Sandra Riggers, and Francis X. Brennan, "Effect of petting a dog on immune system function" (2004), because my dog Jake and I love these studies. In this prospective randomly assigned, but not double-blinded, study, only the treatment group of college students who petted an actual dog (while sitting on a couch, so no exercise involved) showed significantly increased levels of IgA antibodies in their saliva samples, while those who simply sat on the couch and others who petted a stuffed dog did not show these increases.[234]

Lastly, there is this neat little study from 1976, 'an oldie but goodie,' "The Effects of Choice and Enhanced Personal Responsibility for the Aged: A Field Experiment in an Institutional Setting" by Ellen J. Langer and Judith Rodin (1976). This study demonstrated the positive effects of independent decision-making by the elderly in a nursing home. In brief, the results showed that when the elderly were encouraged to make decisions for themselves and take responsibility for a small plant (show love?), they actually did better than the comparison group who had everything done for them, including having their plant watered for them. All other factors were identical for both groups. The authors concluded:

> *Despite the care provided for these (control group) people, 71 % were rated as having become more debilitated over a period of time as short as 3 weeks. In contrast with this group, 93 % of the people who were encouraged to make decisions for themselves (like how their furniture should be arranged), given decisions to make, and given responsibility for something outside of themselves (the plant), actually showed overall improvement. Based on their own judgments and by the judgments of the nurses with whom they interacted on a daily basis, they became more active and felt happier. Perhaps more important was the judged improvement in their mental alertness and increased behavioral involvement in many different kinds of activities.*[235]

Of course, my immediate thought concerning the study done on the nursing home residents was how much of a beneficial role did the plant caretaking play versus the retained sense of control over their lives? I have no doubt that the authors were right about the benefits of staying active and in control of our own lives as we age, but I did go on to find another study involving caring for plants, "Interaction with indoor plants may reduce psychological and physiological stress" by Min-sun Lee, et al. (2015). This was not a closely comparable study because it was done in a group of young men in their mid-20s who were assigned to either take care of indoor plants or do a computer-based word processing task while their vital signs and subjectively reported mood were monitored. Their conclusion was:

> *Our results suggest that active interaction with indoor plants can reduce physiological and psychological stress compared with mental work. This is accomplished through suppression of sympathetic nervous system activity and diastolic blood pressure and promotion of comfortable, soothed, and natural feelings.*[236]

A more comparable study titled "Impact of Horticultural Responsibility the on Health Indicators and Quality of Life in Assisted Living" by Claudia C. Collins and Angela M. O'Callaghan (2008) was done with 18 residents in an assisted living facility (ALF), all of whom were either wheelchair- or walker-users, participating in a voluntary project to grow plants from seeds. Some of the conclusions and comments from that short, four-week, horticultural class study follow. The authors concluded:

> *Class members showed a significant increase in mastery, self-rated health, and self-rated happiness.... Over the 4-week course of the program, the instructors and ALF (assisted living facility) staff noted that class members were walking/sitting taller, dressing better, and smiling more. Their entire demeanor improved as they increased their interaction with each other and any other residents who inquired about their plants. This enthusiasm was reflected as they arrived earlier for each class, anxious to 'get started.'*[237]

Participant comments and other observations included:

> *"Waking up in the morning and knowing the plant made it through the night," was a special joy for one student. Another*

took her responsibility seriously, "moving the plant to find the right light means the plant needs you!" A 102-year-young woman said her plants "depend on my smile" each day. They reported learning patience waiting for the plants to flower or seeds to grow. Plant death was expected, and replacements were available. However, the issue did not arise in this study. Fortunately, even in a short-term situation, changes can be seen as healthy plants thrive and some bloom. Several individuals commented they could not believe how well their plants did, that they did not have green thumbs and thought they would die and how great it was to see them actually living. One student commented, "The assisted living can be a dreary place and the plant adds happiness." Instructors noted that participants showed pride in their plants. They were excited about growing herbs from seeds. Some students left the class with three or four plants. They reported that plant care brought them peace by watching growth and regeneration. They enjoyed learning and sharing with others and said that this class reinforced their prior knowledge about plants. The next stage of horticulture at Silver Sky will be the development of a community garden. When discussing this, participants stated, "I can't wait until we can get started in the garden outside" and "I already have my plot picked out!"[238]

Continuing the theme of a reduced mortality risk related to connectedness, and caring for something outside of yourself, following are four studies on volunteering.

1. "Volunteerism and Mortality among the Community-dwelling Elderly" by Doug Oman, et al. (1999), showed:

   The 44 percent reduction in mortality associated with high volunteerism in this study was larger than the reductions associated with physical mobility (39 percent), exercising four times weekly (30 percent), and weekly attendance at religious services (29 percent) and was only slightly smaller than the reduction associated with not smoking (49 percent).[239]

2. In this study, "Altruistic Social Interest Behaviors Are Associated with Better Mental Health" by Carolyn Schwartz, ScD, et al. (2003), there was the additional finding:

    Our findings suggest that helping others is associated with higher levels of mental health, above and beyond the benefits of receiving help and other known psychospiritual, stress, and demographic factors," (along with the caveat that) *"...feeling overwhelmed by others' demands had a stronger negative relationship with mental health than helping others had a positive one."*[240]

I believe that the mentioned negative effect of 'feeling overwhelmed' is very apropos of what the current healthcare environment constantly subjects us to as healthcare workers, that is, feeling the moral injury of being unable to meet peoples' needs as we would prefer to do, but are systematically prevented from doing by our often-dysfunctional healthcare system.[241]

3. This next study "Providing Social Support May Be More Beneficial Than Receiving It: Results from a Prospective Study of Mortality" by Stephanie L. Brown, et al. (2003) found an association between a reduced risk of dying and giving help but no correlation between receiving help and reduced death risk. They concluded:

    In contrast, all 4 of the different giving measures significantly reduced mortality risk. When the composites for giving support were broken down, 4 of the 6 items were significantly correlated with decreased mortality risk.... Taken together, these findings strongly suggest that giving support, rather than receiving support, accounts for the benefits of social contact, across different domains of support, different targets of support, and different structural features of support....

If giving, rather than receiving, promotes longevity, then interventions that are currently designed to help people feel supported may need to be redesigned so that the emphasis is on what people do to help others. The possibility that giving support accounts for some of the benefits of social contact is a new question and await future research.[242]

4. "The health advantage of volunteering is larger for older and less healthy volunteers in Europe: a mega-analysis" by Arjen de Wit, et al. (2022). This European study used data spanning a period of 33 years, including 952,026 observations from 267,212 respondents in 22 countries, concluding:

Our mega-analysis…provides robust evidence on the association between volunteering and individual health. Volunteering is not a panacea for health. Much of the association is due to self-selection of healthier individuals into volunteering and the selection of less healthy individuals out of volunteering. Nonetheless, taking such selection processes into account, we still find that health improves when Europeans start volunteering and declines when they stop volunteering. Even though the annual advantage is small, it is important because it accumulates over time. The health advantage of volunteering for volunteers is similar in magnitude to the health disadvantage of ageing 1 year. We also find considerable heterogeneity in these changes. The health advantage increases with age, with the most substantial advantages for volunteers aged 60 and over. The health advantage of volunteering among those in worse health is twice as large as the health advantage among the healthiest Europeans.[243]

In one of life's perfect little ironies, there appears to be substantial evidence to suggest that health-wise it is in our own self-interest to strive daily to be less self-interested.

CHAPTER TWELVE

OUT OF THIS WORLD

The reader can be forgiven if at this point they are concluding that I appear to have an unhealthy preoccupation with death, or a fear of it. As it turns out, neither is true. I will admit though that at times I've had the unsettling thought that my immune system appears to be on a 50-year campaign to try to kill me!

Its first attempt was somewhat leisurely in that it appeared to be content with inflicting the daily sufferings of my UC throughout the decade of my 20s, with the accompanying progressively increasing odds of inflicting colon cancer on me. That attempt was stopped in its tracks by my total colectomy. My immune system's second attempt on my life was a much more brazen, full-frontal assault by clotting off that major artery in my brain, again neutralized, this time by Coumadin, a potent blood-thinning medication that I've been taking ever since my 1992 stroke. This current third attempt is the most insidious of the three in that it has left me predominantly asymptomatic, while it goes about more or less silently destroying my liver via primary sclerosing cholangitis and winding up for the possible infliction of a cholangiocarcinoma upon me. I'll admit that this has left me feeling a bit peevish, although not to the point of relinquishing my reflex optimism.

In this chapter, we return once again to the importance of our beliefs and how they affect our end-of-life decision-making. Contemplating our assured ultimate demise inevitably brings up thoughts of, 'What's next?' or 'Is there even a what's next?' There is a burgeoning field of scientific investigation of, and both academic and popular interest in, the ways in which religious involvement and nonreligion-based spirituality affect our health, possibly by helping us to address and cope with these concerns. Religion and spirituality (R/S) and how it potentially affects patients' healthcare decisions and outcomes is now being taught in most medical schools, while it was not ever spoken of in my day (1976-1980).

The default mode in EM is to always 'do everything for everybody to keep them alive.' The unfortunate fact is that although this is the correct course of action in the vast majority of cases, it is regrettably not so in all of them. As emergency physicians we have succeeded remarkably well in pursuit of that primary goal, but we have neither the time nor the experience to navigate that other category of cases. We are rarely involved in slow and deliberate end-of-life decision-making with our patients and their families. What we hope for is that those discussions will have taken place well in advance of the patient requiring our attention in the ED.

Whether or not we believe in God and/or an afterlife, we all have to eventually face end-of-life decisions. We are best served when we acknowledge the certainty of our inevitable physical decline, and that it will involve multiple decisions about how we want to spend that period in our lives. As difficult as it is to contemplate suffering serious illness, losing our independence, and/or our complete nonexistence, these are some of the most important factors that we need to address in a successful physician-patient partnership.

That full court press approach to the dying patient is how it should be if that is your desire, but it devolves into cruel and unusual punishment if your desire had been to be allowed to pass away from a preexisting known-to-be-terminal condition. Even though being placed on a ventilator is one of the more dramatic interventions we can do for you, it is not a death sentence by itself. Many people, even of advanced age with associated serious health issues, successfully regain enough of their health to come off ventilators every single day (some COVID19 survivors spent weeks on ventilators). In the ED, though, we cannot know in advance if you will or will not succeed with that process, or to what degree you will suffer during it, as there are an unlimited number of variations on those themes.

What the patient-physician partnership can achieve, ideally involving pertinent family members as well, is to review the most common sequences and consider how your own particular health details are likely to affect those sequences. Not to imply that these are easy decisions regarding the prognosis of say your advanced cancer, heart, liver, or kidney disease, or any number of other chronic disease states. The difficult decisions on those interventions can and should be addressed in advance with your physician in a calm moment by you and those who care about you. The far too common alternative is that these decisions are made in frantic moments on the spot by emergency personnel, and unfortunately occur without your or your family's input. Here, of course, the COVID19 pandemic, in decimating some nursing homes as it has, has highlighted the importance of this advanced decision-making.

In one memorable pre-COVID patient encounter, I took care of an elderly woman (in her 80s) with metastatic lung cancer who was brought in by ambulance one evening for evaluation of her breathlessness. Her adult daughter had placed the 911 call when feeling at her wits' end in her attempts to make her mother comfortable at home. Fortunately, advanced planning had been completed and the daughter was able to quickly make it clear to both EMS and me in the ED that her mother did not want to be intubated and placed on a ventilator for this judged-to-be clearly terminal condition.

Although the daughter immediately reported that her mother looked much better after having been positioned upright and placed on oxygen by EMS, I still thought that she looked like she was on death's doorstep (lethargic and not conversational, with shallow inadequate respirations, which in any other set of circumstances would have had me instantly intubating her.) Her chest x-ray, of course, looked awful and in somewhat typical fashion it was hard to determine how much of the visible abnormal markings were related to her spreading lung cancer versus possible fluid overload or overlying pneumonia, and the rest of my evaluation and her lab work did not help clarify those questions. The respiratory technician suctioned some of her oral secretions, and we gave her a small amount of IV fluids with not much change, but her daughter felt she appeared better now than she had at home (in my mind I was weighing how much of that might be actual objective improvement or simply some relief of the daughter's anxiety now with the appropriately shared responsibility for her mother's welfare). At any rate, I promptly arranged for her admission to the hospital for 'comfort measures only.'

I would have been very quickly 'on to the next thing' because in emergency medicine there's always 'the next thing.' To clarify, I'm not referring to the patients as 'things' here, but instead to the next something that I might have to address. For example, in this same ED, thankfully on a different shift, 'the next thing' I once had to address was, 'What are we gonna do now that the rainwater is flowing down the hallway in the ED like a small stream?' (The new construction parallel to the ED had diverted this first prominent rainfall in unanticipated directions.)

At any rate, I knew that I needed to move on once her admission to the hospital was initiated, but I wasn't in a mad rush to get out the door, or beyond the curtained cubicle in this patient's case, when the daughter pulled me aside to ask, "How long do you think she has?" That is a question that I hate, and fortunately we don't have to address it often in the ED because it's usually pretty clear that we either successfully resuscitated your relative or we did not. In fact, throughout my career, I always took great pleasure in occasionally hearing from patients that their physician had given them just six months to live and here they were two years later doing quite well, with the occasional added flourish (at times with obvious glee) that their doctor, though, had since passed away!

Therefore, I had taken a silent internal vow to never make a prediction about how long somebody had to live. In this case though, I chose to break my rule since her daughter had added the additional question about whether she should notify other relatives to come now to say goodbye to her mother. Out of earshot of the patient, I said honestly to the daughter that I couldn't imagine her mother making it through the night. After a brief conversation with her on that, I did then move on to the next patients and 'things.'

As it happened, it was a fairly steady evening shift, although not crazy busy, and sometime later while coming up a different hallway, I found that my patient had been appropriately moved into a room of her own. I was amazed to see that she was now fully engaged in conversation with several people I had not yet met. As I'm writing this, I'm kicking myself for not having taken the time away from 'other things' to at least say hello to the patient for the first time and to learn from her and/or her daughter, or her nurse, how things had progressed since I had last spent time at her side.

My biomedical explanation for her improvement consisted then and now of the fact that for some 'reason' she had been able to increase her respiratory rate and, as we refer to it in medicine, had succeeded in 'blowing off more CO_2' (CO_2 or carbon dioxide being the major component of the air that you exhale; inadequate breathing causes you to retain that carbon dioxide which then has what we refer to as a 'narcotizing' or sedating effect). The ultimate 'reason' though was obviously something psychosocial, since I had not initiated any further biomedical interventions. Was it some degree of joy in seeing her other relatives that perked her up enough to breathe more rapidly, a sense of responsibility to 'host' them in her room, or even her having overheard my prediction and wanting to prove me wrong?! In the end, as is typical for EM, I cannot complete this story for you, because I do not know if she died later that night or lived to her hospital discharge.

Quite frequently in the ED, we meet people who have not chosen to address end-of-life issues in advance, and so those decisions default to us. The standard fallback response from you, if you are still able to communicate, or from your family in your stead is, 'I/he would not want to be kept alive as a vegetable on a machine!' This is a universal, admirable, and more often than the layperson might expect, a completely useless piece of information to us. Without advanced consideration of these issues and subsequent legal documentation of your wish NOT to be resuscitated, you will have already been intubated by EMS in transport to my ED, or by me immediately upon your arrival if you're not breathing adequately. We become in essence your 'death panel' (see this Nov. 20, 2015, article "A Quiet End to the 'Death Panels' Debate" from *The New York Times*, for a concise recap of that thankfully transient political foolishness, which reinforced my conviction that partisan politics of any stripe can be a distinct public health hazard).[244]

Here's another very pertinent case that illustrates just this dilemma, some version of which we are all at risk to face as part of our end-of-life care. One day, I was walking down one of the long hallways in 'Zone 2' of a different, even larger and busier, ED (41 beds) to attend to a patient matter on the other end near the ambulance entrance (a psychiatric patient awaiting mental health evaluation for whom I had assumed responsibility at shift change). I was only paying cursory attention when an EMS crew with stretcher was coming down the same hall in the opposite direction having just entered with a new patient. The guy was breathing a little rapidly, but not in a way to make me change my direction, especially since the triage nurse had apparently thought he was well enough to pass through the more acute end of 'Zone 1' to my end of the ED. What was more eye-catching though was the fact that he was nearly bone white in his complexion, with his visible skin being oddly scaly, did not have any appreciable digits attached to his protruding hands or feet, and appeared to be mentally in his own little world. In a self-centered moment I thought to myself, "Boy, I hope I don't have to see that guy." No surprise then that several minutes later when I had returned to my end of the department where he had been heading, a nurse comes up to me and says, "Can you please come see this new guy in room C-5?"

Long story short, it turns out he suffered from some form of congenital developmental delay, exacerbated by additional early dementia plus underlying chronic obstructive pulmonary disease (COPD), and truly did not have a single finger or toe, presumably related to whatever skin condition he had (leprosy would have been a reasonable consideration in the developing world, but not in New England). However, his deteriorating respiratory status, which was the reason that his nursing home had sent him, made that last consideration moot. I immediately looked for his DNR (do not resuscitate) form, which was at least addressed in his paperwork but with the mind-blowing indication that this unfortunate soul was still considered to be a full code (in other words do everything possible to keep him alive). I was incredulous and said to his nurse, "The last thing on earth that I want to do is intubate this guy; that could reasonably be considered cruel and unusual punishment. I can't believe that he would want that for himself in his present condition. In fact, if that were me and I intubated me, I would sue myself for everything that I was worth."

Inexplicably, and inexcusably, the forms did not indicate any next of kin, or even a healthcare power of attorney (HCPOA) for me to contact. Not bothering to anticipate that this would happen someday, his nursing home had apparently taken the approach of, "Well, if it does happen, we'll just send him to the ED." So, of course, I did have to ultimately intubate him, and shockingly he survived that hospitalization. This I learned because I saw him in the ED again several months later, but at that time he was already under somebody else's care and, unfortunately, had already been intubated again. Although what I had done was the correct course under professional ethics and legal considerations, I was left with the thought that it was some form of moral malpractice initiated earlier in his life (when end-of-life planning might have been reasonably addressed) and sustained in his nursing home, with which I had then been made complicit.

Admittedly, it was possible that he still had a rich internal life and had his moments where he could converse and share some of the pleasures of life with his nursing home staff and the fellow residents of his nursing home. This was the driving reason why I had intubated him, despite my reservations about possibly needlessly and unkindly prolonging his suffering. Another, and more likely, possibility was that his nursing home was perfectly content to warehouse him while they were getting paid for his care from whatever reliable source (think back to Chapter Ten with private equity gobbling up nursing homes for their potential profit margins). Then it would be in their best interest financially to keep him alive, no matter how many times they had to send him to the ED to be placed on a ventilator (a simple rinse and repeat process that cost them no money or effort at all).

The fact is that over the course of my long career, many of our EMS patients from nursing homes did arrive without their most pertinent paperwork front and center. The appropriate paperwork would have addressed their code status, next of kin, and/or healthcare power of attorney, and provided a brief clear narrative of what had happened to generate the ED visit at that moment (that is, what was brand new and/or how much changed was that moment's situation from the patient's baseline condition?). That kind of careless and take the easy-way-out decision-making appears to be dangerously common in my experience. If you're overworked and understaffed, there are understandable pressures to choose the three-second-solution of hitting 911, versus the longer time involved in composing a narrative of your concerns, possibly contacting the family or HCPOA of the patient, and also being certain to have all the pertinent paperwork in order. I by no means want to appear to be maligning the professional ethics of nursing home staffs, just highlighting here the pressures that private equity ownership might be bringing to bear that affect their usual skilled, kind, and compassionate decision-making. This magnifies the importance of patients and their families taking a very active and engaged role in guiding their healthcare and repeatedly clarifying and updating their wishes.

The hospice physician and author Dr. Karen M. Wyatt has shared the following insights on these issues on her podcast, with a lengthier discussion on her website and in her book, *7 Lessons for Living from the Dying*:

Dying provides an opportunity for transformation

In my work with hospice patients, I have witnessed over and over the transformative power of love and forgiveness during the last days of life. When dying is respected as a natural part of life and time is allowed for the process to unfold, patients can turn their focus to matters of the heart and soul and find meaning in both life and death. But this does not happen when death is perceived as an enemy that must be resisted until the final breath is taken. Doctors can help their patients change focus by advising them with honesty when the time comes that pursuing further treatment is futile and will cause more harm than benefit. [245]

Now let's take a closer look at a number of medical studies on religion and spirituality (R/S) and mortality. Of course, regarding death itself there can be no objective determination of 'what comes next.' There are a number of publications addressing near-death experiences, which do demonstrate some surprising consistencies, but again these are subjective reports without objective data as a form of proof (though the physician Eben Alexander did title his book *Proof of Heaven: A Neurosurgeon's Journey into the Afterlife,* which I have not read). Also, in 1901 in Haverhill, Massachusetts, there was an attempt to scientifically prove the exit of the soul from the body at the time of death. The study did ultimately get published in 1907. Though I failed to find a copy of the actual publication, there is a *New York Times* article recap, "Soul Has Weight, Physician Thinks" published March 11, 1907. In brief, the physician in Haverhill used a very sensitive scale holding the entire bed occupied by a patient deemed to be quite near death, then compared the predeath and immediate postdeath weight of the bed/patient and derived a measurement change of 21 grams, which he claimed amounted to the weight of the soul leaving the body. However, he was only able to obtain a useful measurement on one of his six study subjects, and this study was never repeated…so not really in the realm of scientific evidence. I mention this for completeness' sake and also to highlight the inherent limitations of getting reliable scientific information in this realm.[246] More details on this study can be found in a concise summary in *Wikipedia* under the heading "21 grams experiment."[247]

More readily available concerning religion and spirituality are survey results as mentioned in the following two articles. This first is a review article involving 125,826 participants.

1. "Religious Involvement and Mortality: A Meta-Analytic Review" by Michael E. McCullough, et al. (2002):

   Substantial numbers of Americans engage in religious activity. More than 90% of American adults are affiliated with a formal religious tradition. Nearly 96% of Americans believe in God or a universal spirit, 42% attend a religious worship service weekly or almost weekly, 67% are members of a local religious body, and 60% feel that religion is very important in their lives.[248]

Further on in this same review article, these authors write:

   Although the strength of the association varied as a function of several moderator variables, the basic finding was robust: Religious involvement is associated with higher odds of survival (or conversely, lower odds of death) during any specified follow-up period. These findings could not be attributed to publication bias.[249]

2. "Spirituality and Medical Practice: Using the HOPE Questions as a Practical Tool for Spiritual Assessment" by Ellen Hight, MD, MPH, and Gowri Anandarajah, MD (2001):

Polls of the U.S. population[6] have consistently shown that 95 percent of Americans believe in God. One study[3] found that 94 percent of patients admitted to hospitals believe that spiritual health is as important as physical health, 77 percent believe that physicians should consider their patients' spiritual needs as part of their medical care, and 37 percent want their physician to discuss their religious beliefs more. However, 80 percent reported that physicians never or rarely discuss spiritual or religious issues with them. ... General spiritual care can be defined as recognizing and responding to the "multifaceted expressions of spirituality we encounter in our patients and their families."[30] It involves compassion, presence, listening and the encouragement of realistic hope,[36] and might not involve any discussion of God or religion.[250]

So, in terms of readiness on this topic, it appears that we patients are ahead of our physicians, at least in terms of recognizing the importance of including a spiritual component to the biopsychosocial model.

These next six studies give more specific mortality data and are representative of the four dozen or so articles that I read, with the last two included to demonstrate the associated dissension among researchers.

1. "Frequent Attendance at Religious Services and Mortality over 28 Years" by William J. Strawbridge, PhD, et al. (1997):

This study demonstrated lower mortality rates over nearly 3 decades for frequent religious attenders (>= once a week) compared with infrequent attenders (twice a month or less), even with adjustments for mental and physical health during follow up. Adjusting for social connections (stable marriages, increased social contacts) had only a modest impact; the association between attendance and mortality was reduced when health practices (exercise, smoking, alcohol use) were added as adjustments, but remained statistically significant.[251]

2. The next several passages come from "Religious Involvement, Spirituality, and Medicine: Implications for Clinical Practice" by Paul S Mueller, MD, et al. (2001):

According to Levin (127) to verify a causal relationship between a variable (e.g., religious involvement) and a health outcome (e.g., mortality), 3 questions must be answered. Is there an association? If so, is the relationship valid? If so, is it causal? Regarding the first question, a majority of nearly 850 studies of mental health and 350 studies of physical health have found a direct relationship between religious involvement and spirituality and better health outcomes (23).... Whether religious involvement and spirituality cause better health outcomes is more difficult to determine.... Even though the association between religious involvement and spirituality and better health outcomes appears valid, clinicians should be careful not to draw erroneous conclusions from the research findings (Table 1). For example, the research does not tell us that religious people do not get sick or that illness is due to lack of religious faith.

Features of spirituality include quest for meaning and purpose, transcendence (i.e., the sense that being human is more than simple material existence), connectedness (e.g., with others, nature, or the divine), and values (e.g., love, compassion, and justice).... In fact, most people report having a spiritual life. Surveys of the general population and of patients have consistently found that more than 90% of people believe in a Higher Being. Another survey found that 94% of patients regard their spiritual health and their physical health as equally important. Most patients want their spiritual needs met and would welcome an inquiry regarding their religious and spiritual needs.[252]

The authors also point out that even when controlling for factors such as age, sex, ethnicity, education, baseline health status, body mass index, health practices, and social connections, there are a number of studies showing a range of mortality reduction from 23% to 29% for those who are frequent church attenders (greater than or equal to once a week) compared to nonattenders. They comment:

Finally, a 9-year study of a nationally representative sample of 22,080 US adults (age, greater than or equal to 20 years) found the risk of death for non-attenders to be 1.87 times the risk of death for frequent attenders (P<.01) after controlling for numerous demographic, baseline health, behavioral, social, and economic variables.[253]

3. "Religion, Spirituality, and Medicine: Application to Clinical Practice" by Harold G. Koenig, MD (2000):

An additional 350 studies have examined religious involvement and health. The majority of these have found that religious people are physically healthier, lead healthier lifestyles, and require fewer health services.[1] *The magnitude of the possible impact on physical health—particularly survival—may approximate that of abstaining from cigarette smoking*[4] *or adding 7 to 14 years to life.*[5] *However, religious practices should not replace allopathic therapies. Also, while many people find that illness spurs them to ask metaphysical questions and helps them rediscover religion, no studies have shown that people who become religious only in anticipation of health benefits will experience better health.*

What does all this mean for clinical practice? While no research exists on the impact of physician-directed religious assessments or interventions, some recommendations based on clinical experience and common sense can be made. First, what should physicians not do? Physicians should not "prescribe" religious beliefs or activities for health reasons. Physicians should not impose their religious beliefs on patients....[254]

4. "Religiousness and Mental Health: A Review" by Alexander Moreira-Almeida, et al. (2006):

With some exceptions, most studies have found a positive association between religiosity and other factors associated with well-being, such as optimism and hope (12 out of 14 studies), self-esteem (16 out of 29 studies but only one with a negative association), sense of meaning and purpose in life (15 out of 16 studies), internal locus of control, social support, (19 out of 20) and being married or having higher marital satisfaction (35 out of 38). As will be discussed later these may be some of the mediating factors between religiousness and well-being.[255]

5. "Religion, Spirituality, and Medicine" by Richard P. Sloan, PhD, et al. (1999):

However, between the extremes of rejecting the idea that religion and faith can bring comfort to some people coping with illness and endorsing the view that physicians should actively promote religious activity among patients lies a vast uncharted territory in which guidelines for appropriate behaviour are needed urgently.[256]

6. "Religion, Spirituality, and Medicine: A Rebuttal to Skeptics" by Harold Koenig, et al. (1999):

Nevertheless, we are strongly convinced, as Sloan et al. are not, that the evidence regarding religion and health, while still

emerging, is neither weak nor inconsistent, and that religion is
a factor that should not be overlooked in describing influences
on the health of populations.[257]

I myself am encouraged by Sloan's comment endorsing the attempt to find a middle ground in the care of patients on the topic of religion and spirituality. However, I also agree with Koenig's objection to Sloan presenting strawmen to attack, as in the conclusion of Sloan's comment. In my experience, having read dozens of articles on this topic (admittedly, only a fraction of the hundreds available) and having had personal contact with many hundreds of physicians in practice, I have never encountered a physician who "actively promoted religious activity among patients." Plus, Koenig himself writes to discourage just that in his article listed at point 3!

I do have the bias of having already read Dr. Koenig's book, *Spirituality in Patient Care: Why, How, When, and What,*[258] which I thoroughly enjoyed. On the other hand, Dr. Sloan's book *Blind Faith: The Unholy Alliance of Religion and Medicine* remains on my 'books to be read' list.

In summary, in researching for this book, it was disappointing to learn that there was no definitive study confirming a causal relationship between adopting religious or spiritual beliefs and/or actions and subsequent health results and longevity. However, there is a preponderance of suggestive studies. Some studies show inconsistent results, while others suffer weaknesses in controlling for the multiple confounders associated with choosing a more religious or spiritual lifestyle such as less or no use of cigarettes, alcohol, and drugs, increased engagement with exercise, and a stable marriage. The presence of these inconsistencies and the confusing confounders is not surprising, given the inherent difficulty of objectively measuring the factors under consideration. Therefore, the study investigators are reliant upon self-report by study participants, which may or may not be accurate. One consistent finding, though, is that the people who make those religious or spiritual choices tend to have healthier lifestyles to begin with, and then go on to adopt even healthier lifestyles, apparently from the association with others who share their beliefs.

On this topic I have to confess to competing biases. I am not an attender of frequent (weekly or even monthly) religious services. I have though had a lifelong commitment to a theistic philosophy. My experiences make it difficult for me to imagine an omnipotent Creator who might be insecure enough to be taking attendance at the doors of places of worship, and then doling out diseases and/or death on the basis of those results! If there were to be such a Creator, I fully expect that following my own death transition, I will be deemed woefully insufficient in reverence. The fact that I'm also going to be chock full of questions about this, that, and the other thing no doubt will magnify this Deity's baseline disappointment in me. It seems to me far more likely that any direct health benefits gained would be from adopting a spiritual point of view with an associated benevolent attitude towards others, versus attending any specific church, temple, synagogue, or mosque in a merely obligatory fashion.

I do have to include here one of several articles referring to the possible negative effects of religiosity, or what is referred to as 'negative religious coping' or the 'religious struggle.' In this study "Religious Struggle as a Predictor of Mortality Among Medically Ill Elderly Patients: A 2-Year Longitudinal Study" by Kenneth I. Pargament, PhD, et al. (2001) of 390 patients, those who reported feeling alienated from, unloved by, or punished by God, or who attributed their illness to 'the work of the devil,' had an associated 19% to 28% increased risk of death.[259]

To summarize, these study findings suggest that our religious or spiritual beliefs can either assist or hinder our coping with health challenges, potentially resulting in either an increase or decrease in our health and/or lifespan. This appears to be an echo of the positive and negative expectations involved in the placebo and nocebo effects that we reviewed in Chapter Seven. Perhaps the physiology might be similar in that each may have the same, as yet to be completely delineated, psychoneuroimmunology pathway. For now, both phenomena remain frustratingly opaque.

I find this next study to be intriguing, though extremely cruel-sounding, with results that do confirm a distinct biomedical pathway for sudden unexpected death in research animals. In the study "The Phenomenon of Sudden Death in Animals and Man" by Curt P. Richter, PhD (1957), the author starts by reviewing the phenomenon of voodoo death in humans, which is well described in a variety of settings but remains unexplained. Briefly, the author compared wild and domesticated rats in different situations of stress, either by being excessively handled and restrained, or by being immersed in a swimming tank after having their whiskers removed. Rats are known to use their whiskers as their primary way of establishing their environmental location (their safe place in the world?). In both cases, the wild rats died much faster than the domesticated ones did. Most of the domesticated rats swam up to 60 hours before drowning, while the whiskerless wild rats died within minutes! There was even heart monitoring in place which showed that, as opposed to the expected adrenaline release and increase in heart rate, the wild rats demonstrated a vagal response (an activation of the vagus nerve, which leads to a slowing of the heart rate and drop in blood pressure) in which the heart slowed to the point of completely stopping. The author writes, "The situation of these rats scarcely seems one demanding fight or flight – it is rather one of hopelessness. ...they seem to literally 'give up.'...after elimination of the hopelessness the rats do not die." The wild rats could be fairly quickly conditioned to this experience by being repeatedly and rapidly released from their dilemma, and the author continues, "In this way the rats quickly learn that the situation is not actually hopeless." [260]

As a confirmed, though sorely tested, optimist, I'm also really encouraged by this next study, "Self-Rated Health: A Predictor of Mortality Among the Elderly" by Jana M. Mossey, MPH, PhD, and Evelyn Shapiro, MA (1982). The subjects were 3,128 residents of Manitoba, Canada, from the noninstitutional population age 65 and over. There are also similar findings when the study population is US residents, but I'll spare you all of those studies. Mossey reports:

> *Analyses of the data revealed that, controlling for OHS (objective health status), age, sex, life satisfaction, income and urban/rural residence, the risk of early mortality (1971-1973) and late mortality (1974-1977) for persons whose SRH (self-rated health) was poor was 2.92 and 2.77 times that of those whose SRH was excellent. This increased risk of death associated with poor self-rated health was greater than that associated with poor OHS, poor life satisfaction, low income and being male. These findings provide empirical support for the long held, but inadequately substantiated, belief that the way a person views his health is importantly related to subsequent health outcomes.... Only age appears to have a more powerful influence on mortality than self-rated health.... It may also be that positive health ratings – even if discordant with objective ratings – are protective because positive, optimistic feelings, in themselves, are protective.*[261]

Continuing with the above optimism comment, is the study "Optimism and Cause-Specific Mortality: A Prospective Cohort Study" by Eric S. Kim (2016):

> *We found strong and statistically significant associations of increasing levels of optimism with decreasing risks of mortality, including mortality due (to) each major cause of death, such as cancer, heart disease, stroke, respiratory disease, and infection. Importantly, findings were maintained after close control for potential confounding factors, including sociodemographic characteristics and depression (both diagnosed depression and depressive symptoms) and were still evident, although attenuated, even after inclusion of health conditions or health behaviors in the models.*[262]

So, is it too big a leap to consider that we might feel equally as hopeless as those study rats if we envisioned ourselves as being in the unrelentingly cruel grip, or drowning tank, of an all-powerful and judgmental God (or voodoo curse?), or that by regaining our hopefulness we can experience or at least envision experiencing a release from our medical suffering? Is it at least sounding a little less soft-headed to consider that our thinking mind and our feeling heart and soul can have a substantial effect on our body and health?

Even with all of the above study results, I don't fault Dr. Sloan for not being completely satisfied with the state of the science on religion and spirituality. I'm not either, but I'm not as dissatisfied as he appears to be with all that we do have to work with. In the absence of any additional hard science to guide us, I don't think that we should be too reluctant to benefit from the guidance of insightful philosophers, writers, and just plain thinkers. I benefited from hearing the following range of thoughts.

Before I leave the medical folks behind, I want to relate this comment from Joseph Rotella, MD, of the Hospice of Louisville, Kentucky, as quoted in "Spirituality, Religion, and Health" by Elaine J. Yuen (2007):

> *Healing is much more than physical comfort or disease remission. It is the restoration of a person's sense of balance, wholeness, meaning, and positive relationship with self, others, God, and the world. It springs from the therapeutic relationships between the patient and care provider. It is windfall, unforced and often unexpected. In the moment of healing, the patient and doctor/healthcare professional share a deep and fulfilling mystery.*[263]

Next consider this statement from Pierre Teilhard de Chardin (1881-1955), the French philosopher and Jesuit priest:

> *We are not human beings having a spiritual experience. We are spiritual beings having a human experience.*[264,265]

Also very worthy of consideration are these additional comments from the Introduction of *The Little Book of Atheist Spirituality* by André Comte-Sponville (2008):

> *Humanity is one; both religion and irreligion are part of it; neither are sufficient unto themselves. ... Spirituality is far too important a matter to be left to fundamentalists. ... Atheists have as much spirit as everyone else; why would they be less interested in spiritual life? ... Atheists have none of these worries (hell/ eternal damnation). We accept our mortality as best we can and try to get used to the idea of nothingness. Can this actually be done? We try not to obsess about it. Death will take everything away with it, including the fear it instills in us. Life on earth is more important to us, and quite sufficient.*
>
> *Far more real, far more painful and unbearable is the death of loved ones. This is where atheists find themselves the most helpless. The person you care about most – your child, parent, spouse, closest friend – has just been torn away from you by death. How not feel bereft?*[266]

That question and experience raises the perpetual paradox of theodicy, which is, how can God be all knowing, all loving, and all powerful? It seems that we can only pick two out of three qualities for God. If all knowing and all loving, then why doesn't he have the power to prevent human suffering? If all powerful and all loving, then why can't he foresee and understand our suffering and stop it? Finally, if all knowing and all powerful, why doesn't he love us enough to prevent us from suffering?

John S. Hatcher, the Bahá'í author and Professor Emeritus of English Literature, University of South Florida, explores this theme more thoroughly and eloquently in his superb book *The Purpose of Physical Reality* (2005), where he writes:

Since God fashioned physical reality and since it is His intention that we develop spiritually, then physical reality must be a benevolent creation that somehow facilitates spiritual development...paradox of why, if we are essentially spiritual beings, we are ordained to take our beginning in a physical environment that most of the time seems antithetical to all we proclaim the Creator to be and to all we proclaim the Creator would have us become.[267]

In reference to common concepts, and what he considers erroneous concepts, of good and evil he adds:

We naturally assume that whatever occurs in God's universe is directly or indirectly His responsibility. He is logically guilty of either malfeasance or nonfeasance while operating heavy machinery (our planet and the rest of the universe).

If God is omnipotent and can create us in any way He wishes, why did He not create us already spiritualized, already in a state of understanding?[268]

In response to those dilemmas, Hatcher proposes the concept that our experience in physical reality functions as prelude and a necessary and 'foundational' experience for the future development of our souls.

If we love the physical temple for itself or come to accept this metaphorical vehicle that is our body as being synonymous with the tenor that is our soul, we quickly lose touch with the foundational purpose which caused God to create physical reality in the first place.[269]

The recurrent question that my personal and professional experiences with illness have led me to be perhaps excessively preoccupied with is how much of our personal experience might be divinely directed versus random? I tend to come down on the side of significant randomness for both accidents and diseases. It strikes me as regressive and pre-Hippocratic to suppose that God causes diseases or injuries. In my work, I'm grateful to have retired at the point where I could still count the number of pediatric fatalities that I had to directly care for on one hand. They were all accidents and in the 5- to 10-year-old age range: three motor vehicle accidents and one smoke inhalation death in a house fire. Of the things they shared in common, one is that they were each already dead when I saw them. By that I mean 'not resuscitable,' which mercifully spared them any more suffering and us the fear of having failed them in our efforts. But the more memorable aspect is the degree to which their freshly dead bodies still appeared peacefully unmarred, their fatal injuries having been internal—unmarred, but also unbreathing. Then comes the appalling moment of their parents' arrival, when they look back and forth from their children to you, trying to will you to say something reassuring... and the stricken look on their faces the moment they realize that you can't provide hope, after you begin to say, "I'm so sorry, but..."

I conclude that for human suffering in all its forms, medical and otherwise, scientific studies appear to show that we would be best served by being kinder to ourselves, and even more so by being kinder to each other! I also believe, based on the preceding demonstrations of benefits derived from showing love to others, that a compelling argument could be made for the fact that Jesus Christ's admonition to "Love thy neighbor as thyself" could possibly be the most effective prescientific piece of health advice ever given.

CODA

AN OBSERVATION

During the Chapter Four discussion on beliefs, I chose to withhold any discussion of my own personal beliefs, and as the book has progressed, I've tried to make it very clear when something I was saying was simply an opinion. This decision was based on the desire to not have my beliefs and opinions interfere with or be a distraction from the logical progression of the argument that I was developing. Having brought that presentation to a conclusion, I will now return to the topic of beliefs and make some comments of a more personal nature. In doing this, I want to definitively clarify that my purpose here is the same as it has been throughout the entire book—merely to present information for consideration, not to 'prescribe' what the reader should think or do in regard to that information, either here or leading up to this point.

To be succinct, my theistic beliefs are based on being a long-time member of the Bahá'í Faith, the fourth and latest Abrahamic religion (Judaism, Christianity, and Islam as precedents), whose Prophet-Founder was Bahá'u'lláh (1817-1892). Bahá'u'lláh appointed his son

'Abdu'l-Bahá to succeed him as head of the Bahá'í Faith, to reflect its principles as an exemplar, and to propagate that revelation. Ironically enough, it was hearing about a specific Bahá'í principle that led me to first consider the writing of this book.

As background, in the summer of 2014 my cousin and fellow Bahá'í, Dr. David Rutstein, and I were having a discussion about medicine-related topics as we often did. He offhandedly said to me, apropos of I can't remember what, "Well Drew, it is my understanding that Bahá'u'lláh made it obligatory that we follow our physicians' advice." My immediate, though unexpressed, thoughts were: "I did not know that" and "That sounds like particularly dangerous and bad advice to me." So that's what sent me to the medical literature, well outside my usual comfort zone in emergency medicine, looking for anything that might support such a notion. I had already experienced firsthand the inherent dangers of the fallibility of physicians' advice, so I had plenty of evidence on the side of rejecting that notion.

> *Whatever competent physicians or surgeons prescribe for a patient should be accepted and complied with, provided that they are adorned with the ornament of justice. If they were to be endued with divine understanding, that would certainly be preferable and more desirable.*[270]

Here I am hoping that even those who reject any notion of a divine origin for humanity will please consider reading just a little bit further. I'm going to refer here to a belief in God as the 'theistic theory,' and the absence or rejection of a belief in God termed the 'just us here theory.'

The phrase 'just us here theory' is not meant in a dismissive way, but as shorthand for there's nobody but us here to rely on, credit, or blame for our predicament, which definitely has some inherent appeal and benefits too. Both of these are viewed as only theories because, as per the proper functioning of science, neither can ever be anything more than conjectural, given that we can never have definitive and reproducible proof of either. The two theories do diverge most prominently at the time of death regarding whether the body is just a temporary vessel for the progress of our soul, and raising the question, does the soul live on or not?

There are two key principles within the Bahá'í Faith's version of the theistic theory that I hold close to my heart (and head). The first is that science and religion must be in harmony, as their natures and observations about reality are complementary and not identical. This is based on the concept that there is only one physical reality, and though science and religion are fundamentally different lenses through which to view that one reality, they should not be allowed to come up with concepts that are in radical disagreement. Here, I am here purposefully setting aside the theoretical concept of a multiverse, which frankly gives me a headache to try to wrap my brain around!

In his thought-provoking book *Rocks of Ages: Science and Religion in the Fullness of Life*, the evolutionary biologist Stephen Jay Gould addresses the science/religion dichotomy with the concept that science and religion are nonoverlapping magisteria (which he terms NOMA) that need to keep their respectful distances from each other.[271]

On this same topic, we have 'Abdu'l-Bahá saying, "If any religion rejected Science and knowledge, that religion was false. Science and Religion should go forward together; indeed, they should be like two fingers of one hand."[272]

And in an interesting echo of 'Abdu'l-Bahá's comment, the famed physicist Albert Einstein some years later said, "Science without religion is lame, religion without science is blind."[273] This is not to say that Einstein believed in a 'personal God,' which by report he stated empathetically that he did not, referring to such beliefs as 'naïve' and 'childlike.' He did, however, elaborate by also saying:

The most beautiful and deepest experience a man can have is the sense of the mysterious. It is the underlying principle of religion as well as of all serious endeavour in art and science. He who

never had this experience seems to me, if not dead, then at least
blind. To sense that behind anything that can be experienced
there is a something that our minds cannot grasp, and whose
beauty and sublimity reaches us only indirectly and as a feeble
reflection: this is religiousness. In this sense I am religious. To
me it suffices to wonder at these secrets and to attempt humbly
to grasp with my mind a mere image of the lofty structure of all
there is.[274, 275]

'Abdu'l-Bahá's historically earlier comment had been:

The difference in station between man and Divine Reality is
thousands upon thousands of times greater than the difference
between vegetable and animal. And that which a human being
would conjure up in his mind is but the fanciful image of his
human condition, it does not encompass God's reality but rather
is encompassed by it.[276]

Although I see a distinct parallel between their descriptions above of
"all there is," 'Abdu'l-Bahá's conception of God does differ dramatically
from that of Einstein's in that 'Abdu'l-Bahá provides reassurance that,
"Thy God is affectionate, compassionate and merciful."[277]

One observation I was able to make fairly quickly in my research
was that Herbert Benson's description of the placebo effect as outlined
in his 1996 article is surprisingly consistent with statements made by
'Abdu'l-Bahá in 1906. To revisit Chapter Seven, Benson proposed that
the following were needed for placebo-effect healing to work:

- Positive beliefs and expectations on the part of the patient
- Positive beliefs and expectations on the part of the physician or
  health care professional
- Good relationship between both parties

'Abdu'l-Bahá's historically earlier comments were:

In brief, a complete and perfect connection between the spiritual physician and the patient—that is, one where the physician concentrates his entire attention on the patient and where the patient likewise concentrates all his attention on the spiritual physician and anticipates healing—causes a nervous excitement whereby health is regained. But this is effective only to a point and not in all cases. For instance, should someone contract a grave illness or be physically injured, these means will neither dispel the illness nor soothe and heal the injury—that is, these means have no sway over grave illnesses unless assisted by the constitution of the patient, for a strong constitution will often ward off an illness.[278]

Although the language varies slightly, the described three-step process sounds otherwise identical, with 'Abdu'l-Bahá's statement preceding Benson's by 90 years. One could say that this is just a simple coincidence, that is, that an unusual phenomenon was separately stumbled upon by two different individuals in two different times in history. Consider though that these individuals were radically different in their upbringing, education, and goals in life. I favor the explanation that 'Abdu'l-Bahá (who had just one year of formal schooling at age seven) was given divine inspiration to reveal this concept, while Benson learned it through long science-based education and hard work.

I've come across no information suggesting that Benson took his inspiration from 'Abdu'l-Bahá's previously published statements. I conclude that this is an apt example of science and religion agreeing on the nature of our one reality. It sounds to me like they're both describing the placebo effect, and please note that 'Abdu'l-Bahá adds in the definitive proviso of not relying on the placebo effect to work if we "contract a grave illness or be physically injured." This is a point on which both the placebo-effect supporters and skeptics seemed to agree.

My second favorite Bahá'í principle that I alluded to above is that we are also under the obligation to independently investigate the truth. This is not in any way to say that the conclusions that we come to through our independent investigation will necessarily have the same validity as Bahá'u'lláh's divine revelation or science's systematic study. However, Bahá'ís are repeatedly discouraged from accepting the conclusions of others without using the power of their own minds. These two principles helped lead me to my conclusion that it is only in a true partnership, with an honest and open give-and-take, that we and our physicians can develop, and make a commitment to, a treatment plan that is in our best interest as patients and also within the physician's best judgment. Yes, this goal is a difficult and time-consuming proposition, but indispensable to achieving and maintaining our health in the face of serious illness.

To repeat here for emphasis, the Bahá'í Faith is a religion with the unique and somewhat radical admonitions that you should not follow religious principles unthinkingly, nor should you reflexively reject science when it appears to disagree with religious principles. Add in the factor that you're not considered a Bahá'í simply by virtue of birth or family of origin because you must commit yourself independently and overtly to become a Bahá'í. Age 15 is considered to be the age of spiritual maturity in the Bahá'í Faith, when one can officially declare their belief in Bahá'u'lláh and desire to become a Bahá'í. By this time it is hoped that the new Bahá'í has developed some independent, critical thinking skills. 'Abdu'l-Bahá commented as follows on this principle of the independent investigation of the truth:

> God has bestowed the gift of mind upon man in order that he may weigh every fact or truth presented to him and adjudge whether it be reasonable. That which conforms to his reason he may accept as true, while that which reason and science cannot sanction may be discarded as imagination and superstition, as a phantom and not reality.[279]

'Abdu'l-Bahá further reinforced the importance of our power of reason and responsibility to investigate reality when he wrote:

> *Furthermore, know ye that God has created in man the power of reason, whereby man is enabled to investigate reality. God has not intended man to imitate blindly his fathers and ancestors. He has endowed him with mind, or the faculty of reasoning, by the exercise of which he is to investigate and discover the truth, and that which he finds real and true he must accept. He must not be an imitator or blind follower of any soul. He must not rely implicitly upon the opinion of any man without investigation; nay, each soul must seek intelligently and independently, arriving at a real conclusion and bound only by that reality.[280]*

In isolation, these statements almost make 'Abdu'l-Bahá sound as much like a scientist as a religious figure, don't they? I believe that these statements are meant to let us know that we are imbued by God with a need to know, a restlessness in not knowing, and are charged with the responsibility to make a concerted effort to try to know. Although He does not mention our physicians explicitly, I hear in His words the caution to not just blindly and unquestioningly comply with our physicians' advice. More intriguingly, I hear the same message from medical science, even more explicitly and emphatically stated, especially when addressing the need for safer and more effective healthcare interventions.

I'm not happy that we cannot have more definitive knowledge on why there is such an overly wide range of medical suffering, but I'm trying to reconcile myself to our mutual limits there. If I had been the one placed in charge of drawing up design plans for our existence here on earth, I certainly would have put pediatric cancer, birth defects, and chronic pain as the top three on my 'Not Needed' list. Fortunately for all of us, I was not in charge, because no doubt I would have gotten the astrophysics all wrong, with the inevitable accompaniment of planets careening out of orbit and catastrophic collisions…thus your not being here to consider these thoughts and my not being here to propose them.

Why is this chapter's discussion relevant to the preceding materials you might ask? As we saw earlier, committing oneself to a treatment plan has been repeatedly shown to have a strong association with a longer and healthier lifespan. Those of us who adhere to the theistic theory might logically conclude that that was one of the intended purposes of these principles in the Bahá'í revelation. In contrast, those who adhere to the 'just us here' theory might choose to point out Freud's conclusion that all religious beliefs are "illusions and insusceptible of proof."[281] I think that adherents of both theories can agree on the "insusceptible of proof" part. But the idea that those who hold or originally espouse divine beliefs are merely suffering illusions and delusions deserves further reflection.

The saying of Jesus that "wherefore by their fruits ye shall know them" (Matthew 7:20, KJV) becomes relevant here. A memorable case in which I was only indirectly involved comes to mind. At a shift change, a colleague I was replacing informed me that in a certain room there was a patient awaiting psychiatric evaluation. My only role was needing to be aware that he might escalate in his agitation to the point where he needed medication to calm him, but ideally to avoid that if possible until he could be seen in his present state by the mental health evaluator. He added the detail that the patient had come in stating very loudly and repeatedly that, "God will kill all of you and all of your families." He was ultimately hospitalized for further psychiatric evaluation.

I consider it pretty easy to conclude that those might be 'tainted fruits.' Some people might be tempted to put 'Abdu'l-Bahá in the same category as the above confused individual, just because they would think anyone claiming to speak divine truth is mentally unsound. However, in contrast, 'Abdu'l-Bahá was uniformly lauded by those whom He encountered. He was, in fact, knighted by the British empire in 1920 for His selfless support in providing food aid to the residents of then Palestine during World War I. The Bahá'í believers at the time wanted to elevate 'Abdu'l-Bahá to the status of a Prophet of God in His own right. However, He repeatedly stated that His role was one of service to God, to His father Bahá'u'lláh's revelation, and to humanity. He chose the name 'Abdu'l-Bahá, which translates to "servant of the glory." He did not go to England after the war and benefit from His knighthood but led an active life of continued service to both humanity and the Bahá'í Faith. Again, not definitive proof of the value and validity of 'Abdu'l-Bahá"s extensive writings explicating Bahá'u'lláh's revelation, but I conclude that there are definitely different fruits there.[282, 283]

Figure 7: 'Abdu'l-Bahá at his investiture ceremony as a Knight Commander of the Order of the British Empire, April 1920

Related to both Einstein's and 'Abdu'l-Bahá's above observations on the 'unknowability' of "the lofty structure of all there is," there is this caution by Alister McGrath, professor of science and religion at Oxford University, in his book *The Big Question*:

> *The danger—and it is a real danger—is that we just reduce our vast and complex world to the intellectually manageable and treat this impoverished and truncated mental representation of reality as if it is reality.*[284]

I hear McGrath's caution as a reminder to us as patients as well to not be too quick to reject medical advice simply because we don't understand it. We, along with our physicians, have to put in the time and effort to learn and understand together all that we can about whatever problem is at hand.

I conclude that the patient-physician relationship is a nearly sacred encounter, and I believe it is designedly so. There was a time, not so very long ago, when the relationship between the patient and physician was all that we had because there were no science-based, effective, diagnostic or therapeutic interventions available to us. The nonscientific interventions that we jointly resorted to were at times harmful, although at other times clearly therapeutic. There is broad agreement among medical historians that the history of medicine is the history of the placebo effect, and evidence for its persistent effectiveness is now becoming science-based and reproducible.

It is perfectly understandable that as the scientific underpinnings of the causes of and treatments for diseases were clarified, we would become less exclusively reliant upon a relationship with our physicians. It is not at all understandable, though, that we would choose to consciously enfeeble this relationship within the therapeutic armamentarium. We are all currently suffering from the unintended side effects of that poor choice.

I believe that we can and should alter that choice. The intent of this book is to promote a dialogue on how we, both medical and nonmedical individuals alike, might do so.

ACKNOWLEDGMENTS

See one, Do one, Teach one: Quite like medical practice, the seeing of the end result, whether it be a book or a well-performed medical procedure, reveals absolutely nothing about its execution. Who knew how many tasks and steps a book passes through and the competencies an editor needs to be able to achieve a worthy creation. Now having had a glimpse into that process, I am extremely grateful that my editor Beth Rule has the full set of necessary skills of observation, perception, analysis, and communication, along with an unfailing commitment to 'get it right,' bordering on the obsessive attention to detail that we want in our physicians. Eileen Maddocks also brought her own parallel editorial skills that greatly facilitated this presentation. My gratitude extends beyond them to the rest of SOOP's team as well for enabling this book to emerge.

When it comes to the medical doing, there are too many to count physicians who have demonstrated their skills to both my own health and professional benefit. Earliest in my career are my Rutgers Medical

School classmates who will remain nameless here, but you know who you are. I do want to name and thank to no end, Dr. Amy Johnson, Dr. Don Middleton, Dr. Henry Kurusz, and Dr. John Romano, with whom as a group we faced the novel challenges of the newborn specialty of emergency medicine as both residents and joint-practice JAFERDs.

Thanks also to Don and John, along with Drs. David Rutstein, Karen Wyatt, Michael Caldwell, Stephen Buglione, and Jeffrey Salloway (the last three being non-MDs, in case you thought only fellow physicians could tolerate me) for being advance readers of the manuscript and providing feedback and support, when I needed it most. Additional thanks to Mark and Marion Remignanti (my older brother and his wife, in case the name sounded familiar), who provided the same advance reader favor.

Dr. Bob Like has graciously contributed the gift of writing this book's insightful Foreword, in addition to keeping me aware of the latest research and articles pertaining to my topic. I deeply value his friendship and admire his lifelong commitment to improving primary care medicine.

As far as teaching, I feel no closer qualified to teach anything about writing or producing a book. Instead, I will once again thank all the patients that I encountered throughout my career who acted, whether by choice or unwillingly, in the role of being my instructors, especially those who had the ill luck to meet me before I had completed either the 'Do one' or even the 'See one' tasks relevant to their predicament. I honor you as my teachers.

To bookend my beginning, I'm most grateful for the initial editorial assistance and loving support of my wife Darby Johnson, and the loving support of, and teenaged distractions from, our son Cooper Remignanti.

GLOSSARY

acute versus **subacute** » dependent on the condition under consideration, with neither having a precise time duration: acute usually indicating minutes to hours, with subacute indicating hours to days

ADL » activities of daily living

ALF » assisted living facility

AM » alternative medicine

AITA » Am I The Asshole

AMA » American Medical Association

ambu bag » a flexible silicon or rubber inflatable, hand squeezable device for forcing air through a patient's mouth/nose or through an inserted endotracheal tube to support their breathing

antibody IgA » a blood protein naturally produced for the purpose of combatting infection

arrhythmia » an abnormal heart rhythm

arteriosclerosis/atherosclerotic » a disease process of fat deposition along inner artery walls causing narrowing

ARTI » abbreviation for acute respiratory tract infection

ASC » ambulatory surgery center

attending physician » senior doctor having completed the hospital training years after medical school

BAFERD » bad ass f#cking emergency room doctor

BNTI » blind nasotracheal intubation or a breathing tube placed through the nose

C diff/C difficile/Clostridium difficile/Clostridioides difficile » a bacterial cause of severe diarrhea often following strong or lengthy antibiotic use

call room » mini room with bed for doctors to catnap when time allows and fatigue demands

cardiac tamponade » when blood or fluid fills the sac surrounding the heart diminishing its ability to pump out blood, causing low blood pressure, shock, and/or death

CAM » complementary and alternative medicine

carotid artery » a pair of large arteries, left and right side of the front of the neck which bring blood to the brain

CAT/CT scan » synonyms for computerized axial tomography which provides very detailed views of internal tissue anatomy, bone or otherwise

CCT » conventional cancer treatment

CDC » Centers for Disease Control and Prevention

central line » a large bore intravenous line providing closer access to larger veins near the heart

chest tube » a large diameter flexible silicone tube placed between the ribs into the space between the lungs and the chest wall to evacuate abnormal blood, fluid or air that is trapped there

CHF » congestive heart failure

cholangiocarcinoma » cancer of the bile ducts in or around the liver

CIM » complementary and integrative medicine

CMS » Centers for Medicare & Medicaid Services

CO/carbon dioxide » one major component of the air that we breathe out

coagulopathy » an abnormality of the body's blood clotting system causing the blood to clot unnecessarily

code » cardiac or respiratory arrest

COPD/chronic obstructive pulmonary disease » a disease characterized by lung tissue loss and airway inflammation/thickening caused by long-term smoking or other chemical irritants

CSF/cerebrospinal fluid » the clear fluid which bathes and circulates around the brain and spinal column

CVP/central venous pressure » measurement of pressure from a central line reflecting degree of hydration and ease of blood flow back into the heart

differential diagnosis » a mental working list of possible medical conditions that might account for a patient's symptoms

dissection » when a blood vessel's walls (artery or less commonly vein) begin to separate longitudinally into its constituent parts creating a separate nonfunctional channel for blood flow, possibly leading to complete rupture

DNR/Do Not Resuscitate » a restriction a patient may choose to designate in cases of a poor prognosis near the end of their life

ED » emergency department

EKG » an electrocardiogram, usually done with twelve simultaneous electrical leads, unlike home or portable devices which display only one lead

EM » emergency medicine

emesis » vomited material

emetic » causing nausea and vomiting

EMR/EHR » electronic medical/health record, a digital version of a patient's paper medical chart

EMS » emergency medical services (ambulance staff)

EMT » emergency medical technicians

encephalopathy » when the brain's normal function is compromised leading to confusion, caused by processes such as infection, trauma, oxygen deprivation or toxins from either excess exposure or progressive accumulation due to advanced liver or kidney disease

endoscopy » any use of a flexible lighted fiberoptic scope to view the body's interior spaces

endotracheal tube » a clear flexible tube for placement within the trachea/'windpipe' to support a patient's breathing

epiglottis » a valve-like flap of tissue deep in the back of the throat that guards the opening of the airway, keeping swallowed objects from 'going down the wrong pipe'

ER » emergency room

ERCP » endoscopic retrograde cholangiopancreatography, an evaluation of the bile ducts within and around the liver

forceps » medical tools designed to grab or clamp off objects (bodily or foreign in origin), the Magill forceps version being long and curved thus ideal for airway related problems

GI » gastrointestinal

GILD » stock market ticker symbol for the pharmaceutical company Gilead Sciences, Inc.

HBV » hepatitis B virus

HCPA/HCPOA » health care power of attorney; legal document outlining your medical treatment wishes and designating a proxy person to act in your best interests if you become incapacitated

heart chambers (four) » the two ventricles, right and left are thick and muscular and pump blood out to the lungs and rest of the body respectively; the two atria are thinner-walled and collect the returning blood before passing it on to the ventricles

heparin » a medication administered intravenously or by injection under the skin that slows down the blood clotting process

hepatic » referring to the liver

hepatitis » inflammation of the liver

HIV » human immunodeficiency virus

HPI » history of the present illness, the conversation meant to elicit the patient's account of their current illness experience

HPV » human papilloma virus

hydrocephalus » an abnormal collection of cerebrospinal fluid enlarging the brain's normal fluid-filled reservoirs

iatrogenic » refers to medical problems that are caused by the medical treatment itself

IBD » inflammatory bowel disease

IBS » irritable bowel syndrome

ICU » intensive care unit

idiopathic » of unknown cause

injury pattern » an EKG tracing suggesting damage to the heart muscle

intern » also called PGY1 for postgraduate year one; refers to physicians in their first year of hospital training after finishing medical school

intra-arterial » within the artery

intracranial » within the cranium/skull

intubate » most commonly the insertion of a tube into the airway to support/control/protect a patient's breathing

JAFERD » just another f#cking emergency room doctor

lateral » to one side or the other of the body's midline

lidocaine » a medication that provides an anesthetic/numbing effect within body tissue, but also can prevent the heart's electrical system from misfiring dangerously

lobotomy » a surgical procedure separating the frontal lobes from the rest of the brain

lumbar vertebrae » the low back portion of the stacked block appearing bones of the spine

mandible » the jawbone

MERS » Middle East Respiratory Syndrome

MRI » magnetic resonance imaging

MUS » medically unexplained symptoms

MVA » motor vehicle accident

narcotizing » any process which simulates the sedating effect of narcotics

neglect » a lack of awareness of, and attention to, one side of the body in the setting of damage to the opposite sided/controlling hemisphere of the brain, most often to the right hemisphere from a stroke, but can occur in infection or injury

nocebo effect » a negative response to a medical intervention which is scientifically believed to be otherwise without specific biological activity, for example, taking a sugar pill

OECD » Organization for Economic Cooperation and Development; an intergovernmental organization with 38 member countries that are democracy-based with high-income market economies

OLP » open label placebos

OR » operating room

papilledema/choked disc » swelling around the large optic nerve as it leaves the central back of the eye/retina caused by increased pressure within the skull against the back wall of the eye

pericardiocentesis » a procedure involving a long needle inserted under the ribcage, perforating the pericardial sac surrounding the heart, in order to withdraw abnormal collections of blood or fluid compressing and compromising the heart's contractions

PET scan » positron emission tomography scan

phocomelia » a malformation of the limbs

placebo effect » a positive response to a medical intervention which is scientifically believed to be otherwise without specific biological activity, for example taking a sugar pill

PNI » psychoneuroimmunology; the study of the interaction between psychological processes and the nervous and immune systems of the human body

posey restraints » a soft medical vest with straps that prevents patients from unsafely exiting their bed or chair without assistance

postictal » the lethargic, unresponsive period which typically follows a seizure

PPE » personal protective equipment

productivity metrics » when administrative staff measure and report the number and speed at which physicians and others can finish one patient evaluation and proceed to the next one (no actual 'product' is 'produced')

PSC » primary sclerosing cholangitis; a condition causing bile duct inflammation resulting in an increased risk of bile duct cancers as well as the risk of progressing to complete liver failure

pulmonary embolism » a blood clot within the lungs

pulse oximetry » when a device is applied to the fingertip or earlobe to obtain a measurement of the blood's oxygen content

PVCs/premature ventricular contractions » abnormal beats of the heart that may indicate that a portion of the heart is not receiving sufficient oxygen, which may lead to V tach or V fib

RCT » randomized clinical trial, the random distribution of medical study participants to different groups to avoid bias when assessing the effectiveness of a medical intervention compared to a placebo

resident » also called PGY for postgraduate years 2-7, denoting the number of hospital training years after medical school graduation

ROS/review of systems » a thorough set of questions asked of the patient about possible symptoms related to each of the organ systems, such as cardiac, pulmonary, gastrointestinal, etc.

SARS » Severe Acute Respiratory Syndrome

seizure » uncontrolled brain electrical activity, most often (but not always) accompanied by uncontrolled muscle contractions and brief unconsciousness

self-limited illness » resolves spontaneously and may lack a precise organic cause

spinal tap/lumbar puncture » a procedure in which a needle is inserted through the low back to obtain cerebrospinal fluid

STEMI » S-T segment elevation myocardial infarction; EKG findings showing a heart attack in progress

subclavian and internal jugular veins » large, centrally-located veins used for IV access, medication administration, and central venous pressure measurement; the subclavian veins are located under the clavicles (collar bones) and the internal jugular veins are on each side of the front of the neck (anterolateral)

submandibular glands » salivary glands located just under the edge of each side of the mandible/jawbone

susceptible versus **resistant bacteria** » bacteria are susceptible when able to be killed by a certain antibiotic, and resistant if unable to be killed

SVC/superior vena cava » the large vein just above the right side of the heart through which blood from the upper body returns to the heart

temporary pacemaker wire » under emergency conditions, a wire placed through a central vein to stimulate cardiac contractions pending the more permanent pacemaker placement

thoracotomy » a large incision in the chest made to get direct access to the heart for stopping bleeding or relieving tamponade

thrombolytic » medications given to dissolve a blood clot

TCM » Traditional Chinese Medicine

trepanation/trephination » the process of creating a hole in the skull

troponin » a protein that lives in muscle cells, most prominently in the heart muscle

ultrasound » a non-invasive radiation free bedside available technique using sound waves to image inside the body

unilateral » one-sided

unremarkable » (medical context) a normal or nearly normal result of a physical examination or medical test, not requiring further evaluation or intervention

USPHS » US Public Health Service

vagal response » an activation of the vagus nerve, which leads to a slowing of the heart rate and drop in blood pressure, a common cause of fainting

V-tach/V-fib » ventricular tachycardia is when the electrical impulses in the heart originate from the ventricle muscle tissue rather than the heart's intrinsic pacemaker, usually excessively fast but can be effective enough to sustain the blood pressure; the risk is deterioration into ventricular fibrillation where the heart muscle is merely wriggling and unable to circulate any blood, causing death, if not immediately treated

ventricles » the two large chambers of the heart; alternatively, the centrally located cerebrospinal fluid-producing/storing chambers in the brain

NOTES

Foreword

1. National Academies Sciences, Engineering, and Medicine, et al., *Implementing High-Quality Primary Care: Rebuilding the Foundation of Health Care* (Washington, DC: The National Academies Press, 2021), 3, https://doi.org/10.17226/25983.

2. Yalda Jabbarpour, et al.,"The Health of US Primary Care: A Baseline Scorecard Tracking Support for High-Quality Primary Care," Millbank Memorial Fund, February 22, 2023, https://www.milbank.org/publications/health-of-us-primary-care-a-baseline-scorecard/.

Introduction

3. "OECD Health Data 2012: U.S. health care system from an international perspective," OECD.org, released June 28, 2012, https://www.oecd.org/health/HealthSpendingInUSA_HealthData2012.pdf.

4. "Majority of Americans Say the Health Care System Needs Fundamental Change or Complete Rebuilding," *Commonwealth Fund Survey of Public Views*

of the U.S. Health Care System, 2011, https://www.commonwealthfund.org/sites/default/files/documents/___media_files_publications_issue_brief_2011_apr_stremikis_public_views_2011_survey_exhibits.pdf.

5.   Robert Pearl, MD, "Physician Burnout is up, Gender inequality is making it worse," LinkedIn, Apr. 26, 2022, https://www.linkedin.com/pulse/physician-burnout-up-gender-inequality-making-worse-pearl-m-d-/.

6.   Maria Rebello-Valdez, MPH, "Is Medical School a Catalyst for Depression, Suicide and Burnout?" Medium, Apr 3, 2019, https://mariavaldez-15080.medium.com/is-medical-school-a-catalyst-for-depression-suicide-and-burnout-2d5c3a5fb645.

7.   "Unnecessary medical tests, treatments cost $200 billion annually, cause harm," Healthcare Finance News, Kaiser Health News, May 24, 2017, https://www.healthcarefinancenews.com/news/unnecessary-medical-tests-treatments-cost-200-billion-annually-cause-harm.

8.   Sara Heath, "Patient Recall Suffers as Patients Remember Half of Health Info," Patient Engagement HIT, Mar. 26, 2018, https://patientengagementhit.com/news/patient-recall-suffers-as-patients-remember-half-of-health-info.

9.   Janice Mara, "Open Minds – International Trepanation Advocacy Group," Brandweek, 2000, https://indexarticles.com/business/brandweek/open-minds-international-trepanation-advocacy-group/.

Chapter One – Where Are We and How Did We Get Here?

10.   Raymond Tallis, MD, *Hippocratic Oaths: Medicine and Its Discontents* (London: Atlantic Books, 2004), 2, 58.

11.   Robert J. Blendon, ScD, John M. Benson, MA, and Joachim O. Hero, MPH, "Public Trust in Physicians — U.S. Medicine in International Perspective." N Engl J Med 2014; 371:1570-1572, http://www.nejm.org/doi/full/10.1056/NEJMp1407373.

12.   Molly Gamble, "11 highest paid CEOs in healthcare," *Becker's Hospital Review*, May 15, 2023, https://www. beckershospitalreview.com/compensation-issues/11-highest-paid-ceos-in-healthcare.html.

13.   Bob Herman, "Seven health insurance CEOs raked in a record $283 million last year," *STAT*, May 12, 2022, https://www. statnews.com/2022/05/12/health-insurance-ceos-raked-in-record-pay-during-covid/.

14. Dave Muoio, "Here's what CEOs at the US' top for-profit health systems earned in 2021," *Fierce Healthcare*, Apr. 26, 2022, https://www.fiercehealth-care.com/providers/heres-what-ceos-us-top-profit-health-systems-earned-2021.

15. Adam Andrzejewski, "Top U.S. 'Non-Profit' Hospitals & CEOs Are Racking Up Huge Profits," *Forbes.com*, June 26, 2019, https://www.forbes.com/sites/adamandrzejewski/2019/06/26/top-u-s-non-profit-hospitals-ceos-are-racking-up-huge-profits/? sh=49581d2719df.

16. "New International Report on Health Care: U.S. Suicide Rate Highest Among Wealthy Nations: U.S. Outspends Other High-Income Countries on Health Care but Has Lowest Life Expectancy," The Commonwealth Fund, Jan. 30, 2020, https://www.commonwealthfund.org/press-release/2020/new-international-report-health-care-us-suicide-rate-highest-among-wealthy#:~:text=The%20United%20States20spends%20substantially%20more%20than%20any,nations%2C%20according%20to%20a%20new%20Commonwealth%20Fund%20report.

17. Melissa Hellmann, "U.S. Health Care Ranked Worst in the Developed World," Time.com, June 17, 2014, https://time.com/2888403/u-s-health-care-ranked-worst-in-the-developed-world/.

18. "U.S. Outspends Other High-Income Countries on Health Care but Has Lowest Life Expectancy," New International Report on Health Care: U.S. Suicide Rate Highest Among Wealthy Nations, The Commonwealth Fund, Jan. 30, 2020, https://www.commonwealthfund.org/press-release/2020/new-international-report-health-care-us-suicide-rate-highest-among-wealthy#:~:text=The%20United%20States20spends%20substantially%20more%20than%20any,nations%2C%20according%20to%20a%20new%20Commonwealth%20Fund%20report.

19. Roosa Tikkanen and Melinda K. Abrams, "U.S. Health Care from a Global Perspective, 2019: Higher Spending, Worse Outcomes?" The Commonwealth Fund, January 2020, https://www.commonwealthfund.org/sites/default/files/2020-01/Tikkanen_US_hlt_care_global_perspective_2019_OECD_db_v2.pdf

20. William H. Shrank, MD, MSHS, Teresa L. Rogstad, MPH, and Natasha Parekh, MD, MS, "Waste in the US Health Care System: Estimated Costs and Potential for Saving." *JAMA*, 2019;322(15):1501-1509, Oct. 7, 2019, https://jamanetwork.com/journals/jama/fullarticle/2752664.

21. Dyfed Loesche, "America Has the Highest Drug-Death Rate in North America - and the World," Statista, June 26, 2017, https://www.statista.com/chart/9973/drug-related-deaths-and-mortality-rate-worldwide/.

22. David Squires and Chloe Anderson, "U.S. Health Care from a Global Perspective," The Commonwealth Fund, Oct. 8, 2015, https://

www.commonwealthfund.org/publications/issue-briefs/2015/oct/us-health-care-global-perspective.

23. Megan Knowles, "Healthcare becomes largest US employer: 6 takeaways," *Becker's Hospital Review*, Jan. 11, 2018, https://www.beckershospitalreview.com/workforce/healthcare-becomes-largest-us-employer-6-takeaways.html.

24. "Blue Cross Blue Shield Association," *Wikipedia*, accessed May 3, 2023, https://en.wikipedia.org/wiki/Blue_Cross_Blue_Shield_Association.

25. David Marcozzi, "Trends in the Contribution of Emergency Departments to the Provision of Hospital-Associated Health Care in the USA," SageJournals, International Journal of Social Determinants of Health and Health Services, Vol. 48, Issue 2, Oct 17, 2017, https://doi.org/10.1177/0020731417734498.

26. Howard K. Koh, MD, MPH and Rima E. Rudd, ScD, MSPH, "The Arc of Health Literacy," *JAMA*, 2015;314(12):1225-1226, Sept. 22/29, 2015, https://jamanetwork.com/journals/jama/fullarticle/10.1001/jama.2015.9978.

27. "History of medicine," *Wikipedia*, accessed Mar. 31, 2023, https://en.wikipedia.org/wiki/History_of_medicine.

28. "Hippocratic Oath," *Wikipedia*, accessed Mar. 31, 2023, https://en.wikipedia.org/wiki/Hippocratic_Oath.

29. "Humorism," *Wikipedia*, accessed June 14, 2023, https://en.wikipedia.org/wiki/Humorism.

30. David Hill, "Ain't No Way To Go," *Panati's Extraordinary Endings*, 1989, http://www.aintnowaytogo.com/charlesII.htm.

31. Arthur K. Shapiro, MD, "A Contribution to a History of the Placebo Effect," *Behavioral Science*, Baltimore, Md. Vol. 5, Issue 2, (Apr. 1, 1960): 109, https://www.proquest.com/docview/1301267155?pq-origsite=gscholar&fromopenview=true&imgSeq=1.

32. Fabrizio Benedetti, "Drugs and placebos: what's the difference?" EMBO Reports (2014)15:329-332, https://www.embopress.org/doi/full/10.1002/embr.201338399.

33. Sandra Blakeslee, "Placebos Prove So Powerful Even Experts Are Surprised; New Studies Explore the Brain's Triumph Over Reality," *The New York Times*, Oct. 13, 1998, https://www.nytimes.com/1998/10/13/science/placebos-prove-so-powerful-even-experts-are-surprised-new-studies-explore-brain.html.

34. Bruno Klopfer, "Psychological Variables In Human Cancer," *Journal of Projective Techniques*, Vol. 12, Issue 4, 1957, https://www.tandfonline.com/doi/abs/10.1080/08853126.1957.10380794.

35. Curtis Jeffrey, MD, MS, MPH, et al. "Placebo Adherence, Clinical Outcomes and Mortality in the Women's Health Initiative Randomized Hormone

Therapy Trials," *Medical Care*, vol. 49,5 2011: 427-35. http://www.ncbi.nlm.
nih.gov/pmc/articles/pmc4217207/.

36. David Wootton, *The Invention of Science: A New History of the Scientific Revolution* (New York: Harper Perennial, 2015).

37. "Bounty Museum," Facebook, Aug. 20, 2019, https://www.facebook.
com/108678780476128/posts/john-norton-quartermaster-bounty-loyalists-
john-norton-quartermaster-aboard-the-/119421856068487/.

Chapter Two –
Illness Versus Disease

38. Eric J. Cassell, MD, "Illness and Disease," *The Hastings Center Report*, 6 (April 1976), https://onlinelibrary.wiley.com/doi/pdf/10.2307/3561497.

39. Eric J. Cassell, MD, *The Nature of Suffering and the Goals of Medicine* (USA: Oxford University Press 1991), 19-20.

40. Richard E. Dixon, MD, FACP, "Economic Costs of Respiratory Tract Infections in the United States," *The American Journal of Medicine*, Vol. 78, Issue 6, Supplement 2, 45-51, June 28, 1985, https://doi.
org/10.1016/0002-9343(85)90363-8.

41. *Antibiotic Resistance Threats in the United States 2019*, U.S. Centers for Disease Control and Prevention (CDC), revised Dec. 2019, https://www.cdc.gov/dru-
gresistance/pdf/threats-report/2019-ar-threats-report-508.pdf.

42. "National Infection & Death Estimates for Antimicrobial Resistance," U.S. Centers for Disease Control and Prevention (CDC), accessed May 5, 2023, https://www.cdc.gov/drugresistance/national-estimates.html.

43. "WHO remains firmly committed to the principles set out in the preamble to the Constitution," World Health Organization, accessed Apr. 1, 2023, https://
www.who.int/about/governance/constitution.

44. George R. Engel, MD, "The Need for a New Medical Model: A Challenge for Biomedicine," *Science*, New Series, Vol. 196, No. 4286. (Apr. 8, 1977), 129-136, https://resspir.org/wp-content/uploads/2018/02/3.-article-Engel-
1977-biopsychosocial-model.pdf.

45. Kurt Kroenke, MD, MACP, "Patients presenting with somatic complaints: epidemiology, psychiatric co-morbidity and management," *International Journal of Methods in Psychiatric Research*, 2003 Feb; 12(1): 34–43, https://www.
ncbi.nlm.nih.gov/pmc/articles/PMC6878426/pdf/MPR-12-34.pdf.

46. "Post hoc ergo propter hoc," *Wikipedia*, accessed June 14, 2023, https://
en.wikipedia.org/wiki/Post_hoc_ergo_propter_hoc.

Chapter Three –
Challenges of the Medical Interaction

47. Leo Tolstoy, *Anna Karenina* (New York: Thomas Y. Crowell and Co. 1886).

48. Renée Onque, "How to recognize 'medical gaslighting' and better advocate for yourself at your next doctor's appointment," CNBC.com – Health and Wellness, Sept. 1, 2022, https://www.cnbc.com/2022/09/01/medical-gaslighting-warning-signs-and-how-to-advocate-for-yourself.html.

49. Jared Diamond, *The World until Yesterday: What Can We Learn from Traditional Societies?* (New York: Viking Press, 2012).

50. Daniel Kahneman, *Thinking Fast and Slow* (New York: Farrar, Straus & Giroux, 2011), 263.

51. Jonathan A. Galli, MD, Ronald Andari Sawaya, MD, and Frank K. Friedenberg, MD, "Cannabinoid Hyperemesis Syndrome," National Library of Medicine, Curr Drug Abuse Rev. 2011;4(4):241-249, https://www.ncbi.nlm.nih.gov/pmc/articles/PMC3576702/.

52. "Hypereosinophilic Syndrome," Cleveland Clinic, accessed June 21, 2023, https://my.clevelandclinic.org/health/diseases/22541-hypereosinophilic-syndrome.

53. Kroenke, MD, MACP, "Patients presenting with somatic complaints: epidemiology, psychiatric co-morbidity and management."

54. Kurt Kroenke, MD, MACP, et al., "Anxiety Disorders in Primary Care: Prevalence, Impairment, Comorbidity, and Detection," ResearchGate.net, https://www.researchgate.net/publication/6466355_Anxiety_Disorders_in_Primary_Care_Prevalence_Impairment_Comorbidity_and_Detection.

55. Madhukar H. Trivedi, MD, "The Link Between Depression and Physical Symptoms," *Prim Care Companion, The Journal of Clinical Psychiatry* 2004;6[suppl 1]:12–16, https://www.psychiatrist.com/read-pdf/25335/.

56. Susan Sontag, *Illness as Metaphor* (New York: Farrar, Straus & Giroux, 1978), https://monoskop.org/images/4/4a/Susan_Sontag_Illness_As_Metaphor_1978.pdf.

57. Dana Gelb Safran, ScD., et al., "Linking Primary Care Performance to Outcomes of Care," *The Journal of Family Practice*, 1998 September;47(3) (1998), 217, https://www.mdedge.com/familymedicine/article/179483/linking-primary-care-performance-outcomes-care.

58. Mary Catherine Beach, MD, MPH, Jeanne Keruly, MS, CNRP, and Richard D. Moore, MD, MHS, "Is the Quality of the Patient-Provider Relationship

Associated with Better Adherence and Health Outcomes for Patients with HIV?" *J GEN INTERN MED (JGIM)* 2006; 21:661–665. https://www.ncbi. nlm.nih.gov/pmc/articles/PMC1924639/pdf/jgi0021-0661.pdf.

59. Patrick O'Brian, *The Nutmeg of Consolation* (New York: W. W. Norton & Company, 1991).

60. "Prescription Painkiller Overdoses in the US," *CDC Vital Signs,* November 2011, https://www.cdc.gov/vitalsigns/pdf/2011-11-vitalsigns.pdf.

61. "Prescription Painkiller Overdoses in the US," *CDC Vital Signs.*

62. Beth Duff-Brown, "Overprescribing of opioids is not limited to a few bad apples," Stanford Medicine Newscenter, Dec. 14, 2015, https://www.npr. org/2020/07/17/887590699/doctors-and-dentists-still-flooding-u-s-with-opioid-prescriptions.

63. "Top 10 Leading Causes of Death for People Ages 18 to 45 in the U.S.," FamiliesAgainstFentanyl.org, accessed May 31, 2023, https://static1. squarespace.com/static/61f366b9dd05336e4a3ce776/t/6305834bc3bafe63 96d12910/1661305675942/Fentanyl+Deaths_Top+10+COD.pdf.

64. Nusaiba Mizan, "Is fentanyl the leading cause of death among American adults?" Politifact.com, Oct. 3, 2022, https://www.politifact.com/article/2022/ oct/03/fact-check-fentanyl-leading-cause-death-among-amer/.

65. Dan MacGuill, "Did Fentanyl Overdose Become Top Cause of Death for Adults Aged 18-45 in the US?" Snopes, Dec. 21, 2021, https://www.snopes. com/fact-check/fentanyl-overdose-death/.

66. Alicia Naspretto, "CDC: Fentanyl overdoses now leading cause of death for Americans aged 18 to 45," KXXV.com, last updated Dec. 20, 2021, https:// www.kxxv.com/cdc-fentanyl-overdoses-now-leading-cause-of-death-for-amer-icans-aged-18-to-45.

Chapter Four – Belief

67. Michael Shermer, MD, *Why People Believe Weird Things* (New York: Henry Holt and Company, 1997).

68. Stanford Research into the Impact of Tobacco Advertising, accessed May 31, 2023, http://tobacco.stanford.edu/.

69. "Thalidomide scandal," *Wikipedia,* accessed Mar. 29, 2023, https:// en.wikipedia.org/wiki/Thalidomide_scandal.

70. "Photos: History of Thalidomide," CNN.com, Sept. 1, 2012, slide 4, http://
    i2.cdn.turner.com/cnnnext/dam/assets/120901013138-thalidomide-7-hori-
    zontal-large-gallery.jpg.

71. "Frances Oldham Kelsey: Medical reviewer famous for averting a public health
    tragedy," FDA.gov, accessed Apr. 23, 2023, https://www.fda.gov/about-fda/
    fda-history-exhibits/frances-oldham-kelsey-
    medical-reviewer-famous-averting-public-health-tragedy.

72. Leila McNeill, "The Woman Who Stood Between America and a Generation
    of 'Thalidomide Babies,'" *Smithsonian Magazine*, May 8, 2017, https://www.
    smithsonianmag.com/science-nature/woman-who-stood-between-
    america-and-epidemic-birth-defects-180963165/.

73. Fred D. Gray, *The Tuskegee Syphilis Study* (Montgomery: New South Books,
    1998), http://image1.slideserve.com/2619443/tuskegee-syphilis-study-
    1932-72-n.jpg.

74. "Rosemary Kennedy," *Wikipedia*, accessed Apr. 2, 2023, https://en.wikipedia.
    org/wiki/Rosemary_Kennedy.

75. Bengt Jansson, "Controversial Psychosurgery Resulted in a Nobel Prize," The
    Nobel Prize, accessed Mar. 30, 2023, https://www.nobelprize.org/prizes/
    medicine/1949/moniz/article/.

76. "'My Lobotomy': Howard Dully's Journey," NPR, Nov. 16, 2005, https://
    www.npr.org/2005/11/16/5014080/my-lobotomy-howard-dullys-journey.

77. *Inside Edition*, "'Icepick Surgeon' Did Over 2000 Lobotomies," *You-
    Tube* video, 10:54, accessed May 31, 2023, https://www.youtube.com/
    watch?v=ZPyxwTC-Lqs.

78. David P. Steensma, MD, "The Farid Fata Medicare Fraud Case and Misplaced
    Incentives in Oncology Care," *JCO Oncology Practice*, Vol. 12, No. 1, Jan. 1,
    2016, https://ascopubs.org/doi/full/10.1200/jop.2015.008557#:~:text=On%20
    Julyc%2010%2C%202015%2C%20in%20a%20health%20care,pay%20
    restitution%20to%20former%20patients%20or%20their%20families.

79. History.com Editors, "Larry Nassar, a former doctor for USA Gymnastics, is
    sentenced to prison for sexual assault," HISTORY, Aug. 28, 2019, https://
    www.history.com/this-day-in-history/larry-nassar-usa-gymnastics-
    doctor-sentenced-prison-sexual-assault.

80. "Christopher Duntsch," *Wikipedia*, accessed May 4, 2023, https://
    en.wikipedia.org/wiki/Christopher_Duntsch.

81. Don S. Dizon, MD, "Some Decisions Aren't Right or
    Wrong; They're Just Devastating," Medscape Emer-
    gency Medicine, Apr. 28, 2003, https://www.medscape.com/

viewarticle/991216?ecd=wnl_tp10_daily_230502_MSCPEDIT_etid5391071
&uac=226947SV&impID=5391071#vp_2.

82. Pamela Wible, MD, "Dealing With Intrusive Thoughts After A Medical Error," Pamela Wible MD: America's leading voice on ideal medical care & doctor suicide, Sept. 24, 2020, https://www.idealmedicalcare.org/what-not-to-do-after-a-medical-error/.

83. Dinah Wisenberg Brin, "Why Don't Patients Follow Their Doctors' Advice?" AAMCNEWS, Jan. 16, 2017, https://www.aamc.org/news-insights/why-don-t-patients-follow-their-doctors-advice.

84. Alexander Fleming, "Penicillin," Nobel Lecture, Dec. 11, 1945, https://www.nobelprize.org/uploads/2018/06/fleming-lecture.pdf.

85. Peter J. Hotez, "The Antiscience Movement Is Esclating, Going Global and Killing Thousands," *Scientific American*, Mar. 29, 2021, https://www.scientificamerican.com/article/the-antiscience-movement-is-escalating-going-global-and-killing-thousands/.

86. Tom Nicols, "The Death of Expertise," *The Federalist*, Jan. 17, 2014, https://thefederalist.com/2014/01/17/the-death-of-expertise/.

Chapter Five – Bias

87. Kahneman, *Thinking Fast and Slow*.

88. Deborah Smith, "Psychologist wins Nobel Prize: Daniel Kahneman is honored for bridging economics and psychology," *American Psychological Association*, Vol. 33, No. 11, December 2002, https://www.apa.org/monitor/dec02/nobel.

89. "The Sveriges Riksbank Prize in Economic Sciences in Memory of Alfred Nobel 2002," NobelPrize.org, Nobel Prize Outreach AB 2023, accessed Mar. 29, 2023, https://www.nobelprize.org/prizes/economic-sciences/2002/summary/.

90. Kendra Cherry, medically reviewed by Amy Morin, LCSW, Editor-in-Chief, "List of Common Cognitive Biases: Common Types of Bias That Influence Thinking," Verywellmind, Nov. 06, 2022, https://www.verywellmind.com/cognitive-biases-distort-thinking-2794763.

91. F. Scott. Fitzgerald, "Essay: The Crack-Up by F. Scott Fitzgerald," American Masters, S16 EP2, Aug. 31, 2005, https://www.pbs.org/wnet/americanmasters/f-scott-fitzgerald-essay-the-crack-up/1028/.

92. Andrew J. Foy, MD, and Edward J. Filippone, MD, "The Case for Intervention Bias in the Practice of Medicine," Yale J Biol Med. 2013;86(2):271-280, Published Jun 13, 2013, https://www.ncbi.nlm.nih.gov/pmc/articles/PMC3670446/.

93. Agile Minds #26. "Tim Minchin – 9 Life Lessons," *YouTube* video, 12:00, accessed May 31, 2023, https://youtu.be/FJ__a4qVE_g.

94. Tim Minchin, "'Confirmation bias' | Tim Minchin: BACK," *YouTube* video, 11:54, accessed May 31, 2023, https://youtu.be/G1juPBoxBdc.

95. Kahneman, *Thinking Fast and Slow.*

96. Pat Croskerry, MD, PhD, "Bias: a normal operating characteristic of the diagnosing brain," Diagnosis 2014; 1(1): 23–27, http://clinical-reasoning.org/resources/pdfs/Bias%20by%20Croskerry.pdf.

Chapter Seven – Placebo Effect

97. Anton J. M. de Craen, et al., "Placebos and placebo effects in medicine: historical overview." *Journal of the Royal Society of Medicine.* 1999 Oct; 92(10): 511–515. https://www.ncbi.nlm.nih.gov/pmc/articles/PMC1297390/pdf/jrsocmed00004-0023.pdf.

98. Henry K. Beecher, MD, "The Powerful Placebo," *JAMA.* 1955;159(17):1602-1606. https://jamanetwork.com/journals/jama/article-abstract/303530.

99. Beecher, MD, "The Powerful Placebo."

100. J. Bruce Mosley, MD, et al., "A Controlled Trial of Arthroscopic Surgery for Osteoarthritis of the Knee," *The New England Journal of Medicine,* Vol. 347, No. 2, July 11, 2002, https://www.nejm.org/doi/pdf/10.1056/NEJMoa013259.

101. Fabrizio Benedetti, Giuliano Maggi, and Leonardo Lopiano, "Open Versus Hidden Medical Treatments: The Patient's Knowledge About a Therapy Affects the Therapy Outcome," *Prevention & Treatment,* Vol. 6, Article 1, June 23, 2003, https://uploads-ssl.webflow.com/59faaf5b01b9500001e95457/5bc5 52c262d1401ce2060bfe_Benedetti%20et%20al.pdf.

102. Franklin G. Miller, PhD, Luana Colloca, MD, PhD, and Ted J. Kaptchuk, "The placebo effect: illness and interpersonal healing," *Perspectives in Biology and Medicine,* 2009;52(4):518-539. https://www.ncbi.nlm.nih.gov/pmc/articles/PMC2814126/#R22.

103. Ted J. Kaptchuk, et al., "Placebos without Deception: A Randomized Controlled Trial in Irritable Bowel Syndrome," *PLOS ONE*, Dec. 22, 2010, https://journals.plos.org/plosone/article?id=10.1371/journal.pone.0015591.

104. Claudia Carvalho, et al., "Open-label placebo treatment in chronic low back pain: a randomized controlled trial," *Pain.* 2016;157(12):2766-2772. https://www.ncbi.nlm.nih.gov/pmc/articles/pmid/27755279/.

105. Sriram Yennurajalingam, et al., "Open-Label Placebo for the Treatment of Cancer-Related Fatigue in Patients with Advanced Cancer: A Randomized Controlled Trial," *The Oncologist*, Vol. 27, Issue 12, December 2022, Pages 1081–1089. https://doi.org/10.1093/oncolo/oyac184.

106. Herbert Benson, MD, and Richard Friedman, PhD, "Harnessing the power of the placebo effect and renaming it 'remembered wellness,'" *Annual Review of Medicine 1996*, 47:193–99, https://sci-hub.ru/10.1146/annurev.med.47.1.193.

107. Benson, MD, and Friedman, PhD, "Harnessing the power of the placebo effect and renaming it 'remembered wellness.'"

108. Jack Kruse, "Have a cold you want to get rid of? Biohack a cold," Reversing Disease for Optimal Health, July 24, 2015, https://forum.jackkruse.com/threads/have-a-cold-you-want-to-get-rid-of-bio-hack-a-cold.16603/.

109. Kruse, "Have a cold you want to get rid of? Biohack a cold."

110. R.I. Horwitz, et al., "Treatment adherence and risk of death after a myocardial infarction," *The Lancet,* 1990 Sep 1;336(8714):542-5, https://pubmed.ncbi.nlm.nih.gov/1975045/.

111. Scot H. Simpson, et al., "A meta-analysis of the association between adherence to drug therapy and mortality," *BMJ*, 2006;333:15, https://doi.org/10.1136/bmj.38875.675486.55.

112. Andrew L. Avins, MD, MPH, et al., "Placebo Adherence and Its Association with Morbidity and Mortality in the Studies of Left Ventricular Dysfunction," *Journal of General Internal Medicine*, 2010;25(12):1275-1281, https://www.ncbi.nlm.nih.gov/pmc/articles/PMC2988150/.

113. Alice Pressman, et al., "Adherence to placebo and mortality in the Beta Blocker Evaluation of Survival Trial (BEST)," *Contemporary Clinical Trials*, Vol. 33, Issue 3, May 2012, Pages 492-498. https://doi.org/10.1016/j.cct.2011.12.003.

114. Miller, PhD, Colloca, MD, PhD, and Kaptchuk, "The placebo effect: illness and interpersonal healing."

115. Robert Ader, PhD, and Nicholas Cohen, PhD, "Behaviorally Conditioned Immunosuppression," *Psychosomatic Medicine* Vol. 37, No. 4 (July-August 1975), https://liberationchiropractic.com/wp-content/uploads/research/1975Ader-Immunosuppression.pdf.

116. Bill Moyers, "Conditioned Responses, Interview with Robert Ader," *Healing and the Mind*, (New York: Broadway Books 1995), 241, https://books.google.com/books?id=G4wHYbyZQF8C&pg=PA241&dq=%E2%80%9CHere+we+had+a+conditioning+effect+that+had+a+major+biologic+impact+on+the+survival+of+the+animal.+That+suggests+that+the+placebo+effect+is+a+learned+response+available+to+anybody+under+the+appropriate+circumstances.%E2%80%9D&hl=en&newbks=1&newbks_redir=1&sa=X&ved=2ahUKEwin7N_F4IH-AhWDMlkFHR0pCagQ6AF-6BAgHEAI.

117. Marion U. Goebel, et al., "Behavioral conditioning of immunosuppression is possible in humans," FASEB J. 2002 Dec;16(14):1869-73, https://pubmed.ncbi.nlm.nih.gov/12468450/.

118. "Bob Ader on Placebos & Psychosomatic Disease," *Health and Stress, The Newsletter of the American Institute of Stress*, Number 8, August 2010, 6, https://stress.org/wp-content/uploads/2011/11/Aug10-NL.pdf.

119. Walter F. M. Chang, MD, FACS, "Complete spontaneous regression of cancer: Four case reports, review of literature, and discussion of possible mechanisms involved," *Hawai'i Medical Journal*, Vol. 59, October 2000, https://evols.library.manoa.hawaii.edu/server/api/core/bitstreams/7e61ed0c-73de-4b1e-8e36-f231cdd60416/content.

120. Skyler B. Johnson, et al., "Use of Alternative Medicine for Cancer and Its Impact on Survival," *JNCI: Journal of the National Cancer Institute*, Volume 110, Issue 1, January 2018, Pages 121–124, https://doi.org/10.1093/jnci/djx145.

121. Tim Minchin, "Storm by Tim Minchin," *YouTube* video, 9:49, accessed May 31, 2023, https://youtu.be/jIWj3tI-DXg.

122. Tallis, MD, *Hippocratic Oath: Medicine and Its Discontents*.

123. David Rutstein, MD, email message to author, Dec. 8, 2022.

Chapter Eight –
How Much Healthcare Is Enough?

124. Staff, "Froedtert CEO Cathy Jacobson: We need to make the health system work for our patients — not the other way around," *Becker's Hospital Review*, July 17, 2018, https://www.beckershospitalreview.com/

hospital-management-administration/froedtert-ceo-cathy-jacobson-not-every-patient-needs-a-primary-care-physician.html.

125. Alexandra Robbins, "The Problem With Satisfied Patients," *The Atlantic,* Apr. 17, 2015, https://www.theatlantic.com/health/archive/2015/04/the-problem-with-satisfied-patients/390684/.

126. Joshua J. Fenton, MD, et al., "The Cost of Satisfaction: A National Study of Patient Satisfaction, Health Care Utilization, Expenditures, and Mortality," *Arch Intern Med.* 2012;172(5):405-411, https://jamanetwork.com/journals/jamainternalmedicine/fullarticle/1108766.

127. "A hospital patient was 'disturbed' by the sound of her 79-year-old roommate's ventilator. So she allegedly shut it off – twice," CBS NEWS, Dec. 2, 2022, https://www.cbsnews.com/news/hospital-patient-arrested-shutting-off-roommates-ventilator-germany/.

128. Molly Gamble, "Room Service with MRIs, IV drips and bloodwork: Luxury hotels go all in on 'wellness,'" *Becker's Hospital Review,* June 27, 2022, https://www.beckershospitalreview.com/strategy/room-service-with-mris-iv-drips-and-bloodwork-luxury-hotels-go-all-in-on-wellness.html.

129. "Americans Spent $30.2 Billion Out-Of-Pocket On Complementary Health Approaches," National Center for Complementary and Integrative Health, June 22, 2016, https://www.nccih.nih.gov/news/press-releases/americans-spent-302-billion-outofpocket-on-complementary-health-approaches.

130. "Americans Spent $30.2 Billion Out-Of-Pocket On Complementary Health Approaches."

131. Dina Halegoua-DeMarzio, MD, et al., "Liver Injury Associated with Turmeric—A Growing Problem: Ten Cases from the Drug-Induced Liver Injury Network [DILIN]," *The American Journal of Medicine*, Vol. 136, Issue 2, P200-206, Oct. 13, 2022, https://doi.org/10.1016/j.amjmed.2022.09.026.

132. Harvard Medical School, "Don't buy into brain health supplements," *Harvard Health Publishing,* Mar. 3, 2022, https://www.health.harvard.edu/mind-and-mood/dont-buy-into-brain-health-supplements.

133. Susan Perry, "Is taxpayer money well spent or wasted on alternative-medicine research?" *MinnPost,* May 3, 2012, https://www.minnpost.com/second-opinion/2012/05/taxpayer-money-well-spent-or-wasted-alternative-medicine-research/.

134. Perry, "Is taxpayer money well spent or wasted on alternative-medicine research?".

135. Erin Brodwin, "The $37 billion supplement industry is barely regulated — and it's allowing dangerous products to slip through the

cracks," *Business Insider*, Nov 8, 2017, https://www.businessinsider.com/supplements-vitamins-bad-or-good-health-2017-8.

136.   Memo Diriker, DBA, MBA, "Up to $935B wasted in health care spending annually," Healio, Oct. 7, 2019, https://www.healio.com/primary-care/practice-management/news/online/%7Bfffdab25-8006-46a9-92d0-5afdae61c2d7%7D/up-to-935b-wasted-in-health-care-spending-annually?utm_source=selligent&utm_medium=email&utm_campaign=primary%20care%20news&m_bt=2313726388190.

137.   David U. Himmelstein, MD, et al., "Health Care Administrative Costs in the United States and Canada, 2017," *Annals of Internal Medicine*, Jan. 21, 2020, https://annals.org/aim/article-abstract/2758511/health-care-administrative-costs-united-states-canada-2017.

138.   John E. Wennberg, MD, MPH, and Alan Gittelsohn, MPH, PhD, "Small Area Variations in Health Care Delivery," *Science*, 14 Dec. 1973, Vol. 182, pp. 1102-1108, https://digitalcommons.dartmouth.edu/cgi/viewcontent.cgi?article=3596&context=facoa.

139.   John E. Wennberg, MD, *Tracking Medicine: A Researcher's Quest to Understand Health Care* (New York: Oxford University Press, 2010), 121.

140.   Wennberg, MD, *Tracking Medicine: A Researcher's Quest to Understand Health Care.*

141.   Francesca Prestinaci, Patrizio Pezzotti, and Annalisa Pantosti, "Antimicrobial resistance: a global multifaceted phenomenon," National Library of Medicine, Pathog Glob Health. October, 2015; 109(7): 309–318., https://www.ncbi.nlm.nih.gov/pmc/articles/PMC4768623/.

142.   Brian J. Zink, MD. *Anyone, Anything, Anytime: A History of Emergency Medicine* (Maryland Heights, Missouri: Mosby Elsevier, 2006).

143.   Zink, MD, *Anyone, Anything, Anytime: A History of Emergency Medicine.*

144.   Zink, MD, *Anyone, Anything, Anytime: A History of Emergency Medicine.*

145.   Zink, MD, *Anyone, Anything, Anytime: A History of Emergency Medicine.*

146.   Jacqueline LaPointe, "1% of People Account for 22% of Total Healthcare Spending," Revcycle Intelligence, Feb. 26, 2020, https://www.revcycleintelligence.com/news/1-of-people-account-for-22-of-total-healthcare-spending.

147.   Carol Ann Campbell, "New Jersey Program Finds Alternatives for ER 'Super Users,'" KHN.org, Mar. 9, 2009, https://khn.org/news/er-super-users/.

148.   Ilene MacDonald, "How hospitals can control Medicaid 'super-users,'" *Fierce Healthcare,* July 26, 2013, https://www.fiercehealthcare.com/healthcare/how-hospitals-can-control-medicaid-super-users.

149. Alison Rodriguez, "Nearly Half of All Medical Care in the US Is in Emergency Departments," *American Journal of Managed Care*, Oct. 24, 2017, https://www.ajmc.com/newsroom/nearly-half-of-all-medical-care-in-the-us-is-in-emergency-departments?sfns=mo.

150. Amy Faith Ho, MD, MPH, FACEP, "Pros and Cons: Waiting Room Medicine," ACEP Now, Apr. 2, 2023, https://www.acepnow.com/article/pros-and-cons-waiting-room-medicine/.

151. Christine Wiebe, MA, "Abraham Verghese: 'Revolution' Starts at Bedside," Medscape Emergency Medicine, Oct. 24, 2017, https://www.medscape.com/viewartiving the acle/887249.

152. TEDTalks, "Abraham Verghese: A doctor's touch," *YouTube* video, 18:32, 2011, https://www.youtube.com/watch?v=sxnlvwprf_c&t=205s.

153. Brett Kelman and Blake Farmer, "Doctors are disappearing from emergency rooms as hospitals look to cut costs," *Salon,* Apr. 10, 2023, https://www.salon.com/2023/04/10/doctors-are-disappearing-from-rooms-as-hospitals-look-to-cut-costs_partner/.

154. Healthline, Contributor, "Hospital CEO Pay Rises While Americans Drown in Medical Debt," *Huffpost,* Aug. 30, 2017, https://www.huffpost.com/entry/hospital-ceo-pay-rises-wh_b_11767768.

155. Joe Cantlupe, "Expert Forum: The rise (and rise) of the healthcare administrator," AthenaHealth, Nov. 7, 2017, https://www.athenahealth.com/knowledge-hub/practice-management/expert-forum-rise-and-rise-healthcare-administrator.

156. Elizabeth Rosenthal, MD, "Medicine's Top Earners Are Not the M.D.s," *The New York Times*, May 17, 2014, https://www.nytimes.com/2014/05/18/sunday-review/doctors-salaries-are-not-the-big-cost.html.

157. Terry Gross, "How U.S. Health Care Became Big Business," NPR.org, Apr. 10, 2017, https://www.npr.org/sections/health-shots/2017/04/10/523005353/how-u-s-health-care-became-big-business.

158. Bob Herman, "Aetna CEO could make $500 million from CVS merger," *Axios,* Dec 5, 2017, https://www.axios.com/2017/12/16/aetna-ceo-could-make-500-million-from-cvs-merger-1513388416.

159. Ahmed Shakeel, MD, "Why Doctors Make The Best Healthcare CEOs," *Forbes.com*, July 27, 2022, https://www.forbes.com/sites/forbesbusinesscouncil/2022/07/27/why-doctors-make-the-best-healthcare-ceos/?sh=2d5295b03b6b#:~:text=Doctors%20are%20uniquely%20positioned%20to%20achieve%20that%20goal.,an%20institution%20that%20puts%20patients%20above%20all%20else.

Chapter Nine – Slow Versus More Medicine

160.   Yung Lie, "Slow Medicine, an international appeal on mindful healthcare," Slow Medicine, Setembro 1, 2022. https://www.slowmedicine.com.br/slow-medicine-an-international-appeal-on-mindful-healthcare/ .

161.   Peter A Ubel, MD, *Critical Decisions: How You And Your Doctor Can Make The Right Medical Choices For You* (San Francisco: HarperOne, 2012).

162.   Bernard Lown, MD, *The Lost Art of Healing: Practicing Compassion in Medicine* (Boston: Houghton Mifflin, 1996).

163.   H. Gilbert Welch, *Less Medicine More Health* (Boston: Beacon Press, 2016).

164.   "Prescription Painkiller Overdoses in the US."

165.   Duff-Brown, "Overprescribing of opioids is not limited to a few bad apples."

166.   Don Winslow, "The Chapo Trap," *VanityFair.com*, March 2019, 81, https://archive.vanityfair.com/article/2019/03/01/the-chapo-trap.

167.   Anthony Mazzarelli and Stephen Trzeciak, *Compassionomics: The Revolutionary Scientific Evidence That Caring Makes a Difference* (Pensacola: Studer Group, 2019).

168.   Mazzarelli and Trzeciak, *Compassionomics: The Revolutionary Scientific Evidence That Caring Makes a Difference.*

169.   Lawrence D. Egbert, MD, et al., "Reduction of Postoperative Pain by Encouragement and Instruction of Patients — A Study of Doctor-Patient Rapport," *The New England Journal of Medicine*, N Engl J Med 1964; 270:825-827, Apr. 16, 1964, https://www.nejm.org/doi/full/10.1056/NEJM196404162701606.

170.   Issidoros Sarinopoulos, et al., "Patient-centered interviewing is associated with decreased responses to painful stimuli: An initial fMRI study," *Patient Education and Counseling*, Vol. 90, Issue 2, February 2013, 220-225, https://www.researchgate.net/publication/233767499_Patient-centered_interviewing_is_associated_with_decreased_responses_to_painful_stimuli_An_initial_fMRI_study.

171.   Jorge Fuentes, et al., "Enhanced therapeutic alliance modulates pain intensity and muscle pain sensitivity in patients with chronic low back pain: an experimental controlled study," *Physical Therapy*, May 2014; 94:477-489, https://www.researchgate.net/publication/279019566_Enhanced_therapeutic_alliance_modulates_pain_intensity_and_muscle_pain_sensitivity_in_patients_with_chronic_low_back_pain_an_experimental_controlled_study_vol_94_pg_477_2013.

172. Linda A Fogarty, et al., "Can 40 Seconds of Compassion Reduce Patient Anxiety?" *Journal of Clinical Oncology*, Vol 17, No 1 (January), 1999, 371-379, https://www.motivationalinterviewing.org/sites/default/files/fogartyjco99.pdf.

173. Jamie M. Stagl, et al., "A randomized controlled trial of cognitive-behavioral stress management in breast cancer: survival and recurrence at 11-year follow-up," National Library of Medicine, 2015 Nov;154(2):319-28, https://pubmed.ncbi.nlm.nih.gov/26518021/.

174. Helen Riess, "Empathy Training for Resident Physicians: A Randomized Controlled Trial of a Neuroscience-Informed Curriculum," J Gen Intern Med 27(10):1280–6, https://www.ncbi.nlm.nih.gov/pmc/articles/PMC3445669/pdf/11606_2012_Article_2063.pdf.

175. John M. Darley and C. Daniel Batson, "'From Jerusalem To Jericho': A Study Of Situational And Dispositional Variables In Helping Behavior," *Journal of Personality and Social Psychology* 1973, Vol. 27, No. 1, 100-108, http://nwkpsych.rutgers.edu/~kharber/selectedtopicsinsocialpsychology/READINGS/Darley%20&%20Batson.1973.%20From%20Jerusalem%20to%20Jericho.pdf.

176. Douglas Farrago, MD, "Time as a Quality Metric," Authentic Medicine, Aug. 12, 2015, https://authenticmedicine.com/2015/08/time-as-a-quality-metric/.

Chapter Ten – It's a Love-Hate Thing

177. Justin Porter, et al., "Revisiting the Time Needed to Provide Adult Primary Care," *J Gen Intern Med* 38, 147–155 (2023), https://link.springer.com/article/10.1007/s11606-022-07707-x.

178. Christine Sinsky, et al., "Allocation of Physician Time in Ambulatory Practice: A Time and Motion Study in 4 Specialties," *Annals of Internal Medicine,* 165(11) September 2016, https://www.researchgate.net/publication/307871565_Allocation_of_Physician_Time_in_Ambulatory_Practice_A_Time_and_Motion_Study_in_4_Specialties.

179. Tait D. Shanafelt, MD, et al., "Burnout and Medical Errors Among American Surgeons," *Annals of Surgery*, Vol. 251, Number 6, June 2010, https://medschool.ucsd.edu/som/hear/resources/Documents/Burnout and medical errors among American Surgeons 2010.pdf.

180. Jennifer L. Lycette, MD, "AITA for Pointing Out to the Insurance Company That I'm the Expert on My Patient? (A parody, except happening everywhere.)," Medscape Emergency Medicine, July 13, 2022, https://www.medscape.com/viewarticle/976690.

181.   Paul E. Sax, MD, "HIV and ID Observations: How to Induce Rage in a Doctor," *NEJM Journal Watch*, Mar. 17, 2020, https://blogs.jwatch.org/hiv-id-observations/index.php/how-to-induce-rage-in-a-doctor/2022/03/07/.

182.   Dr. Glaucomflecken, "Prior Authorizations," *YouTube* video, 0:59, accessed May 31, 2023, https://youtu.be/FVAFfd3oCgA.

183.   Dr. Glaucomflecken, "The Future of Medicine," *YouTube* video, 2:28, accessed May 31, 2023, https://youtu.be/6JMf-U75fTg.

184.   Sarah Jane Tribble, "Buy and Bust: When Private Equity Comes for Rural Hospitals," KHN, June 15, 2022, https://khn.org/news/article/private-equity-rural-hospitals-closure-missouri-noble-health/.

185.   Gretchen Morgenson and Emmanuelle Saliba, "Private equity firms now control many hospitals, ERs and nursing homes. Is it good for health care?" NBC News, May 13, 2020, https://www.nbcnews.com/news/amp/ncna1203161.

186.   "The Deadly Combination of Private Equity and Nursing Homes During A Pandemic: New Jersey Case Study of Coronavirus at Private Equity Nursing Homes." *Americans for Financial Reform Education Fund*, August 2020. https://ourfinancialsecurity.org/wp-content/uploads/2020/08/AFREF-NJ-Private-Equity-Nursing-Homes-Covid.pdf.

187.   Markian Hawryluk, "Death Is Anything but a Dying Business as Private Equity Cashes In," KFF Health News, Sept. 22, 2022, https://khn.org/news/article/funeral-homes-private-equity-death-care/.

188.   Bernard J. Wolfson, "ER Doctors Call Private Equity Staffing Practices Illegal and Seek to Ban Them," KHN, Dec. 22, 2022, https://khn.org/news/article/er-doctors-call-private-equity-staffing-practices-illegal-and-seek-to-ban-them/.

189.   Robert Pearl, MD, "Physician Burnout is up, Gender inequality is making it worse," LinkedIn, Apr. 26, 2022, https://www.linkedin.com/pulse/physician-burnout-up-gender-inequality-making-worse-pearl-m-d-/.

190.   Staff News Writer, "Medical specialties with the highest burnout rates," AMA, Jan 15, 2016, https://www.ama-assn.org/practice-management/physician-health/medical-specialties-highest-burnout-rates.

191.   Christina Maslach and Susan E. Jackson, "The Measurement of Experienced Burnout," *Journal of Occupational Behavior*, 2(2):99 – 113, April 1981, https://onlinelibrary.wiley.com/doi/epdf/10.1002/job.4030020205.

192.   Zbigniew Sablik, et al., "Universality of physicians' burnout syndrome as a result of experiencing difficulty in relationship with patients," *Archives of Medical Science*, https://www.ncbi.nlm.nih.gov/pmc/articles/PMC3701961/#.

193.   Ashley Turner, "Stress and rigorous work schedules push a doctor to commit suicide every day in the US: 'We need them, but they need us,'" CNBC,

May 21, 2019, https://www.cnbc.com/2019/05/21/stress-and-rigorous-work-push-a-doctor-to-commit-suicide-every-day-in-us.html.

194.   "Top 11 Professions with Highest Suicide Rates," Mental Health Daily, Jan. 6, 2015, https://mentalhealthdaily.com/2015/01/06/top-11-professions -with-highest-suicide-rates/.

195.   William Styron, *Darkness Visible: A Memoir of Madness* (New York: Random House, 1990).

196.   Franz Kafka, *The Metamorphosis* (Leipzig: Kurt Wolff, 1915).

197.   Brandon Glenn, "9 out of 10 doctors wouldn't recommend a career in health-care," MedCityNews, Mar. 1, 2012, https://medcitynews.com/2012/03/9-out-of-10-doctors-wouldnt-recommend-a-career-in-healthcare/.

198.   Jane Spencer and Christina Jewett, "12 Months of Trauma: More Than 3,600 US Health Workers Died in Covid's First Year," KFF Health News Lost on the Frontline, Apr. 8, 2021, https://khn.org/news/article/ us-health-workers-deaths-covid-lost-on-the-frontline/.

199.   Simon G. Talbot, MD and Wendy Dean, MD, "Physicians aren't 'burning out.' They're suffering from moral injury." *STAT*, July 26, 2018, https:// www.statnews.com/2018/07/26/physicians-not-burning-out-they-are-suffering-moral-injury/.

200.   Talbot, MD, and Dean, MD, "Physicians aren't 'burning out.' They're suffering from moral injury."

201.   Eyal Press, "The Moral Crisis of America's Doctors," *The New York Times Magazine*, June 15, 2023, https://www.nytimes.com/2023/06/15/magazine/ doctors-moral-crises.html.

202.   Tae Kim, "Goldman Sachs asks in biotech research report: 'Is curing patients a sustainable business model?'" CNBC, Apr. 11 2018, https://www.cnbc. com/2018/04/11/goldman-asks-is-curing-patients-a-sustainable-business-model.html.

203.   Global Citizen, "Could you patent the sun?" *YouTube* video, 1:03, accessed Apr. 25, 2023, https://video.search.yahoo.com/yhs/search?fr=yhs-ima-remarklist&ei=UTF-8&hsimp=yhs-remarklist&hspart=ima&p=patent+the+s un&type=q3020_D3NNQ_asc_bsfq#id=2&vid=fab0f8312e50ee3d6cf668aa a7b8188a&action=click.

204.   Tanita Sandhu, "Capitalism with A Conscience," *Forbes.com*, Feb 12, 2013, https://www.forbes.com/sites/85broads/2013/02/12/ capitalism-with-a-conscience/.

Chapter Eleven – The Power of Connection

205.   Julianne Holt-Lunstad, et al., "Loneliness and Social Isolation as Risk Factors for Mortality: A Meta-Analytic Review," *SAGE Journals*, Vol. 10, Issue 2, Mar. 11, 2015, https://doi.org/10.1177/1745691614568352.

206.   Beverly H. Brummett, PhD, "Characteristics of Socially Isolated Patients With Coronary Artery Disease Who Are at Elevated Risk for Mortality," *Psychosomatic Medicine* 63(2):p 267-272, March 2001, https://journals.lww.com/psychosomaticmedicine/Abstract/2001/03000/Characteristics_of_Socially_Isolated_Patients_With.10.aspx.

207.   John T. Cacioppo and Stephanie Cacioppo. "The growing problem of loneliness." *Lancet*. 2018 February 03; 391(10119): 426, https://www.ncbi.nlm.nih.gov/pmc/articles/PMC6530780/pdf/nihms-1020513.pdf.

208.   Julianne Holt-Lunstad, et al., "Social Relationships and Mortality Risk: A Meta-analytic Review," *PLOS Medicine*, Vol. 7, Issue 7, July 2010, https://www.academia.edu/6273543/Social_Relationships_and_Mortality_Risk_A_metaanalytic_Review#:~:text=Social%20Relationships%20and%20Mortality%20Risk%3A%20A%20Metaanalytic%20Review.,supportive%20social%20network%20and%20thus%20not%20adequately%20relationships.

209.   Amy K. McLennan and Stanley J Ulijaszek, "Beware the medicalisation of loneliness," *The Lancet*, Vol. 391, Issue 10129, P1480, Apr. 14, 2018, https://doi.org/10.1016/S0140-6736(18)30577-4.

210.   Stuart M. Butler, "Social spending, not medical spending, is key to health," BROOKINGS, July 13, 2016, https://www.brookings.edu/opinions/social-spending-not-medical-spending-is-key-to-health/#:~:text=The%20major%20%28OECD%29%20countries%20on%20average%20spend%20about,with%20social%20service%20spending%20than%20with%20health%20spending.

211.   Statista Research Department, "Feeling of loneliness among adults 2021, by country." Statista, Nov. 29, 2022, https://www.statista.com/statistics/1222815/loneliness-among-adults-by-country/.

212.   Lisa F. Berkman and S. Leonard Syme, "Social Networks, Host Resistance, And Mortality: A Nine-Year Follow-Up Study Of Alameda County Residents," *American Journal of Epidemiology*, Vol. 109, Issue 2, February 1979, 186-204, https://doi.org/10.1093/oxfordjournals.aje.a112674.

213.   Bert N. Uchino, "Social Support and Health: A Review of Physiological Processes Potentially Underlying Links to Disease Outcomes," *Journal of Behavioral Medicine*, 29(4):377-87, September 2006, https://www.

researchgate.net/profile/Bert-Uchino/publication/7025419_Social_Support_ and_Health_A_Review_of_Physiological_Processes_Potentially_Underlying_Links_to_Disease_Outcomes/links/0912f5092dca28047b000000/ Social-Support-and-Health-A-Review-of-Physiological-Processes-Potentially-Underlying-Links-to-Disease-Outcomes.pdf.

214. Tristen K. Inagaki, PhD, "The neurobiology of giving versus receiving support: The role of stress-related and social reward-related neural activity," *Psychosom Med,* 2016 May; 78(4): 443–453, https://www.ncbi.nlm.nih.gov/ pmc/articles/PMC4851591/pdf/nihms744752.pdf.

215. Robert M. Nerem, et al., "Social Environment as a Factor in Diet-Induced Atherosclerosis," *Science,* 27 June 1980, Vol. 208, Issue 4451, 1475-1476, https://www.science.org/doi/10.1126/science.7384790.

216. J. P. Henry, et al., "The Role of Psychosocial Stimulation in the Pathogenesis of Hypertension," *Achtzigster Kongress,* (1974). Vol 80, 107–111, https:// link.springer.com/chapter/10.1007/978-3-642-85449-1_17.

217. "Harlow's Classic Studies Revealed the Importance of Maternal Contact," *Psychological Science,* June 20, 2018, https://www.psychologicalscience.org/ publications/observer/obsonline/harlows-classic-studies-revealed-the-importance-of-maternal-contact.html?pdf=true.

218. Vincent J. Felitti, MD, FACP, et al. "Relationship of Childhood Abuse and Household Dysfunction to Many of the Leading Causes of Death in Adults: The Adverse Childhood Experiences (ACE) Study." *Am J Prev Med* 1998;14(4), https://www.ajpmonline.org/action/showPdf?pii=S0749-3797%2898%2900017-8.

219. Vincent J. Felitti, MD, "The Relationship of Adverse Childhood Experiences to Adult Health: Turning gold into lead," *Z Psychsom Med Psychother,* 2002; 48(4): 359-369, http://www.theannainstitute.org/Gold_into_Lead-_Germany1-02_c_Graphs.pdf#:~:text=The%20ACE%20Study%20reveals%20 a%20powerful%20relationship%20between,over%E2%80%99%20 some%20things%2C%20not%20even%20fifty%20years%20later3.

220. David W. Brown, et al., "Adverse childhood experiences are associated with the risk of lung cancer: a prospective cohort study," *BMC Public Health,* 2010; 10: 311, https://www.ncbi.nlm.nih.gov/pmc/articles/PMC2826284/.

221. David W. Brown, DSc, MScPH, MSc, et al., "Adverse Childhood Experiences and the Risk of Premature Mortality," *AJPM Online,* Vol. 37, Issue 5, P389-396, November 2009, https://doi.org/10.1016/j.amepre.2009.06.021.

222. Mazzarelli and Trzeciak, *Compassionomics: The Revolutionary Scientific Evidence That Caring Makes a Difference.*

223. Mazzarelli and Trzeciak, *Compassionomics: The Revolutionary Scientific Evidence That Caring Makes a Difference*.

224. Barbara Starfield, Leiyu Shi, and James Macinko, "Contribution of Primary Care to Health Systems and Health," *The Milbank Quarterly*, Vol. 83, No. 3, 2005, 457-502, https://www.ncbi.nlm.nih.gov/pmc/articles/PMC2690145/pdf/milq0083-0457.pdf.

225. P. Franks and K. Fiscella, "Primary care physicians and specialists as personal physicians. Health care expenditures and mortality experience,"1998 Aug;47(2):105-9, https://pubmed.ncbi.nlm.nih.gov/9722797/.

226. Sven Engström, et al., "Is general practice effective? A systematic literature review," *Scandinavian Journal of Primary Health Care*, 19:2, 131-144, https://www.tandfonline.com/doi/pdf/10.1080/028134301750235394.

227. Atul Gawande, "Overkill: An avalanche of unnecessary medical care is harming patients physically and financially. What can we do about it?" *The New Yorker*, May 4, 2015, https://www.newyorker.com/magazine/2015/05/11/overkill-atul-gawande.

228. Robert L. Phillips, Jr, MD, MSPH, et al., "Case Study of a Primary Care-Based Accountable Care System Approach to Medical Home Transformation," *Journal of Ambulatory Care Management*, Vol. 34, No. 1, 67-77 (2011), https://www.aafp.org/dam/AAFP/documents/patient_care/nrn/1phillipsjacm2010.pdf.

229. Justin Altschuler, et al., "Estimating a Reasonable Patient Panel Size for Primary Care Physicians With Team-Based Task Delegation," *Annals of Family Medicine*, September 2012, 10 (5) 396-400, https://doi.org/10.1370/afm.1400.

230. "AAMC Report Reinforces Mounting Physician Shortage," AAMC.org, June 11, 2021, https://aamc-black.global.ssl.fastly.net/production/media/filer_public/85/d7/85d7b689-f417-4ef0-97fb-ecc129836829/aamc_2018_workforce_projections_update_april_11_2018.pdf.

231. Caroline K. Kramer, MD, PhD, Sadia Mehmood, BSc, and Renée S. Suen, "Dog Ownership and Survival: A Systematic Review and Meta-Analysis," *Circulation: Cardiovascular Quality and Outcomes*, Vol. 12, Issue 10 (October 2019), https://www.ahajournals.org/doi/epub/10.1161/CIRCOUTCOMES.119.005554.

232. Richard Doll, MD, MRCP, and A. Bradford Hill, PhD, DSc, "Smoking and Carcinoma of the Lung: Preliminary Report," *British Medical Journal*, Sept. 30, 1950, https://www.ncbi.nlm.nih.gov/pmc/articles/PMC2038856/pdf/brmedj03566-0003.pdf.

233. Phil Gaetano, "The British Doctors' Study (1951–2001)," *The Embryo Project Encyclopedia*, 2018-01-30, https://embryo.asu.edu/pages/british-doctors-study-1951-2001.

234.   Carl J. Charnetski, Sandra Riggers, and Francis X. Brennan, "Effect of petting a dog on immune system function," *Psychol Rep.* 2004 Dec;95(3 Pt 2):1087-91, https://pubmed.ncbi.nlm.nih.gov/15762389/.

235.   Ellen Langer and Judith Rodin, "The effects of choice and enhanced personal responsibility for the aged: A field experiment in an institutional setting," *Journal of Personality and Social Psychology*, 34(2):191-8, September 1976, https://www.researchgate.net/publication/22144050_The_effects_of_choice_and_enhanced_personal_responsibility_for_the_aged_A_field_experiment_in_an_institutional_setting.

236.   Min-sun Lee, et al., "Interaction with indoor plants may reduce psychological and physiological stress by suppressing autonomic nervous system activity in young adults: a randomized crossover study," *Journal of Physiological Anthropology*, (2015) 34:21, https://www.ncbi.nlm.nih.gov/pmc/articles/PMC4419447/pdf/40101_2015_Article_60.pdf.

237.   Claudia Collins and Angela O'Callaghan, "The Impact of Horticultural Responsibility on Health Indicators and Quality of Life in Assisted Living," *Hort Technology*, 18(4), October 2008, https://www.researchgate.net/publication/279492779_The_Impact_of_Horticultural_Responsibility_on_Health_Indicators_and_Quality_of_Life_in_Assisted_Living.

238.   Collins and O'Callaghan, "The Impact of Horticultural Responsibility on Health Indicators and Quality of Life in Assisted Living."

239.   Doug Oman, MD, et al., "Volunteerism and Mortality among the Community-dwelling Elderly," *Journal of Health Psychology*, Vol. 4, Issue 3, 1999, 310, https://journals.sagepub.com/doi/10.1177/135910539900400301.

240.   Carolyn Schwartz, ScD., et al., "Altruistic Social Interest Behaviors Are Associated With Better Mental Health," *Psychosomatic Medicine*, 65(5):778-785 (2003), 782-783, https://citeseerx.ist.psu.edu/document?repid=rep1&type=pdf&doi=f65b997f27ee341890221551be3adc81570da27a.

241.   Press, "The Moral Crisis of America's Doctors."

242.   Stephanie L. Brown, et al. "Providing Social Support May Be More Beneficial Than Receiving It: Results from a Prospective Study of Mortality," *Psychological Science*, 14(4):320-7, August 2003, 324-326, https://www.researchgate.net/publication/10708396_Providing_Social_Support_May_Be_More_Beneficial_Than_Receiving_It_Results_From_a_Prospective_Study_of_Mortality.

243.   Arjen de Wit, et al., "The health advantage of volunteering is larger for older and less healthy volunteers in Europe: a mega-analysis," *European Journal of Ageing*, Vol. 19,4 1189-1200, 30 Mar. 2022, 1197-1198, http://www.ncbi.nlm.nih.gov/pmc/articles/pmc9729491/.

Chapter Twelve – Out of This World

244.   Paula Span, "A Quiet End to the 'Death Panels' Debate," *The New York Times*, Nov. 20, 2015, https://www.nytimes.com/2015/11/24/health/end-of-death-panels-myth-brings-new-end-of-life-challenges.html.

245.   Karen Wyatt, MD, "Blog: What Doctors Need to learn About Death and Dying," End of Life University, Apr. 18, 2023, https://eolupodcast.com/2023/04/18/blog-what-doctors-need-to-learn-about-death-and-dying/.

246.   "Soul Has Weight, Physician Thinks," *The New York Times*, Mar. 11, 1907, https://timesmachine.nytimes.com/timesmachine/1907/03/11/106743221.html?pageNumber=5.

247.   "21 grams experiment," *Wikipedia*, accessed May 1, 2023, https://en.wikipedia.org/wiki/21_grams_experiment.

248.   Michael E. McCullough, et al., "Religious involvement and mortality: A meta-analytic review," *Health Psychology*, 19(3):211-22, June 2000, 211, https://www.researchgate.net/publication/12449610_Religious_involvement_and_mortality_A_meta-analytic_review.

249.   McCullough, et al., "Religious involvement and mortality: A meta-analytic review," 219.

250.   Gowri Anandarajah, MD, and Ellen Hight, MD, MPH, "Spirituality and Medical Practice: Using the HOPE Questions as a Practical Tool for Spiritual Assessment," *Am Fam Physician,* 2001;63(1):81-89, 81-84, https://www.aafp.org/pubs/afp/issues/2001/0101/p81.html.

251.   William J. Strawbridge, PhD, et al., "Frequent Attendance at Religious Services and Mortality over 28Years," *American Journal of Public Health*, June 1997, Vol. 87 No. 6, 959, https://ajph.aphapublications.org/doi/pdf/10.2105/AJPH.87.6.957.

252.   Mueller, Paul S., MD, et al., "Religious Involvement, Spirituality, and Medicine: Implications for Clinical Practice," *Mayo Clinic Proceedings,* 2001;76:1225-1235, 1230, 1225, https://www.mayoclinicproceedings.org/action/showPdf?pii=S0025-6196(11)62799-7.

253.   Mueller, MD, et al., "Religious Involvement, Spirituality, and Medicine: Implications for Clinical Practice," 1226-1227.

254.   H. G. Koenig, "MSJAMA: religion, spirituality, and medicine: application to clinical practice," *JAMA*, 2000 Oct 4;284(13):1708, https://pubmed.ncbi.nlm.nih.gov/11015808/.

255.   Alexander Moreira-Almeida, et al., "Religiousness and Mental Health: A Review," *Revista Brasileira de Psiquiatria,* 28(3):242-50, October 2006,

https://www.researchgate.net/publication/6864541_Religiousness_and_Mental_Health_A_Review.

256. Richard P. Sloan, PhD, et al., "Religion, spirituality, and medicine," *The Lancet*, Vol. 353, Issue 9153, P664-667, Feb. 20, 1999, https://www.thelancet.com/journals/lancet/article/PIIS0140-6736(98)07376-0/fulltext.

257. Harold Koenig, et al., "Religion, spirituality, and medicine: A rebuttal to skeptics," *The International Journal of Psychiatry in Medicine,* 29(2):123-31, February 1999, https://www.researchgate.net/publication/12713129_Religion_spirituality_and_medicine_A_rebuttal_to_skeptics.

258. Harold G. Koenig, MD, *Spirituality in Patient Care: Why, How, When, and What* (West Conshohocken: Templeton Press, 2013).

259. Kenneth I. Pargament, PhD, et al., "Religious Struggle as a Predictor of Mortality Among Medically Ill Elderly Patients: A 2-Year Longitudinal Study," *Arch Intern Med.* 2001;161(15):1881-1885, *JAMA Network*, Aug. 13/27, 2001, https://jamanetwork.com/journals/jamainternalmedicine/fullarticle/vol/161/pg/1881.

260. Curt P. Richter, PhD, "On the Phenomenon of Sudden Death in Animals and Man," *Psychosomatic Medicine,* Vol. xix, No. 3, 1957, https://www.aipro.info/wp/wp-content/uploads/2017/08/phenomena_sudden_death.pdf.

261. Jana M. Mossey, MPH, PhD, and Evelyn Shapiro, MA, "Self-Rated Health: A Predictor of Mortality Among the Elderly," *AJPH*, Vol. 72, No. 8, August 1982, https://www.ncbi.nlm.nih.gov/pmc/articles/PMC1650365/pdf/amjph00655-0034.pdf.

262. Eric S. Kim, et al., "Optimism and Cause-Specific Mortality: A Prospective Cohort Study," *Am J Epidemiol*, 2017 Jan. 1; 185(1): 21–29, http://www.ncbi.nlm.nih.gov/pmc/articles/pmc5209589/.

263. Elaine Yuen, PhD., et al., "Spirituality, Religion, and Health," *American Journal of Medical Quality*, Vol. 22, Issue 2, March 2007, 78, https://journals.sagepub.com/doi/abs/10.1177/1062860606298872.

264. "Pierre Teilhard de Chardin," *Wikipedia*, accessed May 31, 2023, https://en.wikipedia.org/wiki/Pierre_Teilhard_de_Chardin.

265. "Pierre Teilhard de Chardin Quotes," Goodreads, https://www.goodreads.com/author/quotes/5387.Pierre_Teilhard_de_Chardin.

266. Andre Comte-Sponville, *The Little Book of Atheist Spirituality* (New York: Penguin Books, 2008), x-xi, 7-8.

267. John S. Hatcher, *The Purpose of Physical Reality* (Wilmette: Bahá'í Publishing Trust, 2005), 3.

268.   Hatcher, *The Purpose of Physical Reality*, 170, 180.

269.   Hatcher, *The Purpose of Physical Reality*, 185.

Coda – An Observation

270.   Bahá'u'lláh, 'Abdu'l-Bahá, Shoghi Effendi, and the Universal House of Justice, "Health, Healing, and Nutrition" in *Compilation of Compilations,* Vol. 1
(Mona Vale: Bahá'í Publications Australia, 1991), 459, https://bahai-library.
com/pdf/compilations/health_healing_nutrition.pdf.

271.   Stephen Jay Gould, *Rocks of Ages: Science and Religion in the Fullness of Life*
(New York: Ballantine Books, 1999).

272.   'Abdu'l-Bahá, *'Abdu'l-Bahá in London* (London: Bahá'í Publishing Trust, 1982), 71, https://bahai-library.com/abdul-baha_abdul-
baha_london#71, QUICK REFERENCE (12.13): https://oceanlibrary.com/
abdul-baha-in-london/.

273.   "Albert Einstein Quotes," *Britannica*, accessed May 31, 2023, https://www.
britannica.com/quotes/Albert-Einstein.

274.   Albert Einstein, "My Credo," from a speech given to the German League of
Human Rights, Berlin, 1932, accessed May 31, 2023, https://einsteinandre-
ligion.com/credo.html.

275.   Michael White and John Gribbin, *Einstein: A life in Science*, (New York: E.
P. Dutton 1994), 262.

276.   'Abdu'l-Bahá, *Selections from the Writings of 'Abdu'l-Bahá* (Wilmette: Bahá'í
Publishing Trust, 1978), 47, https://bahai-library.com/abdul-baha_selec-
tions_writings_abdul-baha, QUICK REFERENCE (21.4): https://oceanlibrary.
com/link/LByPY/selections-from-the-writings-of-abdul-baha.

277.   John E. Esslemont, *Bahá'u'lláh and the New Era*, 110, QUICK REFERENCE
(7.54): https://oceanlibrary.com/link/bsHRg/bahaullah-and-the-
new-era_john-esslemont.

278.   'Abdu'l-Bahá, *Some Answered Questions,* Collected and translated from the
Persian by Laura Clifford Barney, 1908 (Newly Revised by a Committee at
the Bahá'í World Centre, 2014), 296, https://bahai-library.com/abdul-baha_
some_answered_questions,
QUICK REFERENCE (72.6): https://oceanlibrary.com/link/ZDYrA/
some-answered-questions_abdul-baha.

279.   'Abdu'l-Bahá, *The Promulgation of Universal Peace* (Wilmette: Bahá'í Publishing Trust, 1982), 374, https://

bahai-library.com/abdul-baha_promulgation_universal_peace, QUICK REFERENCE (113.12): https://oceanlibrary.com/link/78DcJ/ promulgation-of-universal-peace_abdul-baha.

280.   'Abdu'l-Bahá, *The Promulgation of Universal Peace,* 291, QUICK REFERENCE (97.5): https://oceanlibrary.com/link/U7d83/promulgation-of-universal-peace_abdul-baha.

281.   "Sigmund Freud's views on religion," *Wikipedia*, accessed May 2, 2023, https://en.wikipedia.org/wiki/Sigmund_Freud%27s_views_on_religion .

282.   "Abdulbaha knighting.jpg," Wikimedia Commons, accessed May 31, 2023 https://commons.wikimedia.org/wiki/File:Abdulbaha_knighting.jpg.

283.   "The Knighting of 'Abdu'l-Bahá," Bahá'ís of the United States, https://www.bahai.us/the-knighting-of-abdul-baha/.

284.   Alister McGrath, *The Big Question: Why We Can't Stop Talking About Science, Faith and God* (New York: St. Martin's Press, 2015), 204.

BIBLIOGRAPHY

Printed Resources

Cassell, Eric J., MD. *The Nature of Suffering and the Goals of Medicine*. USA: Oxford University Press, 1991.

Comte-Sponville, Andre. *The Little Book of Atheist Spirituality*. New York: Penguin Books, 2008.

Diamond, Jared. *The World Until Yesterday: What Can We Learn from Traditional Societies?* New York: Viking Press, 2012.

Gould, Stephen Jay. *Rocks of Ages: Science and Religion in the Fullness of Life*. New York: Ballantine Books, 1999.

Hatcher, John S. *The Purpose of Physical Reality*. Wilmette: Bahá'í Publishing Trust, 2005.

Kafka, Franz. *The Metamorphosis*. Leipzig: Kurt Wolff, 1915.

Kahneman, Daniel. *Thinking Fast and Slow*. New York: Farrar, Straus & Giroux, 2011.

Koenig, Harold G., MD, *Spirituality in Patient Care: Why, How, When, and What*. West Conshohocken: Templeton Press, 2013.

Lown, Bernard, MD. *The Lost Art of Healing: Practicing Compassion in Medicine*. Boston: Houghton Mifflin, 1996.

Mazzarelli, Anthony and Stephen Trzeciak. *Compassionomics: The Revolutionary Scientific Evidence That Caring Makes a Difference*. Pensacola: Studer Group, 2019.

McGrath, Alister. *The Big Question: Why We Can't Stop Talking About Science, Faith and God*. New York: St. Martin's Press, 2015.

O'Brian, Patrick. *The Nutmeg of Consolation*. New York: W. W. Norton & Company, 1991.

Shermer, Michael, MD. *Why People Believe Weird Things*. New York: Henry Holt and Company, 1997.

Sontag, Susan. *Illness as Metaphor*. New York: Farrar, Straus & Giroux, 1978. ONLINE COPY: https://monoskop.org/images/4/4a/Susan_Sontag_Illness_As_ Metaphor_1978.pdf.

Styron, William. *Darkness Visible: A Memoir of Madness*. New York: Random House, 1990.

Tallis, Raymond, MD. *Hippocratic Oaths: Medicine and Its Discontents*. London: Atlantic Books, 2004.

Tolstoy, Leo. *Anna Karenina*. New York: Thomas Y. Crowell and Co., 1886.

Ubel, Peter A., MD. *Critical Decisions: How You And Your Doctor Can Make The Right Medical Choices For You*. San Francisco: HarperOne, 2012.

Welch, H. Gilbert. *Less Medicine More Health*. Boston: Beacon Press, 2016.

Wennberg, John E., MD. *Tracking Medicine: A Researcher's Quest to Understand Health Care*. New York: Oxford University Press, 2010.

White, Michael and John Gribbin. *Einstein: A life in Science*. New York: E. P. Dutton, 1994.

Wootton, David. *The Invention of Science: A New History of the Scientific Revolution*. New York: Harper Perennial, 2015.

Zink, Brian J., MD. *Anyone, Anything, Anytime: A History of Emergency Medicine*. Maryland Heights, Missouri, Mosby Elsevier, 2006.

Digital Resources

AAMC.org. "AAMC Report Reinforces Mounting Physician Shortage." June 11, 2021. https://aamc-black.global.ssl.fastly.net/production/media/filer_public/85/ d7/85d7b689-f417-4ef0-97fb-ecc129836829/aamc_2018_workforce_ projections_update_april_11_2018.pdf.

'Abdu'l-Bahá. *Some Answered Questions*. Collected and translated from the Persian by Laura Clifford Barney, 1908. Newly Revised by a Committee at the Baháʼí World Centre, 2014. https://bahai-library.com/abdul-baha_some_answered_ questions. QUICK REFERENCE (72.6): https://oceanlibrary.com/link/ZDYrA/ some-answered-questions_abdul-baha.

'Abdu'l-Bahá. *Selections from the Writings of 'Abdu'l-Bahá*. Wilmette: Baháʼí Publishing Trust, 1978. https://bahai-library.com/abdul-baha_selections_writings_abdul-baha/. QUICK REFERENCE (21.4): https://oceanlibrary.com/link/LByPY/ selections-from-the-writings-of-abdul-baha.

'Abdu'l-Bahá. *'Abdu'l-Bahá in London*. London: Baháʼí Publishing Trust, 1982. QUICK REFERENCE (12.13): https://oceanlibrary.com/abdul-baha-in-london/.

'Abdu'l-Bahá. *The Promulgation of Universal Peace*. Wilmette: Baháʼí Publishing Trust, 1982. https://bahai-library.com/abdul-baha_promulgation_universal_peace. QUICK REFERENCE (113.12): https://oceanlibrary.com/link/78DcJ/promulgation-of-universal-peace_abdul-baha. QUICK REFERENCE (97.5): https://oceanlibrary.com/ link/U7d83/promulgation-of-universal-peace_abdul-baha.

Ader, Robert, PhD, and Nicholas Cohen, PhD. "Behaviorally Conditioned Immunosuppression." *Psychosomatic Medicine* Vol. 37, No. 4 (July-August 1975). https://liberationchiropractic.com/wp-content/uploads/ research/1975Ader-Immunosuppression.pdf.

Agile Minds #26. "Tim Minchin – 9 Life Lessons." *YouTube* video, 12:00. Accessed May 31, 2023. https://youtu.be/FJ__a4qVE_g.

Altschuler, Justin, et al. "Estimating a Reasonable Patient Panel Size for Primary Care Physicians With Team-Based Task Delegation." Annals of Family Medicine, September 2012, 10 (5) 396-400. https://doi.org/10.1370/afm.1400.

Anandarajah, Gowri, MD, and Ellen Hight, MD, MPH. "Spirituality and Medical Practice: Using the HOPE Questions as a Practical Tool for Spiritual Assessment." *Am Fam Physician*, 2001;63(1):81-89. https://www.aafp.org/pubs/ afp/issues/2001/0101/p81.html.

Andrzejewski, Adam. "Top U.S. 'Non-Profit' Hospitals & CEOs Are Racking Up Huge Profits." *Forbes.com*, June 26, 2019. https://www.forbes.com/sites/ adamandrzejewski/2019/06/26/top-u-s-non-profit-hospitals-ceos- are-racking-up-huge-profits/?sh=49581d2719df.

Avins, Andrew L. MD, MPH, et al. "Placebo Adherence and Its Association with Morbidity and Mortality in the Studies of Left Ventricular Dysfunction." *Journal of General Internal Medicine*. 2010;25(12):1275-1281. https://www. ncbi.nlm.nih.gov/pmc/articles/PMC2988150/.

Baháʼís of the United States. "The Knighting of 'Abdu'l-Bahá," https://www.bahai.us/ the-knighting-of-abdul-baha/.

Bahá'u'lláh, 'Abdu'l-Bahá, Shoghi Effendi, and the Universal House of Justice. "Health, Healing, and Nutrition." In *Compilation of Compilations* Vol. 1 (Mona Vale: Bahá'í Publications Australia, 1991). https://bahai-library.com/pdf/compilations/health_healing_nutrition.pdf.

Beach, Mary Catherine, MD, MPH, Jeanne Keruly, MS, CNRP, and Richard D. Moore, MD, MHS. "Is the Quality of the Patient-Provider Relationship Associated with Better Adherence and Health Outcomes for Patients with HIV?" *J GEN INTERN MED (JGIM)*2006; 21:661–665. https://www.ncbi. nlm.nih.gov/pmc/articles/PMC1924639/pdf/jgi0021-0661.pdf.

Beecher, Henry K, MD. "The Powerful Placebo." *JAMA*. 1955;159(17):1602-1606. https://jamanetwork.com/journals/jama/article-abstract/303530.

Benedetti, Fabrizio, Giuliano Maggi, and Leonardo Lopiano. "Open Versus Hidden Medical Treatments: The Patient's Knowledge About a Therapy Affects the Therapy Outcome." *Prevention & Treatment*, Vol. 6, Article 1, June 23, 2003. https://uploads-ssl.webflow.com/59faaf5b01b9500001e95457/5bc552c262d14 01ce2060bfe_Benedetti%20et%20al.pdf.

Benedetti, Fabrizio. "Drugs and placebos: what's the difference?" EMBO Reports (2014)15:329-332. https://www.embopress.org/doi/full/10.1002/embr.201338399.

Benson, Herbert, MD and Richard Friedman, PhD. "Harnessing the power of the placebo effect and renaming it 'remembered wellness.'" *Annual Review of Medicine 1996*, 47:193–99. https://sci-hub.ru/10.1146/annurev.med.47.1.193.

Berkman, Lisa F. and S. Leonard Syme. "Social Networks, Host Resistance, And Mortality: A Nine-Year Follow-Up Study Of Alameda County Residents." *American Journal of Epidemiology*, Vol. 109, Issue 2, February 1979, 186-204. https://doi.org/10.1093/oxfordjournals.aje.a112674.

Blakeslee, Sandra. "Placebos Prove So Powerful Even Experts Are Surprised; New Studies Explore the Brain's Triumph Over Reality." *The New York Times*. Oct. 13, 1998. https://www.nytimes.com/1998/10/13/science/placebos-prove-so-powerful-even-experts-are-surprised-new-studies-explore-brain.html.

Blendon, Robert J., ScD, John M. Benson, MA, and Joachim O. Hero, MPH. "Public Trust in Physicians — U.S. Medicine in International Perspective." *N Engl J Med* 2014; 371:1570-1572. http://www.nejm.org/doi/full/10.1056/NEJMp1407373.

"Bob Ader on Placebos & Psychosomatic Disease." *Health and Stress, The Newsletter of the American Institute of Stress*, Number 8, August 2010. https://stress.org/wp-content/uploads/2011/11/Aug10-NL.pdf.

Brin, Dinah Wisenberg. "Why Don't Patients Follow Their Doctors' Advice?" AAMCNEWS, Jan. 16, 2017. https://www.aamc.org/news-insights/why-don-t-patients-follow-their-doctors-advice.

Britannica. "Albert Einstein Quotes." Accessed May 31, 2023. https://www.britannica.com/quotes/Albert-Einstein.

Brodwin, Erin. "The $37 billion supplement industry is barely regulated — and it's allowing dangerous products to slip through the cracks." *Business Insider,* Nov 8, 2017. https://www.businessinsider.com/supplements-vitamins-bad-or-good-health-2017-8.

Brown, David W., DSc, MScPH, MSc, et al. "Adverse Childhood Experiences and the Risk of Premature Mortality." *AJPM Online,* Vol. 37, Issue 5, P389-396, November 2009. https://doi.org/10.1016/j.amepre.2009.06.021.

Brown, David W., et al. "Adverse childhood experiences are associated with the risk of lung cancer: a prospective cohort study." *BMC Public Health,* 2010; 10: 311. https://www.ncbi.nlm.nih.gov/pmc/articles/PMC2826284/.

Brown, Stephanie L., et al. "Providing Social Support May Be More Beneficial Than Receiving It: Results from a Prospective Study of Mortality." *Psychological Science,* 14(4):320-7, August 2003. https://www.researchgate.net/publication/10708396_Providing_Social_Support_May_Be_More_Beneficial_Than_Receiving_It_Results_From_a_Prospective_Study_of_Mortality.

Brummett, Beverly H., PhD. "Characteristics of Socially Isolated Patients With Coronary Artery Disease Who Are at Elevated Risk for Mortality." *Psychosomatic Medicine* 63(2):p 267-272, March 2001. https://journals.lww.com/psychosomaticmedicine/Abstract/2001/03000/Characteristics_of_Socially_Isolated_Patients_With.10.aspx.

Butler, Stuart M. "Social spending, not medical spending, is key to health." BROOKINGS, July 13, 2016. https://www.brookings.edu/opinions/social-spending-not-medical-spending-is-key-to-health/#:~:text=The%20major%20%28OECD%29%20countries%20on%20average%20spend%20about,with%20social%20service%20spending%20than%20with%20health%20spending.

Cacioppo, John T. and Stephanie Cacioppo. "The growing problem of loneliness." *Lancet.* 2018 February 03; 391(10119): 426. https://www.ncbi.nlm.nih.gov/pmc/articles/PMC6530780/pdf/nihms-1020513.pdf.

Campbell, Carol Ann. "New Jersey Program Finds Alternatives for ER 'Super Users.'" KHN.org, Mar. 9, 2009. https://khn.org/news/er-super-users/.

Cantlupe, Joe. "Expert Forum: The rise (and rise) of the healthcare administrator." AthenaHealth, Nov. 7, 2017. https://www.athenahealth.com/knowledge-hub/practice-management/expert-forum-rise-and-rise-healthcare-administrator.

Carvalho, Claudia, et al. "Open-label placebo treatment in chronic low back pain: a randomized controlled trial." *Pain*. 2016;157(12):2766-2772. https://www.ncbi.nlm.nih.gov/pmc/articles/pmid/27755279/.

Cassell, Eric J., MD. "Illness and Disease." *The Hastings Center Report*. 6 (April 1976), https://onlinelibrary.wiley.com/doi/pdf/10.2307/3561497.

CBS NEWS. "A hospital patient was "disturbed" by the sound of her 79-year-old roommate's ventilator. So she allegedly shut it off – twice." Dec. 2, 2022. https://www.cbsnews.com/news/hospital-patient-arrested-shutting-off-roommates-ventilator-germany/.

Chang, Walter F. M., MD, FACS. "Complete spontaneous regression of cancer: Four case reports, review of literature, and discussion of possible mechanisms involved." *Hawai'i Medical Journal*. Vol. 59, October 2000. https://evols.library.manoa.hawaii.edu/server/api/core/bitstreams/7e61ed0c-73de-4b1e-8e36-f231cdd60416/content.

Charnetski, Carl J., Sandra Riggers, and Francis X. Brennan. "Effect of petting a dog on immune system function." *Psychol Rep*. 2004 Dec;95(3 Pt 2):1087-91. https://pubmed.ncbi.nlm.nih.gov/15762389/.

Cherry, Kendra, medically reviewed by Amy Morin, LCSW, Editor-in-Chief. "List of Common Cognitive Biases: Common Types of Bias That Influence Thinking." Verywellmind, Nov. 06, 2022. https://www.verywellmind.com/cognitive-biases-distort-thinking-2794763.

Cleveland Clinic. "Hypereosinophilic Syndrome." Accessed June 21, 2023. https://my.clevelandclinic.org/health/diseases/22541-hypereosinophilic-syndrome.

CNN.com. "Photos: History of Thalidomide." Sept. 1, 2012. http://i2.cdn.turner.com/cnnnext/dam/assets/120901013138-thalidomide-7-horizontal-large-gallery.jpg.

Collins, Claudia and Angela O'Callaghan. "The Impact of Horticultural Responsibility on Health Indicators and Quality of Life in Assisted Living." *Hort Technology*, 18(4), October 2008. https://www.researchgate.net/publication/279492779_The_Impact_of_Horticultural_Responsibility_on_Health_Indicators_and_Quality_of_Life_in_Assisted_Living.

Croskerry, Pat, MD, PhD. "Bias: a normal operating characteristic of the diagnosing brain" Diagnosis 2014; 1(1): 23–27. http://clinical-reasoning.org/resources/pdfs/Bias%20by%20Croskerry.pdf.

Curtis, Jeffrey, MD, MS, MPH, et al. "Placebo Adherence, Clinical Outcomes and Mortality in the Women's Health Initiative Randomized Hormone Therapy Trials." *Medical Care* vol. 49,5 2011: 427-35. http://www.ncbi.nlm.nih.gov/pmc/articles/pmc4217207/.

Darley, John M. and C. Daniel Batson. "'From Jerusalem To Jericho': A Study Of Situational And Dispositional Variables In Helping Behavior." *Journal of Personality and Social Psychology* 1973, Vol. 27, No. 1, 100-108. http://nwkpsych.rutgers.edu/~kharber/selectedtopicsinsocialpsychology/READINGS/Darley%20&%20Batson.1973.%20From%20Jerusalem%20to%20Jericho.pdf.

de Craen, Anton J. M., et al. "Placebos and placebo effects in medicine: historical overview." *Journal of the Royal Society of Medicine.* 1999 Oct; 92(10): 511–515. https://www.ncbi.nlm.nih.gov/pmc/articles/PMC1297390/pdf/jrsocmed00004-0023.pdf.

de Wit, Arjen, et al. "The health advantage of volunteering is larger for older and less healthy volunteers in Europe: a mega-analysis." *European Journal of Ageing*, Vol. 19,4 1189-1200, 30 Mar. 2022. http://www.ncbi.nlm.nih.gov/pmc/articles/pmc9729491/.

Dina, Halegoua-DeMarzio, MD, et al. "Liver Injury Associated with Turmeric—A Growing Problem: Ten Cases from the Drug-Induced Liver Injury Network [DILIN]." *The American Journal of Medicine*, Vol. 136, Issue 2, P200-206, Oct. 13, 2022. https://doi.org/10.1016/j.amjmed.2022.09.026.

Diriker, Memo, DBA, MBA. "Up to $935B wasted in health care spending annually." Healio, Oct. 7, 2019. https://www.healio.com/primary-care/practice-management/news/online/%7Bfffdab25-8006-46a9-92d0-5afdae61c2d7%7D/up-to-935b-wasted-in-health-care-spending-annually?utm_source=selligent&utm_medium=email&utm_campaign=primary%20care%20news&m_bt=2313726388190.

Dixon, Richard E., MD, FACP. "Economic Costs of Respiratory Tract Infections in the United States." *The American Journal of Medicine.* Vol. 78, Issue 6, Supplement 2, 45-51, June 28, 1985. https://doi.org/10.1016/0002-9343(85)90363-8.

Dizon, Don S., MD. "Some Decisions Aren't Right or Wrong; They're Just Devastating." Medscape Emergency Medicine, Apr. 28, 2003. https://www.medscape.com/viewarticle/991216?ecd=wnl_tp10_daily_230502_MSCPEDIT_etid5391071&uac=226947SV&impID=5391071#vp_2.

Doll, Richard, MD, MRCP, and A. Bradford Hill, PhD, DSc. "Smoking and Carcinoma of the Lung: Preliminary Report." *British Medical Journal,* Sept. 30, 1950, https://www.ncbi.nlm.nih.gov/pmc/articles/PMC2038856/pdf/brmedj03566-0003.pdf.

Dr. Glaucomflecken. "Prior Authorizations." *YouTube* video, 0:59. Accessed May 31, 2023. https://youtu.be/FVAFfd3oCgA.

Dr. Glaucomflecken. "The Future of Medicine." *YouTube* video, 2:28. Accessed May 31, 2023. https://youtu.be/6JMf-U75fTg.

Duff-Brown, Beth. "Overprescribing of opioids is not limited to a few bad apples." Stanford Medicine Newscenter, Dec. 14, 2015. https://www.npr. org/2020/07/17/887590699/doctors-and-dentists-still-flooding-u-s-with-opioid-prescriptions.

Egbert, Lawrence D., MD, et al. "Reduction of Postoperative Pain by Encouragement and Instruction of Patients — A Study of Doctor-Patient Rapport." *The New England Journal of Medicine*, N Engl J Med 1964; 270:825-827, Apr. 16, 1964. https://www.nejm.org/doi/full/10.1056/ NEJM196404162701606.

Einstein, Albert. "My Credo." From a speech given to the German League of Human Rights, Berlin, 1932. Accessed May 31, 2023. https://einsteinandreligion.com/ credo.html.

Engel, George R., MD. "The Need for a New Medical Model: A Challenge for Biomedicine." *Science*, New Series, Vol. 196, No. 4286. (Apr. 8, 1977). https:// resspir.org/wp-content/uploads/2018/02/3.-article-Engel-1977-biopsychosocial-model.pdf.

Engström, Sven, et al. "Is general practice effective? A systematic literature review." *Scandinavian Journal of Primary Health Care*, 19:2, 131-144. https://www. tandfonline.com/doi/pdf/10.1080/028134301750235394.

Esslemont, John E. *Bahá'u'lláh and the New Era*. QUICK REFERENCE (7.54): https:// oceanlibrary.com/link/bsHRg/bahaullah-and-the-new-era_john-esslemont.

Facebook. "Bounty Museum." Aug. 20, 2019. https://www.facebook. com/108678780476128/posts/john-norton-quartermaster-bounty-loyalists-john-norton-quartermaster-aboard-the-/119421856068487/.

FamiliesAgainstFentanyl.org. "Top 10 Leading Causes of Death for People Ages 18 to 45 in the U.S." Accessed May 31, 2023. https://static1. squarespace.com/static/61f366b9dd05336e4a3ce776/t/6305834bc3bafe639 6d12910/1661305675942/Fentanyl+Deaths_Top+10+COD.pdf.

Farrago, Douglas, MD. "Time as a Quality Metric." Authentic Medicine, Aug. 12, 2015. https://authenticmedicine.com/2015/08/time-as-a-quality-metric/.

FDA.gov. "Frances Oldham Kelsey: Medical reviewer famous for averting a public health tragedy." Accessed Apr. 23, 2023. https://www.fda.gov/about-fda/ fda-history-exhibits/frances-oldham-kelsey-medical-reviewer-famous-averting-public-health-tragedy.

Felitti, Vincent J., MD, FACP, et al. "Relationship of Childhood Abuse and Household Dysfunction to Many of the Leading Causes of Death in Adults: The Adverse Childhood Experiences (ACE) Study." *Am J*

Prev Med 1998;14(4). https://www.ajpmonline.org/action/showPdf?pii
=S0749-3797%2898%2900017-8.

Felitti, Vincent J., MD. "The Relationship of Adverse Childhood Experiences to
Adult Health: Turning gold into lead." *Z Psychsom Med Psychother*, 2002; 48(4):
359-369. http://www.theannainstitute.org/Gold_into_Lead-_Germany1-02_c_
Graphs.pdf#:~:text=The%20ACE%20Study%20reveals%20a%20powerful%20
relationship%20between,over%E2%80%99%20some%20things%2C%20
not%20even%20fifty%20years%20later3.

Fenton, Joshua J., MD, et al. "The Cost of Satisfaction: A National Study of
Patient Satisfaction, Health Care Utilization, Expenditures, and Mortality."
Arch Intern Med. 2012;172(5):405-411. https://jamanetwork.com/journals/
jamainternalmedicine/fullarticle/1108766.

Fitzgerald, F. Scott. "Essay: The Crack-Up by F. Scott Fitzgerald." American Masters,
S16 EP2, Aug. 31, 2005. https://www.pbs.org/wnet/americanmasters/f-scott-
fitzgerald-essay-the-crack-up/1028/.

Fleming, Alexander. "Penicillin." Nobel Lecture, Dec. 11, 1945. https://www.
nobelprize.org/uploads/2018/06/fleming-lecture.pdf.

Fogarty, Linda A, et al. "Can 40 Seconds of Compassion Reduce Patient Anxiety?"
Journal of Clinical Oncology, Vol 17, No 1 (January), 1999, 371-379. https://
www.motivationalinterviewing.org/sites/default/files/fogartyjco99.pdf.

Foy, Andrew J., MD, and Edward J. Filippone, MD. "The Case for Intervention Bias
in the Practice of Medicine." Yale J Biol Med. 2013;86(2):271-280. Published
June 13, 2013. https://www.ncbi.nlm.nih.gov/pmc/articles/PMC3670446/.

Franks, P. and K. Fiscella. "Primary care physicians and specialists as personal
physicians. Health care expenditures and mortality experience."1998
Aug;47(2):105-9. https://pubmed.ncbi.nlm.nih.gov/9722797/.

Fuentes, Jorge, et al. "Enhanced therapeutic alliance modulates pain intensity and
muscle pain sensitivity in patients with chronic low back pain: an experimental
controlled study." *Physical Therapy*, May 2014; 94:477-489. https://www.
researchgate.net/publication/279019566_Enhanced_therapeutic_alliance_
modulates_pain_intensity_and_muscle_pain_sensitivity_in_patients_
with_chronic_low_back_pain_an_experimental_controlled_study_vol_94_
pg_477_2013.

Gaetano, Phil. "The British Doctors' Study (1951–2001)." *The Embryo Project
Encyclopedia*, 2018-01-30. https://embryo.asu.edu/pages/british-doctors-
study-1951-2001.

Galli, Jonathan A., MD, Ronald Andari Sawaya, MD, and Frank K. Friedenberg,
MD. "Cannabinoid Hyperemesis Syndrome." National Library of Medicine,

Curr Drug Abuse Rev. 2011;4(4):241-249. https://www.ncbi.nlm.nih.gov/pmc/articles/PMC3576702/.

Gamble, Molly. "Room Service with MRIs, IV drips and bloodwork: Luxury hotels go all in on 'wellness.'" *Becker's Hospital Review*, June 27, 2022. https://www.beckershospitalreview.com/strategy/room-service-with-mris-iv-drips-and-bloodwork-luxury-hotels-go-all-in-on-wellness.html.

Gamble, Molly. "11 highest paid CEOs in healthcare." *Becker's Hospital Review*, May 15, 2023. https://www. beckershospitalreview.com/compensation-issues/11-highest-paid-ceos-in-healthcare.html.

Gawande, Atul. "Overkill: An avalanche of unnecessary medical care is harming patients physically and financially. What can we do about it?" *The New Yorker*, May 4, 2015. https://www.newyorker.com/magazine/2015/05/11/overkill-atul-gawande.

Glenn, Brandon. "9 out of 10 doctors wouldn't recommend a career in healthcare." MedCityNews, Mar. 1, 2012. https://medcitynews.com/2012/03/9-out-of-10-doctors-wouldnt-recommend-a-career-in-healthcare/.

Global Citizen. "Could you patent the sun?" *YouTube* video, 1:03. Accessed Apr. 25, 2023. https://video.search.yahoo.com/yhs/search?fr=yhs-ima-remarklist&ei=UTF-8&hsimp=yhs-remarklist&hspart=ima&p=patent+the+sun&type=q3020_D3NNQ_asc_bsfq#id=2&vid=fab0f8312e50ee3d6cf668aaa7b8188a&action=click.

Goebel, Marion U., et al. "Behavioral conditioning of immunosuppression is possible in humans." FASEB J. 2002 Dec;16(14):1869-73. https://pubmed.ncbi.nlm.nih.gov/12468450/.

Goodreads. "Pierre Teilhard de Chardin Quotes." https://www.goodreads.com/author/quotes/5387.Pierre_Teilhard_de_Chardin.

Gray, Fred D. *The Tuskegee Syphilis Study*. Montgomery: New South Books, 1998. http://image1.slideserve.com/2619443/tuskegee-syphilis-study-1932-72-n.jpg.

Gross, Terry. "How U.S. Health Care Became Big Business." NPR.org. Apr. 10, 2017. https://www.npr.org/sections/health-shots/2017/04/10/523005353/how-u-s-health-care-became-big-business.

"Harlow's Classic Studies Revealed the Importance of Maternal Contact." *Psychological Science*, June 20, 2018. https://www.psychologicalscience.org/publications/observer/obsonline/harlows-classic-studies-revealed-the-importance-of-maternal-contact.html?pdf=true.

Harvard Medical School. "Don't buy into brain health supplements." *Harvard Health Publishing*, Mar. 3, 2022. https://www.health.harvard.edu/mind-and-mood/dont-buy-into-brain-health-supplements.

Hawryluk, Markian. "Death Is Anything but a Dying Business as Private Equity Cashes In." KFF Health News, Sept. 22, 2022. https://khn.org/news/article/funeral-homes-private-equity-death-care/.

Healthcare Finance News. "Unnecessary medical tests, treatments cost $200 billion annually, cause harm." Kaiser Health News. May 24, 2017. https://www.healthcarefinancenews.com/news/unnecessary-medical-tests-treatments-cost-200-billion-annually-cause-harm.

Healthline, Contributor. "Hospital CEO Pay Rises While Americans Drown in Medical Debt." *Huffpost*, Aug 30, 2017. https://www.huffpost.com/entry/hospital-ceo-pay-rises-wh_b_11767768.

Heath, Sara. "Patient Recall Suffers as Patients Remember Half of Health Info." Patient Engagement HIT. Mar. 26, 20218. https://patientengagementhit.com/news/patient-recall-suffers-as-patients-remember-half-of-health-info.

Hellman, Melissa. "U.S. Health Care Ranked Worst in the Developed World." *Time.* June 17, 2014. https://time.com/2888403/u-s-health-care-ranked-worst-in-the-developed-world/.

Henry, J. P., et al. "The Role of Psychosocial Stimulation in the Pathogenesis of Hypertension." *Achtzigster Kongress,* (1974). Vol 80, 107–111. https://link.springer.com/chapter/10.1007/978-3-642-85449-1_17.

Herman, Bob. "Aetna CEO could make $500 million from CVS merger." Axios, Dec 5, 2017. https://www.axios.com/2017/12/16/aetna-ceo-could-make-500-million-from-cvs-merger-1513388416.

Herman, Bob. "Seven health insurance CEOs raked in a record $283 million last year." *STAT,* May 12, 2022. https://www.statnews.com/2022/05/12/health-insurance-ceos-raked-in-record-pay-during-covid/.

Hill, David. "Ain't No Way To Go." *Panati's Extraordinary Endings,* 1989. http://www.aintnowaytogo.com/charlesII.htm.

Himmelstein, David U., MD, et al. "Health Care Administrative Costs in the United States and Canada, 2017." *Annals of Internal Medicine,* Jan. 21, 2020. https://annals.org/aim/article-abstract/2758511/health-care-administrative-costs-united-states-canada-2017.

History.com Editors. "Larry Nassar, a former doctor for USA Gymnastics, is sentenced to prison for sexual assault." HISTORY, Aug. 28, 2019. https://www.history.com/this-day-in-history/larry-nassar-usa-gymnastics-doctor-sentenced-prison-sexual-assault.

Ho, Amy Faith, MD, MPH, FACEP. "Pros and Cons: Waiting Room Medicine." ACEP Now, Apr. 2, 2023. https://www.acepnow.com/article/pros-and-cons-waiting-room-medicine/.

Holt-Lunstad, Julianne, et al. "Loneliness and Social Isolation as Risk Factors for Mortality: A Meta-Analytic Review." SAGE Journals, Vol. 10, issue 2, Mar. 11, 2015. https://doi.org/10.1177/1745691614568352.

Holt-Lunstad, Julianne, et al. "Social Relationships and Mortality Risk: A Meta-analytic Review." PLOS Medicine, Vol. 7, Issue 7, July 2010. https://www.academia.edu/6273543/Social_Relationships_and_Mortality_Risk_A_metaanalytic_Review#:~:text=Social%20Relationships%20and%20Mortality%20Risk%3A%20A%20Metaanalytic%20Review.,supportive%20social%20network%20and%20thus%20not%20adequately%20relationships.

Horwitz, R.I., et al. "Treatment adherence and risk of death after a myocardial infarction." The Lancet, 1990 Sep 1;336(8714):542-5. https://pubmed.ncbi.nlm.nih.gov/1975045/.

Inagaki, Tristen K., PhD. "The neurobiology of giving versus receiving support: The role of stress-related and social reward-related neural activity." Psychosom Med, 2016 May; 78(4): 443–453. https://www.ncbi.nlm.nih.gov/pmc/articles/PMC4851591/pdf/nihms744752.pdf.

Inside Edition. "'Icepick Surgeon' Did Over 2000 Lobotomies." YouTube video, 10:54. Accessed May 31, 2023. https://www.youtube.com/watch?v=ZPyxwTC-Lqs.

Jabbarpour, Yalda, et al. "The Health of US Primary Care: A Baseline Scorecard Tracking Support for High-Quality Primary Care." Millbank Memorial Fund, February 22, 2023. https://www.milbank.org/publications/health-of-us-primary-care-a-baseline-scorecard/ .

Jansson, Bengt. "Controversial Psychosurgery Resulted in a Nobel Prize." The Nobel Prize. Accessed Mar. 30, 2023. https://www.nobelprize.org/prizes/medicine/1949/moniz/article/.

Johnson, Skyler B, et al. "Use of Alternative Medicine for Cancer and Its Impact on Survival." JNCI: Journal of the National Cancer Institute, Vol. 110, Issue 1, Jan. 2018, Pages 121–124. https://doi.org/10.1093/jnci/djx145.

Kaptchuk, Ted J., et al. "Placebos without Deception: A Randomized Controlled Trial in Irritable Bowel Syndrome." PLOS ONE, Dec. 22, 2010. https://journals.plos.org/plosone/article?id=10.1371/journal.pone.0015591.

Kelman, Brett and Blake Farmer. "Doctors are disappearing from emergency rooms as hospitals look to cut costs." Salon, Apr. 10, 2023. https://www.salon.

com/2023/04/10/doctors-are-disappearing-from-rooms-as-hospitals-look-to-cut-costs_partner/.

Kim, Eric S., et al., "Optimism and Cause-Specific Mortality: A Prospective Cohort Study." *Am J Epidemiol,* 2017 Jan 1; 185(1): 21–29. http://www.ncbi.nlm.nih.gov/pmc/articles/pmc5209589/.

Kim, Tae. "Goldman Sachs asks in biotech research report: 'Is curing patients a sustainable business model?'" CNBC, Apr. 11 2018. https://www.cnbc.com/2018/04/11/goldman-asks-is-curing-patients-a-sustainable-business-model.html.

Klopfer, Bruno. "Psychological Variables In Human Cancer." *Journal of Projective Techniques.* Vol. 12, Issue 4, 1957. https://www.tandfonline.com/doi/abs/10.1080/08853126.1957.10380794.

Knowles, Megan. "Healthcare becomes largest US employer: 6 takeaways." *Becker's Hospital Review.* Jan. 11, 2018. https://www.beckershospitalreview.com/workforce/healthcare-becomes-largest-us-employer-6-takeaways.html.

Koenig, H. G. "MSJAMA: religion, spirituality, and medicine: application to clinical practice." *JAMA,* 2000 Oct 4;284(13):1708. https://pubmed.ncbi.nlm.nih.gov/11015808/.

Koenig, Harold, et al. "Religion, spirituality, and medicine: A rebuttal to skeptics." *The International Journal of Psychiatry in Medicine,* 29(2):123-31, February 1999. https://www.researchgate.net/publication/12713129_Religion_spirituality_and_medicine_A_rebuttal_to_skeptics.

Koh, Howard K., MD, MPH, and Rima E. Rudd, ScD, MSPH. "The Arc of Health Literacy." *JAMA.* 2015;314(12):1225-1226, Sept. 22/29, 2015. https://jamanetwork.com/journals/jama/fullarticle/10.1001/jama.2015.9978.

Kramer, Caroline K. MD, PhD, Sadia Mehmood, BSc, and Renée S. Suen. "Dog Ownership and Survival: A Systematic Review and Meta-Analysis." *Circulation: Cardiovascular Quality and Outcomes,* Vol. 12, Issue 10, October 2019. https://www.ahajournals.org/doi/epub/10.1161/CIRCOUTCOMES.119.005554.

Kroenke, Kurt, MD, MACP, et al. "Anxiety Disorders in Primary Care: Prevalence, Impairment, Comorbidity, and Detection." ResearchGate.net. https://www.researchgate.net/publication/6466355_Anxiety_Disorders_in_Primary_Care_Prevalence_Impairment_Comorbidity_and_Detection.

Kroenke, Kurt, MD, MACP. "Patients presenting with somatic complaints: epidemiology, psychiatric co-morbidity and management." *International Journal of Methods in Psychiatric Research,* 2003 Feb; 12(1): 34–43. https://www.ncbi.nlm.nih.gov/pmc/articles/PMC6878426/pdf/MPR-12-34.pdf.

Kruse, Jack. "Have a cold you want to get rid of? Biohack a cold." Reversing Disease for Optimal Health, July 24, 2015. https://forum.jackkruse.com/threads/have-a-cold-you-want-to-get-rid-of-bio-hack-a-cold.16603/.

Langer, Ellen and Judith Rodin. "The effects of choice and enhanced personal responsibility for the aged: A field experiment in an institutional setting." *Journal of Personality and Social Psychology,* 34(2):191-8, September 1976. https://www.researchgate.net/publication/22144050_The_effects_of_choice_and_enhanced_personal_responsibility_for_the_aged_A_field_experiment_in_an_institutional_setting.

LaPointe, Jacqueline. "1% of People Account for 22% of Total Healthcare Spending." Revcycle Intelligence, February 26, 2020. https://www.revcycleintelligence.com/news/1-of-people-account-for-22-of-total-healthcare-spending.

Lee, Min-sun, et al. "Interaction with indoor plants may reduce psychological and physiological stress by suppressing autonomic nervous system activity in young adults: a randomized crossover study." *Journal of Physiological Anthropology,* (2015) 34:21. https://www.ncbi.nlm.nih.gov/pmc/articles/PMC4419447/pdf/40101_2015_Article_60.pdf.

Lie, Yung. "Slow Medicine, an international appeal on mindful healthcare." Slow Medicine, Setembro 1, 2022. https://www.slowmedicine.com.br/slow-medicine-an-international-appeal-on-mindful-healthcare/.

Loesche, Dyfed. "America Has the Highest Drug-Death Rate in North America - and the World." Statista, June 26, 2017. https://www.statista.com/chart/9973/drug-related-deaths-and-mortality-rate-worldwide/.

Lycette, Jennifer L., MD. "AITA for Pointing Out to the Insurance Company That I'm the Expert on My Patient? (A parody, except happening everywhere.)." Medscape Emergency Medicine, July 13, 2022. https://www.medscape.com/viewarticle/976690.

MacDonald, Ilene. "How hospitals can control Medicaid 'super-users.'" *Fierce Healthcare,* July 26, 2013. https://www.fiercehealthcare.com/healthcare/how-hospitals-can-control-medicaid-super-users.

MacGuill, Dan. "Did Fentanyl Overdose Become Top Cause of Death for Adults Aged 18-45 in the US?" Snopes, Dec. 21, 2021, https://www.snopes.com/fact-check/fentanyl-overdose-death/.

"Majority of Americans Say the Health Care System Needs Fundamental Change or Complete Rebuilding." *Commonwealth Fund Survey of Public Views of the U.S. Health Care System, 2011.* https://www.commonwealthfund.org/sites/default/files/documents/___media_files_publications_issue_brief_2011_apr_stremikis_public_views_2011_survey_exhibits.pdf.

Mara, Janice. "Open Minds – International Trepanation Advocacy Group."
Brandweek, 2000. https://indexarticles.com/business/brandweek/open-minds-international-trepanation-advocacy-group/.

Marcozzi, David. "Trends in the Contribution of Emergency Departments to
the Provision of Hospital-Associated Health Care in the USA." SageJournals,
International Journal of Social Determinants of Health and Health Services,
Vol. 48, Issue 2, Oct. 17, 2017. https://doi.org/10.1177/0020731417734498.

Maslach, Christina and Susan E. Jackson. "The Measurement of Experienced
Burnout." Journal of Occupational Behavior, 2(2):99 – 113, April 1981. https://
onlinelibrary.wiley.com/doi/epdf/10.1002/job.4030020205.

McCullough, Michael E., et al. "Religious involvement and mortality: A meta-
analytic review." Health Psychology, 19(3):211-22, June 2000. https://www.
researchgate.net/publication/12449610_Religious_involvement_and_
mortality_A_meta-analytic_review.

McLennan, Amy K. and Stanley J Ulijaszek. "Beware the medicalisation of
loneliness." The Lancet, Vol. 391, Issue 10129, P1480, Apr. 14, 2018. https://
doi.org/10.1016/S0140-6736(18)30577-4.

McNeill, Leila. "The Woman Who Stood Between America and a Generation of
'Thalidomide Babies.'" Smithsonian Magazine, May 8, 2017. https://www.
smithsonianmag.com/science-nature/woman-who-stood-between-america-and-
epidemic-birth-defects-180963165/.

Mental Health Daily. "Top 11 Professions with Highest Suicide Rates." 2015/01/06.
https://mentalhealthdaily.com/2015/01/06/top-11-professions-with-highest-
suicide-rates/.

Miller, Franklin G. PhD, Luana Colloca, MD, PhD, and Ted J. Kaptchuk. "The
placebo effect: illness and interpersonal healing." Perspectives in Biology and
Medicine, 2009;52(4):518-539. https://www.ncbi.nlm.nih.gov/pmc/articles/
PMC2814126/#R22.

Mizan, Nusaiba. "Is fentanyl the leading cause of death among American adults?"
Politifact.com, Oct. 3, 2022. https://www.politifact.com/article/2022/oct/03/
fact-check-fentanyl-leading-cause-death-among-amer/

Moreira-Almeida, Alexander, et al. "Religiousness and Mental Health: A Review."
Revista Brasileira de Psiquiatria, 28(3):242-50, October 2006. https://www.
researchgate.net/publication/6864541_Religiousness_and_Mental_Health_A_
Review.

Morgenson, Gretchen and Emmanuelle Saliba. "Private equity firms now control
many hospitals, ERs and nursing homes. Is it good for health care?" NBC News,
May 13, 2020. https://www.nbcnews.com/news/amp/ncna1203161.

Mosley, J. Bruce, MD, et al. "A Controlled Trial of Arthroscopic Surgery for Osteoarthritis of the Knee." *The New England Journal of Medicine*, Vol. 347, No. 2, July 11, 2002. https://www.nejm.org/doi/pdf/10.1056/NEJMoa013259.

Mossey, Jana M., MPH, PhD, and Evelyn Shapiro, MA. "Self-Rated Health: A Predictor of Mortality Among the Elderly." *AJPH*, Vol. 72, No. 8, August 1982. https://www.ncbi.nlm.nih.gov/pmc/articles/PMC1650365/pdf/amjph00655-0034.pdf.

Moyers, Bill. "Conditioned Responses, Interview with Robert Ader." *Healing and the Mind*, New York: Broadway Books 1995. https://books.google.com/books?id=G4wHYbyZQF8C&pg=PA241&dq=%E2%80%9CHere+we+had+a+conditioning+effect+that+had+a+major+biologic+impact+on+the+survival+of+the+animal.+That+suggests+that+the+placebo+effect+is+a+learned+response+available+to+anybody+under+the+appropriate+circumstances.%E2%80%9D&hl=en&newbks=1&newbks_redir=1&sa=X&ved=2ahUKEwin7N_F4IH-AhWDMlkFHR0pCagQ6AF6BAgHEAI.

Mueller, Paul S., MD, et al. "Religious Involvement, Spirituality, and Medicine: Implications for Clinical Practice." *Mayo Clinic Proceedings*, 2001;76:1225-1235. https://www.mayoclinicproceedings.org/action/showPdf?pii=S0025-6196(11)62799-7.

Muoio, Dave. "Here's what CEOs at the US' top for-profit health systems earned in 2021." *Fierce Healthcare*, Apr. 26, 2022. https://www.fiercehealthcare.com/providers/heres-what-ceos-us-top-profit-health-systems- earned-2021.

Naspretto, Alicia. "CDC: Fentanyl overdoses now leading cause of death for Americans aged 18 to 45." KXXV.com, last updated Dec. 20, 2021. https://www.kxxv.com/cdc-fentanyl-overdoses-now-leading-cause-of-death-for-americans-aged-18-to-45.

National Academies of Sciences, Engineering, and Medicine, et al. *Implementing high-quality primary care: Rebuilding the foundation of health care*. Washington, DC: The National Academies Press, 2021. https://doi.org/10.17226/25983.

National Center for Complementary and Integrative Health. "Americans Spent $30.2 Billion Out-Of-Pocket On Complementary Health Approaches." June 22, 2016. https://www.nccih.nih.gov/news/press-releases/americans-spent-302-billion-outofpocket-on-complementary-health-approaches.

Nerem, Robert M., et al. "Social Environment as a Factor in Diet-Induced Atherosclerosis." *Science*, 27 June 1980, Vol. 208, Issue 4451, 1475-1476. https://www.science.org/doi/10.1126/science.7384790.

Nichols, Tom. "The Death of Expertise." *The Federalist*, Jan. 17, 2014. https://thefederalist.com/2014/01/17/the-death-of-expertise/.

NobelPrize.org. "The Sveriges Riksbank Prize in Economic Sciences in Memory of Alfred Nobel 2002." Nobel Prize Outreach AB 2023. Accessed Mar. 29, 2023. https://www.nobelprize.org/prizes/economic-sciences/2002/summary/.

NPR. "'My Lobotomy': Howard Dully's Journey." Nov. 16, 2005. https://www.npr.org/2005/11/16/5014080/my-lobotomy-howard-dullys-journey.

OECD.org. "OECD Health Data 2012: U.S. health care system from an international perspective." Released June 28, 2012. https://www.oecd.org/health/HealthSpendingInUSA_HealthData2012.pdf.

Oman, Doug, MD, et al. "Volunteerism and Mortality among the Community-dwelling Elderly." *Journal of Health Psychology*, Vol. 4, Issue 3, 1999. https://journals.sagepub.com/doi/10.1177/135910539900400301.

Onque, Renée. "How to recognize 'medical gaslighting' and better advocate for yourself at your next doctor's appointment." CNBC.com – Health and Wellness, Sept. 1, 2022. https://www.cnbc.com/2022/09/01/medical-gaslighting-warning-signs-and-how-to-advocate-for-yourself.html.

Pargament, Kenneth I., MD, et al. "Religious Struggle as a Predictor of Mortality Among Medically Ill Elderly Patients: A 2-Year Longitudinal Study." *Arch Intern Med.* 2001;161(15):1881-1885, *JAMA Network*, Aug. 13/27, 2001. https://jamanetwork.com/journals/jamainternalmedicine/fullarticle/vol/161/pg/1881.

Pearl, Robert, MD. "Physician Burnout is up, Gender inequality is making it worse." LinkedIn. Apr. 26, 2022. https://www.linkedin.com/pulse/physician-burnout-up-gender-inequality-making-worse-pearl-m-d-/.

Perry, Susan. "Is taxpayer money well spent or wasted on alternative-medicine research?" *MinnPost*, May 3, 2012. https://www.minnpost.com/second-opinion/2012/05/taxpayer-money-well-spent-or-wasted-alternative-medicine-research/.

Peter J. Hotez. "The Antiscience Movement Is Esclating, Going Global and Killing Thousands." *Scientific American*, Mar. 29, 2021. https://www.scientificamerican.com/article/the-antiscience-movement-is-escalating-going-global-and-killing-thousands/.

Phillips, Jr, Robert L., MD, MSPH, et al. "Case Study of a Primary Care-Based Accountable Care System Approach to Medical Home Transformation." *Journal of Ambulatory Care Management*, Vol. 34, No. 1, 67-77 (2011). https://www.aafp.org/dam/AAFP/documents/patient_care/nrn/1phillipsjacm2010.pdf.

Porter, Justin, et al. "Revisiting the Time Needed to Provide Adult Primary Care." *J Gen Intern Med* 38, 147–155 (2023). https://link.springer.com/article/10.1007/s11606-022-07707-x.

"Prescription Painkiller Overdoses in the US," *CDC Vital Signs,* November 2011. https://www.cdc.gov/vitalsigns/pdf/2011-11-vitalsigns.pdf.

Press, Eyal. "The Moral Crisis of America's Doctors." *The New York Times Magazine,* June 15, 2023. https://www.nytimes.com/2023/06/15/magazine/doctors-moral-crises.html.

Pressman, Alice, et al. "Adherence to placebo and mortality in the Beta Blocker Evaluation of Survival Trial (BEST)." *Contemporary Clinical Trials,* Vol. 33, Issue 3, May 2012, Pages 492-498. https://doi.org/10.1016/j.cct.2011.12.003.

Prestinaci, Francesca, Patrizio Pezzotti, and Annalisa Pantosti. "Antimicrobial resistance: a global multifaceted phenomenon." National Library of Medicine, Pathog Glob Health. October, 2015; 109(7): 309–318. https://www.ncbi.nlm.nih.gov/pmc/articles/PMC4768623/.

Rebello-Valdez, Maria, MPH. "Is Medical School a Catalyst for Depression, Suicide and Burnout?" Medium. Apr 3, 2019. https://mariavaldez-15080.medium.com/is-medical-school-a-catalyst-for-depression-suicide-and-burnout-2d5c3a5fb645.

Richter, Curt P., PhD. "On the Phenomenon of Sudden Death in Animals and Man." *Psychosomatic Medicine,* Vol. xix, No. 3, 1957. https://www.aipro.info/wp/wp-content/uploads/2017/08/phenomena_sudden_death.pdf.

Riess, Helen. "Empathy Training for Resident Physicians: A Randomized Controlled Trial of a Neuroscience-Informed Curriculum." *J Gen Intern Med* 27(10):1280–6. https://www.ncbi.nlm.nih.gov/pmc/articles/PMC3445669/pdf/11606_2012_Article_2063.pdf.

Robbins, Alexandra. "The Problem With Satisfied Patients." *The Atlantic,* Apr. 17, 2015. https://www.theatlantic.com/health/archive/2015/04/the-problem-with-satisfied-patients/390684/.

Rodriguez, Alison. "Nearly Half of All Medical Care in the US is in Emergency Departments." *American Journal of Managed Care.* Oct. 24, 2017. https://www.ajmc.com/newsroom/nearly-half-of-all-medical-care-in-the-us-is-in-emergency-departments?sfns=mo.

Rosenthal, Elizabeth, MD. "Medicine's Top Earners Are Not the M.D.s." *The New York Times,* May 17, 2014. https://www.nytimes.com/2014/05/18/sunday-review/doctors-salaries-are-not-the-big-cost.html.

Sablik, Zbigniew, et al. "Universality of physicians' burnout syndrome as a result of experiencing difficulty in relationship with patients." *Archives of Medical Science.* https://www.ncbi.nlm.nih.gov/pmc/articles/PMC3701961/#.

Safran, Dana Gelb ScD., et.al. "Linking Primary Care Performance to Outcomes of Care." *The Journal of Family Practice.* 1998 September;47(3) (1998), 213-220.

https://www.mdedge.com/familymedicine/article/179483/linking-primary-care-performance-outcomes-care.

Sandhu, Tanita. "Capitalism with A Conscience." *Forbes.com*, Feb 12, 2013. https://www.forbes.com/sites/85broads/2013/02/12/capitalism-with-a-conscience/.

Sarinopoulos, Issidoros, et al. "Patient-centered interviewing is associated with decreased responses to painful stimuli: An initial fMRI study." *Patient Education and Counseling*, Vol. 90, Issue 2, February 2013, 220-225. https://www.researchgate.net/publication/233767499_Patient-centered_interviewing_is_associated_with_decreased_responses_to_painful_stimuli_An_initial_fMRI_study.

Sax, Paul E., MD. "HIV and ID Observations: How to Induce Rage in a Doctor." *NEJM Journal Watch*, Mar. 17, 2020. https://blogs.jwatch.org/hiv-id-observations/index.php/how-to-induce-rage-in-a-doctor/2022/03/07/.

Schwartz, Carolyn, ScD., et al. "Altruistic Social Interest Behaviors Are Associated With Better Mental Health." *Psychosomatic Medicine*, 65(5):778-785 (2003). https://citeseerx.ist.psu.edu/document?repid=rep1&type=pdf&doi=f65b997f27ee341890221551be3adc81570da27a.

Shakeel, Ahmed, MD. "Why Doctors Make The Best Healthcare CEOs." *Forbes.com*, July 27, 2022. https://www.forbes.com/sites/forbesbusinesscouncil/2022/07/27/why-doctors-make-the-best-healthcare-ceos/?sh=2d5295b03b6b#:~:text=Doctors%20are%20uniquely%20positioned%20to%20achieve%20that%20goal.,an%20institution%20that%20puts%20patients%20above%20all%20else.

Shanafelt, Tait D., MD, et al. "Burnout and Medical Errors Among American Surgeons." *Annals of Surgery*, Vol. 251, Number 6, June 2010. https://medschool.ucsd.edu/som/hear/resources/Documents/Burnout and medical errors among American Surgeons 2010.pdf.

Shapiro, Arthur K., MD. "A Contribution to a History of the Placebo Effect." *Behavioral Science*, Baltimore, Md. Vol. 5, Issue 2, (Apr. 1, 1960): 109. https://www.proquest.com/docview/1301267155?pq-origsite=gscholar&fromopenview=true&imgSeq=1.

Shrank, William H., MD, MSHS, Teresa L. Rogstad, MPH, and Natasha Parekh, MD, MS. "Waste in the US Health Care System: Estimated Costs and Potential for Saving." *JAMA*. 2019;322(15):1501-1509, Oct. 7, 2019. https://jamanetwork.com/journals/jama/fullarticle/2752664.

Simpson, Scot H., et al. "A meta-analysis of the association between adherence to drug therapy and mortality." *BMJ*, 2006;333:15. https://doi.org/10.1136/bmj.38875.675486.55.

Sinsky, Christine, et al. "Allocation of Physician Time in Ambulatory Practice: A Time and Motion Study in 4 Specialties." *Annals of Internal Medicine*, 165(11) September 2016. https://www.researchgate.net/publication/307871565_Allocation_of_Physician_Time_in_Ambulatory_Practice_A_Time_and_Motion_Study_in_4_Specialties.

Sloan, Richard P., PhD, et al. "Religion, spirituality, and medicine." *The Lancet*, Vol. 353, Issue 9153, P664-667, Feb. 20, 1999. https://www.thelancet.com/journals/lancet/article/PIIS0140-6736(98)07376-0/fulltext.

Smith, Deborah. "Psychologist wins Nobel Prize: Daniel Kahneman is honored for bridging economics and psychology." *American Psychological Association*, Vol. 33, No. 11, December 2002. https://www.apa.org/monitor/dec02/nobel.

"Soul Has Weight, Physician Thinks." *The New York Times*, Mar. 11, 1907. https://timesmachine.nytimes.com/timesmachine/1907/03/11/106743221.html?pageNumber=5.

Span, Paula. "A Quiet End to the 'Death Panels' Debate." *The New York Times*, Nov. 20, 2015. https://www.nytimes.com/2015/11/24/health/end-of-death-panels-myth-brings-new-end-of-life-challenges.html.

Spencer, Jane and Christina Jewett. "12 Months of Trauma: More Than 3,600 US Health Workers Died in Covid's First Year." KFF Health News Lost on the Frontline, Apr. 8, 2021. https://khn.org/news/article/us-health-workers-deaths-covid-lost-on-the-frontline/.

Squires, David and Chloe Anderson. "U.S. Health Care from a Global Perspective." The Commonwealth Fund, Oct. 8, 2015. https://www.commonwealthfund.org/publications/issue-briefs/2015/oct/us-health-care-global-perspective.

Staff News Writer. "Medical specialties with the highest burnout rates." AMA, Jan 15, 2016. https://www.ama-assn.org/practice-management/physician-health/medical-specialties-highest-burnout-rates.

Staff. "Froedtert CEO Cathy Jacobson: We need to make the health system work for our patients — not the other way around." *Becker's Hospital Review*, July 17th, 2018. https://www.beckershospitalreview.com/hospital-management-administration/froedtert-ceo-cathy-jacobson-not-every-patient-needs-a-primary-care-physician.html.

Stagl, Jamie M., et al. "A randomized controlled trial of cognitive-behavioral stress management in breast cancer: survival and recurrence at 11-year follow-up." National Library of Medicine, 2015 Nov;154(2):319-28. https://pubmed.ncbi.nlm.nih.gov/26518021/.

Stanford Research into the Impact of Tobacco Advertising. Accessed May 31, 2023. http://tobacco.stanford.edu/.

Starfield, Barbara, Leiyu Shi, and James Macinko. "Contribution of Primary Care to Health Systems and Health." *The Milbank Quarterly*, Vol. 83, No. 3, 2005 (pp. 457–502). https://www.ncbi.nlm.nih.gov/pmc/articles/PMC2690145/pdf/milq0083-0457.pdf.

Statista Research Department. "Feeling of loneliness among adults 2021, by country." Statista, Nov. 29, 2022. https://www.statista.com/statistics/1222815/loneliness-among-adults-by-country/.

Steensma, David P., MD. "The Farid Fata Medicare Fraud Case and Misplaced Incentives in Oncology Care." *JCO Oncology Practice,* Vol. 12, No. 1, Jan. 1, 2016. https://ascopubs.org/doi/full/10.1200/jop.2015.008557#:~:text=On%20Julyc%2010%2C%202015%2C%20in%20a%20health%20care,pay%20restitution%20to%20former%20patients%20or%20their%20families.

Strawbridge, William J., PhD, et al. "Frequent Attendance at Religious Services and Mortality over 28Years." *American Journal of Public Health*, June 1997, Vol 87 No 6, 957-961. https://ajph.aphapublications.org/doi/pdf/10.2105/AJPH.87.6.957.

Talbot, Simon G., MD, and Wendy Dean, MD. "Physicians aren't 'burning out.' They're suffering from moral injury." *STAT*, July 26, 2018. https://www.statnews.com/2018/07/26/physicians-not-burning-out-they-are-suffering-moral-injury/.

TEDTalks. "Abraham Verghese: A doctor's touch." *YouTube* video, 18:32. 2011. https://www.youtube.com/watch?v=sxnlvwprf_c&t=205s.

The Commonwealth Fund. "New International Report on Health Care: U.S. Suicide Rate Highest Among Wealthy Nations: U.S. Outspends Other High-Income Countries on Health Care but Has Lowest Life Expectancy." Jan. 30, 2020. https://www.commonwealthfund.org/press-release/2020/new-international-report-health-care-us-suicide-rate-highest-among-wealthy#:~:text=The%20United%20States%20spends%20substantially%20more%20than%20any,nations%2C%20according%20to%20a%20new%20Commonwealth%20Fund%20report.

"The Deadly Combination of Private Equity and Nursing Homes During A Pandemic: New Jersey Case Study of Coronavirus at Private Equity Nursing Homes." Americans for Financial Reform Education Fund, August 2020. https://ourfinancialsecurity.org/wp-content/uploads/2020/08/AFREF-NJ-Private-Equity-Nursing-Homes-Covid.pdf.

Tikkanen, Roosa and Melinda K. Abrams. "U.S. Health Care from a Global Perspective, 2019: Higher Spending, Worse Outcomes?" The Commonwealth Fund, January 2020. https://www.commonwealthfund.org/sites/default/files/2020-01/Tikkanen_US_hlt_care_global_perspective_2019_OECD_db_v2.pdf.

Tim Minchin. "Storm by Tim Minchin." *YouTube* video, 9:49. Accessed May 31, 2023. https://youtu.be/jIWj3tI-DXg.

Tim Minchin. "'Confirmation bias' | Tim Minchin: BACK." *YouTube* video, 11:54. Accessed May 31, 2023. https://youtu.be/G1juPBoxBdc.

Tribble, Sarah Jane. "Buy and Bust: When Private Equity Comes for Rural Hospitals." KHN, June 15, 2022. https://khn.org/news/article/private-equity-rural-hospitals-closure-missouri-noble-health/.

Trivedi, Madhukar H., MD. "The Link Between Depression and Physical Symptoms." Prim Care Companion J Clin Psychiatry 2004;6[suppl 1]:12–16. https://www.psychiatrist.com/read-pdf/25335/.

Turner, Ashley. "Stress and rigorous work schedules push a doctor to commit suicide every day in the US: 'We need them, but they need us.'" CNBC, May 21, 2019. https://www.cnbc.com/2019/05/21/stress-and-rigorous-work-push-a-doctor-to-commit-suicide-every-day-in-us.html.

U.S. Centers for Disease Control and Prevention (CDC). "National Infection & Death Estimates for Antimicrobial Resistance." Accessed May 5, 2023. https://www.cdc.gov/drugresistance/national-estimates.html.

U.S. Centers for Disease Control and Prevention (CDC). *Antibiotic Resistance Threats in the United States 2019.* Revised Dec. 2019. https://www.cdc.gov/drugresistance/pdf/threats-report/2019-ar-threats-report-508.pdf.

Uchino, Bert N. "Social Support and Health: A Review of Physiological Processes Potentially Underlying Links to Disease Outcomes." *Journal of Behavioral Medicine*, 29(4):377-87, September 2006. https://www.researchgate.net/profile/Bert-Uchino/publication/7025419_Social_Support_and_Health_A_Review_of_Physiological_Processes_Potentially_Underlying_Links_to_Disease_Outcomes/links/0912f5092dca28047b000000/Social-Support-and-Health-A-Review-of-Physiological-Processes-Potentially-Underlying-Links-to-Disease-Outcomes.pdf.

Wennberg, John, MD, MPH, and Alan Gittelsohn, MPH, PhD. "Small Area Variations in Health Care Delivery." *Science*, 14 Dec. 1973, Vol. 182, pp. 1102-1108. https://digitalcommons.dartmouth.edu/cgi/viewcontent.cgi?article=3596&context=facoa.

Wible, Pamela, MD. "Dealing With Intrusive Thoughts After A Medical Error." Pamela Wible MD: America's leading voice on ideal medical care & doctor suicide, Sept. 24, 2020. https://www.idealmedicalcare.org/what-not-to-do-after-a-medical-error/.

Wiebe, Christine, MA. "Abraham Verghese: 'Revolution' Starts at Bedside." Medscape Emergency Medicine, Oct. 24, 2017. https://www.medscape.com/viewarticle/887249.

Wikimedia Commons. "Abdulbaha knighting.jpg." Accessed May 31, 2023. https://commons.wikimedia.org/wiki/File:Abdulbaha_knighting.jpg

Wikipedia. "21 grams experiment." Accessed May 1, 2023. https://en.wikipedia.org/wiki/21_grams_experiment.

Wikipedia. "Blue Cross Blue Shield Association." Accessed May 3, 2023. https://en.wikipedia.org/wiki/Blue_Cross_Blue_Shield_Association.

Wikipedia. "Christopher Duntsch." Accessed May 4, 2023. https://en.wikipedia.org/wiki/Christopher_Duntsch.

Wikipedia. "Hippocratic Oath." Accessed Mar. 31, 2023. https://en.wikipedia.org/wiki/Hippocratic_Oath.

Wikipedia. "History of medicine." Accessed Mar. 31, 2023. https://en.wikipedia.org/wiki/History_of_medicine.

Wikipedia. "Humorism." Accessed June 14, 2023. https://en.wikipedia.org/wiki/Humorism

Wikipedia. "Pierre Teilhard de Chardin." Accessed May 31, 2023. https://en.wikipedia.org/wiki/Pierre_Teilhard_de_Chardin.

Wikipedia. "Post hoc ergo propter hoc." Accessed June 14, 2023. https://en.wikipedia.org/wiki/Post_hoc_ergo_propter_hoc.

Wikipedia. "Rosemary Kennedy." Accessed Apr. 2, 2023. https://en.wikipedia.org/wiki/Rosemary_Kennedy.

Wikipedia. "Sigmund Freud's views on religion," Accessed May 2, 2023, https://en.wikipedia.org/wiki/Sigmund_Freud%27s_views_on_religion.

Wikipedia. "Thalidomide scandal." Accessed Mar. 29, 2023. https://en.wikipedia.org/wiki/Thalidomide_scandal.

Winslow, Don. "The Chapo Trap." *VanityFair.com*, March 2019. https://archive.vanityfair.com/article/2019/03/01/the-chapo-trap.

Wolfson, Bernard J. "ER Doctors Call Private Equity Staffing Practices Illegal and Seek to Ban Them." KHN, Dec. 22, 2022. https://khn.org/news/article/er-doctors-call-private-equity-staffing-practices-illegal-and-seek-to-ban-them/.

World Health Organization. "WHO remains firmly committed to the principles set out in the preamble to the Constitution." Accessed Apr. 1, 2023. https://www.who.int/about/governance/constitution.

Wyatt, Karen, MD. "Blog: What Doctors Need to learn About Death and Dying." End of Life University, Apr. 18, 2023. https://eolupodcast.com/2023/04/18/blog-what-doctors-need-to-learn-about-death-and-dying/.

Yennurajalingam, Sriram, et al. "Open-Label Placebo for the Treatment of Cancer-Related Fatigue in Patients with Advanced Cancer: A Randomized Controlled Trial."

The Oncologist, Vol. 27, Issue 12, December 2022, Pages 1081–1089. https://doi.org/10.1093/oncolo/oyac184.

Yuen, Elaine, PhD, et al. "Spirituality, Religion, and Health." *American Journal of Medical Quality*, Vol. 22, Issue 2, March 2007. https://journals.sagepub.com/doi/abs/10.1177/1062860606298872.

ABOUT THE AUTHOR

A New Jersey native, Drew Remignanti received a Bachelor of Arts (AB) degree from Dartmouth College and a Doctor of Medicine (MD) degree from Rutgers Medical School. A board-certified emergency medicine physician, Dr. Remignanti spent his 40-year career working in a number of New England hospitals. At age 19, he was diagnosed with ulcerative colitis. This disease led to 15 hospitalizations, 7 abdominal operations and, ultimately, a major stroke at age 38 which sidelined his emergency medical career for five years. During this time, Dr. Remignanti earned his Master of Public Health (MPH) degree from the Medical College of Wisconsin and joined a number of international public health projects focused on rural health center development and polio eradication. This work took him to the Federated States of Micronesia, Honduras, Kenya, Pakistan, and Ghana. He was also part of a team providing medical assistance after the 2010 earthquake in Haiti. In 1997, Dr. Remignanti returned to full-time emergency medicine practice. He retired in 2020.

Dr. Remignanti's complex journey as both patient and physician inspired him to write *The Healing Connection*, which explores how dollar-driven decisions are wielding too much influence over our decisions as patients and, sadly, as physicians as well.

Figure 8: Drew Remignanti, MD, MPH
(photo by Cooper Remignanti)

To Julie,

All Good Health to you
Enjoy the read,

Drew

9 781954 102156